A
SOURCEBOOK
FOR
RESPONDING
TO STUDENT WRITING

Edited by

Richard Straub
Florida State University

HAMPTON PRESS, INC.
CRESSKILL, NEW JERSEY

Printed in the United States of America

Library of Congress Cataloging-in-Publication Data

A sourcebook for responding to student writing / edited by Richard
 Straub
       p.   cm.
    Includes bibliographic references.
    ISBN 1-57273-236-9 (pbk.)
    1. English language--Rhetoric--Study and teaching. 2. Report
 writing--Study and teaching. 3. Grading and marking (Students).
 4. College prose--Evaluation.   I. Straub, Richard.
 PE1404.S683   1999
 808'.042'0711--dc21   99-39341
                                                               CIP

Reprinted by permission of NCTE: "On Students' Rights to Their Own Texts: A Model of Teacher Response" by Lil Brannon and C.H. Knoblauch, 1982; "Learning to Praise" by Donald Daiker, 1989; "Ranking, Evaluating, and Liking: Sorting Out Three Forms of Judgment" by Peter Elbow, 1993; "Responding to Student Writing" by Nancy Sommers, 1982; "The Concept of Control in Teacher Response: Defining the Varieties of 'Directive' and 'Facilitative' Response" by Richard Straub, 1996; "Post-Structural Literary Criticism and the Response to Student Writing" by Edward M. White, 1984. Reprinted by permission of Jossey-Bass: "Talking About Text: The Use of Recorded Commentary in Response to Student Writing" by Chris Anson, 1989. Used by permission of author: "Options for Responding to Student Writing" by Peter Elbow; "Using Scoring Guides to Assess Writing" by Edward M. White.

Hampton Press, Inc.
23 Broadway
Cresskill, NJ 07626

For you, Kelly

Contents

Acknowledgments

First of all, I'd like to thank Ronald F. Lunsford, for all the work on *Twelve Readers Reading* that has shown up, one way and another, here; for his direct contributions to this book; and, more than I can say, for his support and guidance and friendship across the years.

I'd like to thank, again, the 12 teachers who contributed to the original study: Chris Anson, Peter Elbow, Anne Gere, Glynda Hull, Richard Larson, Ben McClelland, Frank O'Hare, Jane Peterson, the late Donald Stewart, Patricia Stock, Tilly Warnock, and Edward White. They did an astonishing amount of work for this project, work that has been rich to mine. I'd also like to thank the other teachers whose responses are presented here: Rebecca Mark, Pat McMahon, and Cheryl Nims.

One of the highest compliments you can extend to those who review your work is that they have led you to think more fully, more critically, more expansively about the project. The reviewers of this book—Peter Elbow, Richard Fulkerson, and Susan Taylor—have done all this for me and more. I appreciate the work they have put into this project, all the thought and concern. I think they will see the impact they've had in the book ahead.

I'd like to thank the authors for granting permission to reprint their articles. I'd like to extend special thanks to Peter Elbow for allowing me to reproduce handouts on response he has used in teacher training at the University of Massachusetts at Amherst; Chris Anson, for revising his article on taped response for the audience of this book; and Edward White, for writing an article to spec for the book and for offering suggestions across the project.

Finally, I'd like to thank Barbara Bernstein for letting me run with this book where I would—and being behind it all the way.

Introduction

The best way to develop our ways of responding to student writing is to look at what good teachers do in their responses: see what they focus on, look at how much they write and where they write it, listen to how they sound and notice how they create themselves on the page, and then try out some of these strategies in our own responses. Good models are as important to teachers as they are to writers. They give us an immediate sense of certain strategies and help us, intuitively, to connect practices with goals. They help us look beyond our habits of experience, beyond the feelings, concepts, and expectations that we routinely bring to the task. They help us picture the possibilities and imagine what we might try to do. They offer direction. They provide alternatives. They inspire. Don't most of us who have a propensity for teaching, after all, have some urge to find ways of doing what we do better?

This book derives from a lengthy research study that Ronald F. Lunsford and I conducted on the ways that 12 well-recognized composition specialists and noted teachers of writing respond to student writing. The study is *Twelve Readers Reading: Responding to College Student Writing* (Hampton Press, 1995), and the teachers are a diverse group who advocate a variety of approaches to teaching writing: Edward White, Tilly Warnock, Patricia Stock, Donald Stewart, Jane Peterson, Frank O'Hare, Ben McClelland, Richard Larson, Glynda Hull, Anne Gere, Peter Elbow, and Chris Anson. The study examines the ways that these teachers respond to a common sampling of 12 essays that Ron and I put together with the aim of representing different kinds of writing that are done in first-year composition. The sampling included personal writing and academic writing, rough drafts and final drafts, on topics close to the writers' first-hand experience and those outside their experience. Each of the papers was presented with a hypothetical context—a scenario that presented the writing assignment, the stage of drafting, the point in the course the writing was handed in, some information about the work being done in class, and, as often as not, a short profile of the student writer. Originally, we had asked the 12 readers to respond to the student papers as they would if they had received them in their own classes. However, after we devised the contexts for the writings and thought more fully about the difficulty of commenting on papers from someone else's classes, to faceless students, we revised the assignment. We asked them, how would you respond to these essays, in these hypothetical contexts, in ways that would illustrate your best responding style?

Twelve Readers Reading displays some 60 sets of these teachers' responses to the sample student papers, constructs a detailed method of analyzing comments, analyzes 113 sets of responses, describes the response styles of the 12 teachers, and defines the strategies they use in responding to student writing. Some 500 pages, it may be better suited for researchers and compositionists than it is for teachers. The book before you is a practical guide. *A Sourcebook for Responding to Student Writing* offers models of teacher comments and discussions about response, from a variety of voices and perspectives, with the aim of helping teachers develop their responding styles. It will help you:

- get a feel for the voices that experienced teachers use when they respond to student writing, and the various ways they present themselves on the page;

- clarify what to look for and value when you read student writing—and know which concerns to emphasize or de-emphasize (or defer) in your commentary;

- develop a repertoire of response strategies that might be useful to try in different situations, with different students;

- get a sense of your own responding style, by looking at what you do in relation to other teachers' styles and in relation to current composition theory and practice;

- learn how your responses may be made to work hand-in-hand with your teaching style and your overall goals of instruction.

This book is predicated on the belief that there is no single best way of teaching writing and no single best way of responding to student writing. Different teachers, in different settings, with different students, different kinds of writing, different course goals, and alas! with different time constraints may do different things with their comments, and do them well. Ultimately it comes down to what works best for us as individual teachers and what can be made to work best for this particular student, with this paper, in this setting, at this time. This is not to say that anything goes. Or that whatever we come up with in a set of comments will do. There are some principles that we would do well always to put into practice. There are some ways of responding that are better than others. And there are some ways of responding that may simply be unhelpful, if not harmful, to students' development as writers. Regardless of how much experience we have or how much we have put into honing our methods, I believe that each of us could benefit from examining the ways we respond, looking at the ways other teachers go about making comments on student writing, and expanding our repertoire of response strategies. The best teachers are not those who know the most or have all the answers or do all the right things; the best teachers are those who keep on teaching themselves and continually find new ways to help students learn.

Response is not just one of the things we do as writing teachers, just another task that comes with the territory. Response is integral to the teaching of writing and to any improvement in writing, no less for student writers than for experienced adult writers. Getting responses from others helps writers see how their writing is experienced by readers, where it is and is not working, and how it might be made to work better. It helps them revisit what they think and envision how they might shape their texts in ways that more aptly instantiate their intentions and share their ideas and experience with others. In the long term, getting responses from others helps writers develop their sense of how texts work and how their own texts can be made to do even more.

This book, then, is designed first of all to be a sourcebook for teachers, one that relies on good models as its main resource. It displays 25 sets of teacher comments, half of them published here for the first time. They are all written in response to five sample student essays. The essays—two of them rough drafts, three of them final drafts—take the diverse forms of narrative, expressive, explanatory, evaluative, and argumentative writing. Two of the essays deal with subjects that go beyond the writer's first-hand experience, two of them discuss a familiar subject from the writer's own experiences and perspectives, and one is a highly personal account about the death of the writer's father.

The sample comments are arranged in sections, one for each of the five student essays—first the rough drafts, then the final drafts. Each section begins with an overview about the context of the student writing, the hypothetical circumstances under which the essay was written. Next, a clean copy of the student essay is provided, without any markings. You are invited first to read and respond to the essay on your own, before going on to see how other teachers have responded to the writing. With this ground prepared, the section then presents several sets of teacher responses to the featured essay.

Twenty of the 25 sets of responses were written by the 12 composition specialists from the original study. Of the remaining responses, three were written as part of a follow-up study to *Twelve Readers Reading* that examined how noncomposition specialists—those who are responsible for teaching the vast majority of college writing classes across the country—

would respond to these same writings. One was written by Pat McMahon, a professor of English at Tallahassee Community College; one by Rebecca Mark, an instructor at Tulane University; and one by Cheryl Nims, who at the time was a graduate student at New Mexico State University. Two sets of comments were written by Ronald Lunsford and me. Having assumed the role of fairly detached researchers in *Twelve Readers Reading*, Ron and I studied the responses of others; we did not include any of our responses to the sample student writings. It seemed like a good time—and a good place—to put up our own comments for review.

I selected responses for each essay that would show the range of commentary these teachers gave to the writing: positive and critical, detailed and spare, directive and nondirective, accepting and demanding. I looked to present only those comments that were representative of the teacher's responding style. I also looked to display responses that I've found interesting and useful to work with—in groups that I thought would work well together. The responses are not arranged in any repeated pattern; I arranged them from paper to paper in ways that I thought would bring out the different voices, nuances, and styles of each response.

All of the comments have been refitted into a common format. I have accepted the loss in the original appearance of the comments for a gain in space and readability. The only resulting change in format I regret is the loss of displaying the marks and comments that these teachers made, exactly as they made them, in the margins and between the lines of a student's text. All the comments they made on the students' texts are now displayed in a common area in an extended right-hand margin, which sometimes makes a page look busier than it did in the original and sometimes does not capture graphically how extensively a teacher marked up a student's text. I used two techniques to capture something of these teachers' interlinear editings and commentaries. I inserted a caret (^) where the responder layered his or her own words or corrections between the lines of the student's text, and I underlined words that the teacher underlined or circled. I tried to replicate the responders' use of lines and arrows to identify passages they were addressing and indicate changes they proposed. I also standardized all end comments and letters to the student.

Beyond the sampling of teacher comments, the book provides an anthology of nine articles on response, covering a range of topics from a variety of perspectives. Most of them are reprints of articles that have become staples in the scholarship on responding to student writing. All of them are immediately connected to the practical work of response.

In "Post-Structural Literary Criticism and the Response to Student Writing," Edward White traces connections between the ways poststructural theorists view literary texts and the ways contemporary composition teachers have come to view student writing. By working against the New Critics' emphasis on the text itself, these literary critics offer a theory of reading that supports writing teachers' interests in teaching writing as a process, viewing writing as a means of discovery, and acknowledging the roles that readers play in the making of meaning.

In her pioneering article, "Responding to Student Writing," Nancy Sommers reports on the disappointing but eye-opening results she found in a study comparing the developing theory of response with teachers' actual practice. Among her many findings, Sommers notes that teachers in her study often "appropriated" student texts by taking students' attention away from their own purposes in writing and focusing attention instead on the teachers' purposes in commenting. The teachers presented contradictory messages in their comments, asking students to take on very different orders of revision in the same passages, at the same time. They did not distinguish between more important and less important concerns. They did not help students understand the dynamics of revising or engage them in substantive revision. Teachers in the study also frequently made comments that were vague and not text-specific—that were not "anchored in the particulars of the students' texts." The practices that Sommers advocates as alternatives to these conventional practices are the foundation of contemporary teacher response.

In another highly influential article, "On Students' Rights to Their Own Texts: A Model of Teacher Response," Lil Brannon and C.H. Knoblauch examine one of the central problems of conventional teacher response: how teachers take control over the writing when they read student papers in terms of their "ideal texts"–their own idealized versions of how the writing should look–and overlook the writer's purposes for writing. Asserting that incentive is vital to students' work as writers, Brannon and Knoblauch urge teachers to adopt the roles of readers and facilitators when they read student writing, rather than the conventional roles of critics and judges. Instead of directing changes in student writing, they should try to negotiate meaning and facilitate revision to help students realize their own intentions as writers.

In "The Concept of Control in Teacher Response," I point to the limitations in viewing teacher response as either directive or facilitative. As I try to demonstrate through an analysis of sample responses, teachers have a full range of styles that they may enact, including a number of "facilitative" styles of commentary. In my view, all teacher response is somehow directive inasmuch as it leads the student to attend to one area of the text or another, or to view his writing in one way or another. Directiveness itself is not a problem; it becomes problematic when it is taken to extremes and the teacher takes control over the student's writing choices and becomes authoritarian. The opposite extreme is equally problematic—commentary that is so brief and general that it fails to engage issues of revision.

Donald Daiker focuses his attention on a strategy that has received as much attention as any other across the years of research on response: the use of praise. In "Learning to Praise," Daiker presents findings of a study he conducted on how a group of teachers responded to a sample student essay. He found, not surprisingly, just how error-oriented teacher comments tend to be. In place of this traditional orientation, Daiker proposes a pedagogy of encouragement. Through positive reinforcement, he argues, teachers can reduce students' apprehension and increase their motivation to write. Because praise commentary is easier said than done, Daiker provides some strategies for getting more praise into our comments.

The next article expands the scope and methods of teacher response. Chris Anson shows teachers how they can make their exchanges with students more alive and get students more involved in the activities of response and revision: by exchanging audio tapes and *talking* with each other about the writing. In "Talking About Text: The Use of Recorded Commentary," Anson recounts how he came to use taped responses in his own classroom and explains the differences they made on his attitudes as a responder and hence on the tone and style of his comments. He offers practical advice on how teachers might employ taperecorded commentary as a way to make their responses more communicative, more open-ended, and more interactive.

In "Ranking, Evaluating, and Liking: Sorting Out Three Forms of Judgment," Peter Elbow tries to come to terms—not with teacher response—but with the related act of evaluation. Resisting the age-old tendency to allow grading to control teaching and yet unwilling to dismiss the importance—or the uses—of evaluation in the classroom, Elbow explores ways to develop what he sees as a more constructive approach to evaluation. He does so by distinguishing three forms of assessing students' classroom writing: *ranking*, or placing conventional number or letter grades on student papers; *evaluating*, or making specific judgments about the strengths and weaknesses of particular features of writing; and *liking*, or bringing an appreciative attitude or expectation to reading student writing. He advocates that we do as little ranking and grading as possible; that when we do make judgments about the quality of student writing that those judgments be less like labels and more like explanations; that we allow more room for writing that is not evaluated; and that we learn to bring a more receptive, positive posture to our reading of student writing.

The last two pieces in the anthology are printed here for the first time. "Options for Responding to Student Writing" is actually a series of handout that Peter Elbow has presented to teachers on various strategies and goals for commenting on student writing—many of them interesting alternatives to standard teacher response. Edward White's "Using Scoring Guides to Assess Writing" explains how teachers and student readers might make use of well-articulated criteria when they respond to student writing across the writer's drafts and revisions. Parting ways with Elbow, he argues for a method that foregrounds evaluation and grading and that sees both as indispensable for writing instruction. For White, scoring guides can help make responding and grading fairer and more productive; they can help students gain a clearer sense of how their writing is and is not yet working; they can help teachers and students come to understand the objectives and goals of writing assignments; and finally they can make instruction more effective.

The anthology of readings closes with a fairly detailed bibliography on teacher response—one that I put together with an eye to the needs and interests of teachers. The final section of the book offers two additional student essays, without any sample comments, so that teachers might use them to experiment with and put into practice their own (evolving) response styles, unencumbered by the anxiety of immediate influence.

These articles are not like parts of a puzzle; they do not derive from the same substance and do not form a coherent whole. Often the claims of one article are countered and richly complicated by another. Readers would do well at first simply to try on various ideas and practices and see how they fit, but they would be well-advised not to take everything home and put it in their closet. Optimally, they would consider suggested strategies in light of these teachers' principles and assumptions, and reflect on how they might be used to enhance—or complicate or even challenge—their own approach to teaching and responding to student writing. The goal eventually is to integrate, not simply adopt.

Ultimately, this book will be as useful as it leads us as teachers to reflect on our ways of responding, to connect our comments with our own teaching styles and classroom goals, and, when we turn to each new piece of writing before us, to consider the student behind that text and, in Roethke's words, learn by going where we have to go.

PART ONE

A Sampling of
Teacher Responses

Street Gangs: One Point of View
Context

BACKGROUND

This informative paper is the third paper of the course, the third time students have taken an assignment through several drafts with in-draft commentary. The class has been studying the principles of informative writing and paying special attention to the use of examples. Students have already completed invention activities and a first rough draft toward this paper, neither of which you have made written responses to. They will take the assignment through two more drafts.

Rusty is the kind of student who comes into writing classes apprehensive and expecting not to do well, largely because, as he wrote in his journal at the beginning of the course, his "grammar and structure are not too good." He keeps to himself in class, and he has not talked with you after class or in conference about his writing or his performance in the class, even though your written responses on his first two papers indicated that you expected more from him—in substance and correctness—in his future papers. Now he hands in this paper.

THE ASSIGNMENT

For your third paper, I'd like you to write about a hobby or activity in which you regularly engage and in which you have some level of authority or proficiency. In an informative essay of 600-900 words, inform or advise a general audience (say, the members of this class) about an aspect of this hobby or activity. As you write, try to say as best you can what precisely you mean, in a way that will spark your readers' interest in the subject.

In our work on this paper, we will pay special attention to the use, as distinct from the mere *citation*, of examples to examine and illustrate a point. As you write, keep this objective in mind.

We will take this paper through four drafts. The first is an exploratory draft, a place where you should try to get some words and ideas produced and begin to get them into some general shape. It may well be sketchy and rough. Do what you can to make it a place where you think through and discover what you want to say. You need not concern yourself with being neat and orderly—this is not a draft for readers, but for you as a writer at work. The second and third drafts are working drafts, places where you begin to do more careful shaping and crafting, and perhaps some more discovering and producing, some more experimenting. The fourth is a "final draft"—not in the sense that it is complete and forever done with, but in the sense that you can "finally" let it go now that your writing is ready for readers.

Street Gangs: One Point of View
Rough Draft

Rusty S.
Second Rough Draft

Street Gangs: One Point of View

I'm writing this paper on street gangs because I was once part of one, and I feel that this gives me some authority to write a legitimate opinion.

I never asked or set out to join a gang, it just happened by association. I knew some guys who were members of the Cripps and by hanging around them I was sort of "taken in" by the gang and generally thought to be a part of them by everyone else.

Unlike some members I tried to maintain a low profile. I didn't provoke fights or do destructive things on purpose, but we had a strong bond. If one person was in trouble, no matter who or what kind it was, everyone was there regardless.

This sticking together almost always occured in a physical sense. If one of our guys were to be beaten up, the rest of us would take a revenge of some sort, whether it be by beating someone up or vandalizing someones property, we always got even. That was a basic rule, nobody could "be one up on us", we always had to get even.

Except for this one occasion, I can't really remember us actually going out and starting trouble for no "reason". We were at the pool, and what we did was single out one person at a time. Once we had a target, one of us would go up to that certain someone and "sucker punch" him and before he could retaliate the rest of the gang would break it up.

Being a member had its ups and downs. The worst part was being paranoid about something happening to you. It wasn't a frightening feeling, but more like a burden. You knew something, somehow, somewhere would eventually happen, either to you or the gang. Many times I paid the price for being part of the Cripps with black eyes or broken noses. I even had my windshield busted once.

The good side was the family type atmosphere between us, we were more than friends, almost like cousins or even brothers. That sense of support that I got from being part of that gang was unmeasurable. Walking down the halls of school and having everyone know that your in this gang was great, almost like an "ego-trip". For it did make some of the guys cocky. This overall feeling is hard to explain, it deals a lot with acceptance and friendship. I guess these two things were what kept me in the gang so long. I liked the feeling of being part of something that (where I come from) is almost like a status symbol. My parents called this insecurity, this may be, but more importantly it gave me a purpose and an identity.

During the time I spent in the gang, we were more a "party" gang. We got into trouble and fights, but not with other gangs. Gangs at the time were more friendly and were only gangs by name. I mean everyone knew each other and it was only the name of the gang and their symbols that separated us.

Our symbols were one, a blue and red hankerchief worn around the right ankle, a diamond stud earring in the left ear and most important the thin white cane each member had. This was in relation with our name: "THE CRIPPS".

I left the gang last year because it started getting to violent, especially the growing conflicts between gangs. Many gang fights started to break out in the streets, schools and school related events. I just couldn't handle this, somebody could get really hurt or killed. I also felt I didn't need the ego boost anymore. I felt I could be my own person, with my own traits and characteristics. To sum it up, I grew up.

Street Gangs: One Point of View
Anne Gere's Comments

Rusty S.
Second Rough Draft

Street Gangs: One Point of View

I'm writing this paper on street gangs because I was once part of one, and I feel that this gives me some authority to write a legitimate opinion.

Can you start with one specific experience drawn from your life with street gangs?

I never asked or set out to join a gang, it just happened by association. I knew some guys who were members of the Cripps and by hanging around them I was sort of "taken in" by the gang and generally thought to be a part of them by everyone else.

Unlike some members I tried to maintain a low profile. I didn't provoke fights or do destructive things purpose, but we had a strong bond. If one person was in trouble, no matter who or what kind it was, everyone was there regardless.

These prghs seem to deal with the issue of "membership." What else can you say about membership in the gang? Is there a way to make connections among these prghs?

This sticking together almost always occured in a physical sense. If one of our guys were to be beaten up, the rest of us would take a revenge of some sort, whether it be by beating someone up or vandalizing someones property, we always got even. That was a basic rule, nobody could "be one up on us", we always had to get even.

Except for this one occasion, I can't really remember us actually going out and starting trouble for no "reason". We were at the pool, and what we did was single out one person at a time. Once we had a target, one of us would go up to that certain someone and "sucker punch" him and before he could retaliate the rest of the gang would break it up.

What does this "exception" show? What do you want your readers to draw from this?

Being a member had its ups and downs. The worst part was being paranoid about something happening to you. It wasn't a frightening feeling, but more like a burden. You knew something, somehow, somewhere would eventually happen, either to you or the gang. Many times I paid the price for being part of the Cripps with black eyes or broken noses. I even had my windshield busted once.

This section sets up a nice contrast. Can you say more about advantages and disadvantages of membership?

The good side was the family type atmosphere between us, we were more than friends, almost like cousins or even brothers. That sense of support that I got from being part of that gang was unmeasurable. Walking down the halls of school and having everyone know that your in this gang was great, almost like an "ego-trip". For it did make some of the guys cocky. This overall feeling is hard to explain, it deals a lot with acceptance and friendship. I guess these two things were what kept me in the gang so long. I liked the feeling of being part of something that (where I come from) is almost like a status symbol. My parents called this insecurity, this may be, but more importantly it gave me a purpose and an identity.

How does this relate to your conclusion?

During the time I spent in the gang, we were more a "party" gang. We got into trouble and fights, but not with other gangs. Gangs at the time were more friendly and were only gangs by name. I mean everyone knew each other and it was only the name of the gang and their symbols that separated us.

Is this related to your point about not starting trouble for no reason?

Our symbols were one, a blue and red hankerchief worn around the right ankle, a diamond stud earring in the left ear and most important the thin white cane each member had. This was in relation with our name: "THE CRIPPS".

Does this belong with your discussion of membership?

I left the gang last year because it started getting to violent, especially the growing conflicts between gangs. Many gang fights started to break out in the streets, schools and school related events. I just couldn't handle this, somebody could get really hurt or killed. I also felt I didn't need the ego boost anymore. I felt I could be my own person, with my own traits and characteristics. To sum it up, I grew up.

This last sentence is really interesting. What does the issue of growing up say about gangs? What, finally, is your point of view about gangs?

Rusty—

I think you have the makings of a very good paper here. You clearly know a great deal about gangs, and you have a rich store of illustrations and examples to draw upon. At this stage you should give some thought to how you want to shape your material. A good beginning is to try to summarize your "point of view" in a sentence. What advice or information do you want to give your audience about gangs? Then think about how you can convey this advice/information most effectively.

As my marginal questions indicate, I wonder if you can rearrange parts of your paper to bring related ideas together. What connections do you see among issues of membership, identity and growing up? Does the topic of gangs raise other issues for you?

Don't worry about sentence structure, spelling and punctuation in the next draft. Just concentrate on what you want to tell your audience.

Street Gangs: One Point of View
Edward White's Comments

Rusty S.
Second Rough Draft

Street Gangs: One Point of View

I'm writing this paper on street gangs because I was once part of one, and I feel that this gives me some authority to write [a legitimate opinion]. *about them from the inside.*

I never asked or set out to join a gang, | it just happened by association. I knew some guys who were members of the Cripps and by hanging around them I was sort of "taken in" by the gang and generally thought to be a part of them by everyone else.

Unlike some members ^ I tried to maintain a low profile. I didn't provoke fights or do destructive things purpose, but we had a strong bond. If one person was in trouble, no matter who or what kind it was, everyone was there regardless ☉ *of the cause. (?)*

This sticking together almost always occured in a physical sense. If one of our guys were ~~to be~~ beaten up, the rest of us would take a revenge of some sort, ^whether ~~it be~~ by beating someone up or vandalizing someones property, we always got even. That was a basic rule, ^ nobody could "be one up on us", we always had to get even.

Except for this one occasion, I can't really remember us actually going out and starting trouble for no "reason". We were at the pool, and what we did was single out one person at a time. Once we had a target, one of us would go up to that certain someone and "sucker punch" him and before he could retaliate the rest of the gang would break it up.

,

;

:

This sentence makes us expect something else. Begin with "On one occasion . . . "

This is the kind of detail we need. But we need more, even here.

Being a member had its ups and downs. The worst part was being paranoid about something happening to you. It wasn't a frightening feeling, but more like a burden. You knew something, somehow, somewhere would eventually happen, either to you or the gang. Many times I paid the price for being part of the Cripps with black eyes or broken noses. I even had my windshield busted once.

This sign (⎵) means you are using a comma to connect sentences. Review the handbook, chap 4, on this. We will talk about it at our next conference.

Oral tone

The good side was the family type⎵atmosphere between us, we were more than friends, almost like cousins or even brothers. That sense of support that I got from being part of that gang was [unmeasurable]. Walking down the halls of school and having everyone know that your in this gang was great, almost like an "ego-trip". For it did make some of the guys cocky. This overall feeling is hard to explain,⎵it deals a lot with acceptance and friendship. I guess these two things were what kept me in the gang so long. I liked the feeling of being part of something that (where I come from) is almost like a status symbol. My parents called this insecurity,⎵this may be, but more importantly it gave me a purpose and an identity.

"very important to me" (?)

What did they do when "cocky"? Detail.

During the time I spent in the gang, we were more a "party" gang. We got into trouble and fights, but not with other gangs. Gangs at the time were more friendly and were only gangs by name. I mean everyone knew each other and it was only the name of the gang and their symbols that separated us.

More than what?

More than when?

Our symbols were one, a blue and red hankerchief worn around the right ankle, a diamond stud earring in the left ear and most important the thin white cane each member had. This was in relation with our name: "THE CRIPPS".

I left the gang last year because it started getting [to]
violent,^ especially the growing conflicts between gangs.   ^ "I especially disliked"
Many gang fights started to break out in the streets,
^schools and ^school related events. I just couldn't handle   ^ "in..." ^ "at..."
this, somebody could get really hurt or killed. I also felt
I didn't need the ego boost anymore. I felt I could be my
own person, with my own traits and characteristics. To
sum it up, I grew up.

> *This is an interesting paper that promises to become very good. Your
> major idea is solid: gangs are an "ego boost" for immature kids. Notice that
> you don't get around to saying this until the last paragraph. You need now
> to put this idea up front and to arrange your experiences and details so
> they all show this idea. Remember: we need lots of details and descriptions,
> so we can see what you mean.*
>
> *Remember to edit the next draft, with a particular eye to sentence
> punctuation.*
>
> *I want to know more about your subject and about your experiences.
> You have certainly "sparked my interest," as the assignment called for.*

Street Gangs: One Point of View
Frank O'Hare's Comments

Rusty–

I get the feeling that you are still thinking through your experiences with the gang and that you haven't yet decided the significance of this experience.

In the first paragraph, you seem hesitant about your right to write about this subject. Of course, your opinion about this subject is of value. Your opinion will be not only legitimate but authoritative.

This hesitancy has, I think, caused you to neglect focusing on your purpose in this paper. It would probably be useful for you to sketch quickly an informal outline of your draft. What major points do you want to establish?

Why did you talk about keeping a low profile?

You seem to be combining the bonding issue with "starting trouble."

You claim that your gang didn't look for trouble, and yet the fifth paragraph discusses the only time you did.

Paragraph six needs specifics. What incident or incidents led you to use the terms "paranoia" and "burden"? You suffered black eyes and broken noses and yet weren't afraid. Please explain.

Paragraph seven does a good job of establishing your sense of identity.

Paragraph eight is confused and confusing. Are you saying that gang rivalries weren't as nasty as they appear to be? If so, the point is interesting and well worth explaining to your readers.

Paragraph nine: what point are you establishing here?

This subject is well worth writing about, but you must decide what your major points will be.

Two comments about code:

1.   The level of your vocabulary is just a little too informal.

2.   I have marked six places where you failed to recognize sentence boundaries. Please examine these examples and see if you can rewrite them correctly. Please come in for a conference and we'll discuss this problem. All six are, in reality, examples of just one problem.

Street Gangs: One Point of View
Peter Elbow's Comments

Dear Rusty,

This is interesting to read and sometimes has a strong impact on me.

What I noticed first are the places where you talk about your feelings while being in the gang: the oddly, interestingly, low-key "burden" as you put it. I would feel flat out *fear*. Also the feeling of comfort and support and family quality. Seems important. I would enjoy getting a bit more exploration here: but not just finding more words for it but more *examples*: what does all that look like in events or scenes?

At the bottom of 1 you give the example of picking on people at the pool. You tell it in a kind of deadpan way, but it's kind of horrifying for me. I think *I* was the kind of person who was picked on—or always felt I was about to be. There's something intriguing or even moving about your low key tone here, but I'm also curious to know a bit more how you actually felt—and feel. Something mysterious here: perhaps it's more interesting this way, despite my unsatisfied curiosity. But I do know I'd like you to flesh it out more as an example: it's a specific scene or incident, but you don't let us see any particulars.

The symbols of the gang are nice and concrete. I had the thought of somehow starting with them—or at least finding some way to start that has some zip to it; it's a little bit of a soggy opening as you have it. And the ending sentence is very sudden—though now I see you were building to it. I need some kind of help here; not sure what; don't want some abstract discussion of "growing up"—but somehow this important point (I really like it) needs something.

The heart and strength is your investment and relation; the weakness is need for more concretes and specifics.

Best,

Peter

Street Gangs: One Point of View
Richard Straub's Comments

Rusty S.
Second Rough Draft

Street Gangs: One Point of View

I'm writing this paper on street gangs because I was once part of one, and I feel that this gives me some authority to write a legitimate opinion.

I can see how this is helping you get into your subject and discover what you want to say. Will you be able to use it as is on the next draft?

I never asked or set out to join a gang, it just happened by association. I knew some guys who were members of the Cripps and by hanging around them I was sort of "taken in" by the gang and generally thought to be a part of them by everyone else.

Unlike some members I tried to maintain a low profile. I didn't provoke fights or do destructive things purpose, <u>but we had a strong bond</u>. If one person was in trouble, no matter who or what kind it was, everyone was there regardless.

This idea about bonding is interesting. Is it a subject you want to go further with on your next draft?

<u>This sticking together</u> almost always occured in a physical sense. If one of our guys were to be beaten up, the rest of us would take a revenge of some sort, whether it be by beating someone up or vandalizing someones property, we always got even. That was a basic rule, nobody could "be one up on us", we always had to get even.

Except for this one occasion, I can't really remember us actually going out and starting trouble for no "reason". We were at the pool, and what we did was single out one person at a time. Once we had a target, one of us would go up to that certain someone and "sucker punch" him and before he could retaliate the rest of the gang would break it up.

You come back to this idea about troublemaking. How much did the gang get together to make trouble? Is it something you want to get into in this paper?

Being a member had its ups and downs. The worst part was being paranoid about something happening to you. It wasn't a frightening feeling, but more like a burden. You knew something, somehow, somewhere would eventually happen, either to you or the gang. Many times I paid the price for being part of the Cripps with black eyes or broken noses. I even had my windshield busted once.

I like the way you go back over these ideas, to describe them—and then go on to try to get an even better hold on them in the next sentence. Now that you've got me with you, do you want to tell me more? How did you deal with this burden?

The good side was the family type atmosphere between us, we were more than friends, almost like cousins or even brothers. That sense of support that I got from being part of that gang was unmeasurable. Walking down the halls of school and having everyone know that your in this gang was great, almost like an "ego-trip". For it did make some of the guys cocky. This overall feeling is hard to explain, it deals a lot with acceptance and friendship. I guess these two things were what kept me in the gang so long. I liked the feeling of being part of something that (where I come from) is almost like a status symbol. My parents called this insecurity, this may be, but more importantly it gave me a purpose and an identity.

The writing comes alive here—I like the way you open this subject up.

Notice the way you make "great" mean something here—good thoughtful writing.

I like the way you search for the words to explain this feeling. You're using your writing as a way of thinking, of saying something that is yours, not just everyone else's. Keep it up.

These terms seem full of potential. I'd like to hear more about them.

During the time I spent in the gang, we were more a "party" gang. We got into trouble and fights, but not with other gangs. Gangs at the time were more friendly and were only gangs by name. I mean everyone knew each other and it was only the name of the gang and their symbols that separated us.

Our symbols were one, a blue and red hankerchief worn around the right ankle, a diamond stud earring in the left ear and most important the thin white cane each member had. This was in relation with our name: "THE CRIPPS".

How do you see these prghs fitting in with the material before about the burden and benefits of being in the gang? How will they fit into your next draft?

I left the gang last year because it started getting to violent, especially the growing conflicts between gangs. Many gang fights started to break out in the streets, schools and school related events. I just couldn't handle this, somebody could get really hurt or killed. I also felt I didn't need the ego boost anymore. I felt I could be my own person, with my own traits and characteristics. To sum it up, I grew up.

To say "in sum, you grew up" is to close off what otherwise might be an interesting and revealing issue: How did your feeling that you could "be your own person" get you over the need to be in the gang?

Rusty—

This paper is rich with your experience, your language, and your thinking. It seems to come alive especially on page 2, where you get into your sense of the burdens and benefits of being in the gang, and talk about the sense of identity and status the gang offered you. I like the way you use this writing to search for what you have to say on the subject, for what membership in this gang meant for you. You've clearly got something to say—something that is distinctive and interesting, something that is <u>yours</u>.

I think now it's time to get a better handle on what you want to do in the paper and to work these materials into a draft that will help me and your other readers see what you have to say about gangs. What do you want to focus on? How much do you want us to know about gangs? How much do you want us to know about your experience with this particular gang? What else can you say that will help us see what you want us to see about gangs or about your participation in this gang? As you get a sense of what the central point is, you will be more able to see what can stay and what can go, what needs to be elaborated on and what needs to go where.

It is your best paper to date, and it shows me what you're capable of doing in your writing. A pleasure to read. And interesting to think about how you might do more with it in revision. Let's see what you can do.

What If Drugs Were Legal?
Context

BACKGROUND

This is the first rough draft of an argumentative response essay. Through the first several weeks of the course, the class has focused on various kinds of expressive writing, and students have been writing essays mostly from their personal experience. Now the class is moving into transactional writing on topics which may include, but which must extend beyond, their firsthand experience. As a bridge into the second half of the course, students are to write a response essay in which they express their views on what another writer has to say about an issue. In anticipation of this assignment, students have been given practice in summarizing and paraphrasing the ideas of others. Although they have written several essays up to this point, this is the first paper that they will take through several drafts and receive another's comments on before they hand in the final draft.

This particular student, Nancy, sees herself as a "good writer." As she has told you a few times already (both verbally and in her course journal), she "has always gotten A's in English." Evidently, she is confused, or even put off, by your view of writing and, particularly, your assessment of her work thus far in the course. She has been somewhat resistant to changing her style and process of writing, and has not been very responsive to your comments on the four previous course papers.

THE ASSIGNMENT

Select from a journal, magazine, or newspaper, a recent article on an issue you are interested in, one that presents a view you disagree with or that you find some problem with. In an essay intended for the same publication, write a response to the article. You may respond to the article as a whole or to parts of it. Your task is not to review the article for its own sake but to express your views on what this writer has to say. Your final draft should identify the author, title, and publication information somewhere in the opening, define the topic or issue you are responding to and summarize what the author says about it, and then present your response.

We'll take this essay through two rough drafts before the final draft is due, two weeks from today. I will respond to both the first rough draft and the second rough draft.

Legalize Drugs

By John LeMoult

As a trial lawyer with some 20 years' experience, I have followed the battle against drugs with a keen interest. Month after month, we have read stories of how the Government has made a major seizure of drugs and cracked an important drug ring. It is reassuring to know that for more than 20 years our Federal, state and local governments have been making such headway against drugs. It reminds me of the body counts during the Vietnam War, when every week we heard of large numbers of North Vietnamese and Vietcong soldiers killed in battle. Somehow, they kept coming, and they finally forced us out and overwhelmed their enemies.

Every elected official from President Reagan on down goes through the ritual of calling for stiffer enforcement of drug and trafficking laws. The laws get stricter, and more and more billions of dollars are spent on the police, courts, judges, jails, customs inspectors and informants. But the drugs keep coming, keep growing, leaking into this country through thousands of little holes. Traffic is funded by huge financial combines and small entrepreneurs. Drugs are carried by organized crime figures and ordinary people. The truth is, the stricter the enforcement, the more money there is in smuggling.

Legalization is not a new idea. But perhaps it is time to recognize that vigorous drug enforcement will not plug the holes. Perhaps it is time to think the unthinkable. What would happen if we legalized heroin, cocaine, marijuana and other drugs? What if they were regulated like liquor and with the protections provided for over-the-counter drugs? Would we turn into a nation of spaced-out drug addicts?

Drugs have been a part of our society for some time. The first antidrug laws in the United States were passed in 1914. They were really anti-Chinese laws, because people on the West Coast were alarmed at the rise of opium dens among Chinese immigrants. Before that, there were plenty of opium addicts in the United States, but they were mostly white middle-class women who took laudanum (then available over the counter) because it was considered unacceptable for women to to drink alcohol.

After the first laws were passed, and more drugs added to the forbidden list, the sale of heroin and other drugs shifted to the ghettos, where men desperate for money were willing to risk prison to make a sale. Middle-class addicts switched to alcohol. Today, one in 10 Americans is an alcohol addict.

It is accepted. The number of addicts of heroin and other drugs is tiny compared with the number of alcoholics. But these drugs cause 10 times the amount of crime caused by alcohol.

What would happen if the other drugs were legal? Many experts believe there would be no increase in the number of drug addicts. They speak of an addictive personality and say that if such a person cannot easily obtain one drug he will become addicted to another. Many feel that the legalization of heroin and other drugs would mean that such addictive types would change from alcohol to other drugs. A 1972 Ford Foundation study showed that addiction to these other drugs is no more harmful than addiction to alcohol.

But what about crime? Overnight it would, be dealt a shattering blow. Legal heroin and cocaine sold in drugstores, only to people over 21, and protected by our pure food and drug laws, would sell at a very small fraction of its current street value. The adulterated and dangerous heroin concoctions available today for $20 from your friendly pusher would, in clean form with proper dosage on the package, sell for about 50 cents in a drugstore. There would be no need for crime.

With addicts no longer desperate for money to buy drugs, mugging and robbery in our major cities would be more than cut in half. The streets would be safer. There would be no more importers, sellers and buyers on the black market. It would become uneconomical. Huge crime rings would go out of business.

More than half the crime in America is drug related. But drugs themselves do not cause crime. Crime is caused by the laws against drugs and the need of addicts to steal money for their purchase. Overnight the cost of law enforcement, courts, judges, jails and convict rehabilitation would be cut in half. The savings in taxes would be mom than $50 billion a year.

We may not be ready for a radical step of this kind. Perhaps we are willing to spend $50 billion a year and suffer the unsafe streets to express our moral opposition to drugs. But we should at least examine the benefits of legalization. We should try to find out whether drug use would dramatically increase, what the tax savings would be. I do not suggest that we legalize drugs immediately. I ask only that we give it some thought.

— *New York Times 1984*

What If Drugs Were Legal?
Rough Draft

Nancy S.
First Rough Draft

What If Drugs Were Legal?

What if drugs were legal? Could you imagine what it would do to our society? Well according to John E. LeMoult, a lawyer with twenty years of experience on the subject, feels we should at least consider it. I would like to comment on his article "Legalize Drugs" in the June 15, 1984, issue of the New York Times. I disagree with LeMoult's idea of legalizing drugs to cut the cost of crime.

LeMoult's article was short and sweet. He gives the background of the legalization of drugs. For example, the first antidrug laws of the United States were passed in 1914. The laws were put in effect because of the threat of the Chinese imagrants. In addition, he explains how women were the first to use laudanun, an over the counter drug, as a substitute for drinking; it was unacceptable for women to drink. By explaining this he made the reader feel that society was the cause of women using the substitute, laudanun, for drinking. LeMoult proceeded from there to explain how the money to buy drugs comes from us as society. Since drug addicts turn to crime to get money we become a corrupt society. Due to this we spend unnecessary money protecting inocent citizens by means of law enforcment, jails, and ect. LeMoult says that if we legalize drugs that "Overnight the cost of law enforcement, courts, judges, jails and convict rehabilitation would be cut in half. The savings in tax would be more than $50 billion a year."

LeMoult might be correct by saying that our cost of living in society would be cut in half if drugs were legalized, however, he is justifying a wrong to save money. In my opinion legalizing drugs is the easy man's way out. Just because crime is high due to the fact that the cost of drugs is unbeleivable it doesn't make legalizing them right. We all know drugs are dangerous to the body and society without any explanation, therefore, you shouldn't legalize something that is dangerous.

My only and most important argument to LeMoult is the physical harm it would bring by legalizing drugs. People abuse their right to use alcoholic beverages because they are legal. For example, LeMoult himself says the amount of drug addicts is small compared to alcoholics. Why?–of course it is because of the legalization of alcohol. When you make something legal it can and will be done with little hassel. Why allow something to be done with ease when it is wrong? LeMoult's points are good and true but I believe he is approaching the subject in the wrong manner. Drugs are wrong, therefore, should not be legal!

What If Drugs Were Legal?
Pat McMahon's Comments

Nancy S.
First Rough Draft

What If Drugs Were Legal?

What if drugs were legal? Could you imagine what it would do to our society? Well according to John E. LeMoult, a lawyer with twenty years of experience on the subject, feels we should at least consider it. I would like to comment on his article "Legalize Drugs" in the June 15, 1984, issue of the New York Times. I disagree with LeMoult's idea of legalizing drugs to cut the cost of crime.

Try an expanded lead in. Imagine scenes from such a society.

LeMoult's article was short and sweet. He gives the background of the legalization of drugs. For example, the first antidrug laws of the United States were passed in 1914. The laws were put in effect because of the threat of the Chinese imagrants. In addition, he explains how women were the first to use laudanun, an over the counter drug, as a substitute for drinking; it was unacceptable for women to drink. By explaining this he made the reader feel that society was the cause of women using the substitute, laudanun, for drinking. LeMoult proceeded from there to explain how the money to buy drugs comes from us as society. Since drug addicts turn to crime to get money we become a corrupt society. Due to this we spend unnecessary money protecting inocent citizens by means of law enforcment, jails, and ect. LeMoult says that if we legalize drugs that "Overnight the cost of law enforcement, courts, judges, jails and convict rehabilitation would be cut in half. The savings in tax would be more than $50 billion a year."

Here you've just renamed a few disjointed points. You need to sum up his major arguments for legalization. That way you can refute them one at a time.

The only real point you grant him is that we would save money. I don't feel that you have understood and/or expressed his major arguments.

LeMoult might be correct by saying that our cost of living in society would be cut in half if drugs were legalized, however, he is justifying a wrong to save money. In my opinion legalizing drugs is the easy man's way out. Just because crime is high due to the fact that the cost of drugs is unbeleivable it doesn't make legalizing them right. We all know drugs are dangerous to the body and society without any explanation, therefore, you shouldn't legalize something that is dangerous. *Circular reasoning*

Good logic on your part, but you've reduced his argument in order to make your point.

Don't use cliché phrases as substitutes for logic.

You've missed his point— Drugs are only dangerous because laws make their use illegal.

My only and most important argument to LeMoult is the physical harm it would bring by legalizing drugs. People abuse their right to use alcoholic beverages because they are legal. For example, LeMoult himself says the amount of drug addicts is small compared to alcoholics. Why? —of course it is because of the legalization of alcohol. When you make something legal it can and will be done with little hassel. Why allow something to be done with ease when it is wrong? LeMoult's points are good and true but I believe he is approaching the subject in the wrong manner. Drugs are wrong, therefore, should not be legal!

Good 2nd point.

Try to refute his major point.

Put conclusion in separate prgh.

Good start – Now add a better intro, clearer summary of his points, better logic and more points to your side. Try an outline now – your development seems random in this draft. Arguments need to have some control. Free associating is helpful in this kind of discovery draft—but now grab your best points and build a real essay.

What If Drugs Were Legal?
Edward White's Comments

Nancy S.
First Rough Draft

What If Drugs Were Legal?

What if drugs were legal? Could you imagine what it would do to our society? Well according to John E. LeMoult, a lawyer with twenty years of experience on the subject, feels we should at least consider it. I would like to comment on his article "Legalize Drugs" in the June 15, 1984, issue of the <u>New York Times</u>. I disagree with LeMoult's idea of legalizing drugs to cut the cost of crime.

Now that you are clear on what you have to say (see your last prgh), revise the opening to begin your argument.

LeMoult's article was short and sweet. He gives the background of the legalization of drugs. For example, the first antidrug laws of the United States were passed in 1914. The laws were put in effect because of the threat of the Chinese imagrants. In addition, he explains how women were the first to use laudanun, an over the counter drug, as a substitute for drinking; it was unacceptable for women to drink. By explaining this he made the reader feel that society was the cause of women using the substitute, laudanun, for drinking. LeMoult proceeded from there to explain how the money to buy drugs comes from us as society. Since drug addicts turn to crime to get money we become a corrupt society. Due to this we spend unnecessary money protecting inocent citizens by means of law enforcment, jails, and ect. LeMoult says that if we legalize drugs that "Overnight the cost of law enforcement, courts, judges, jails and convict rehabilitation would be cut in half. The savings in tax would be more than $50 billion a year."

Select the parts of LeMoult's article that are appropriate for your paper and omit the rest. Be sure to quote accurately.

LeMoult might be correct by saying that our cost of living in society would be cut in half if drugs were legalized, however, he is justifying a wrong to save money. In my opinion legalizing drugs is the easy man's way out. Just because crime is high due to the fact that the cost of drugs is unbeleivable it doesn't make legalizing them right. We all know drugs are dangerous to the body and society without any explanation, therefore, you shouldn't legalize something that is dangerous.

Your first argument: the financial reasons are not good enough for legalization. Focus this prgh on this argument and develop your case.

My only and most important argument to LeMoult is the physical harm it would bring by legalizing drugs. People abuse their right to use alcoholic beverages because they are legal. For example, LeMoult himself says the amount of drug addicts is small compared to alcoholics. Why? —of course it is because of the legalization of alcohol. When you make something legal it can and will be done with little hassle. Why allow something to be done with ease when it is wrong? LeMoult's points are good and true but I believe he is approaching the subject in the wrong manner. Drugs are wrong, therefore, should not be legal!

Not so. Look at the previous prgh.

Second argument: Now develop this one.

Make this into a full closing prgh.

The paper is a good discovery draft that could become a good paper. As you revise, be sure you focus each prgh on its central idea. I enjoy the energy of your style.

What If Drugs Were Legal?
Jane Peterson's Comments

Nancy S.
First Rough Draft

What If Drugs Were Legal?

What if drugs were legal? Could you imagine what it would do to our society? Well according to John E. LeMoult, a lawyer with twenty years of experience on the subject, feels we should at least consider it. I would like to comment on his article "Legalize Drugs" in the June 15, 1984, issue of the New York Times. I disagree with LeMoult's idea of legalizing drugs to cut the cost of crime.

LeMoult's article was short and sweet. He gives the background of the legalization of drugs. For example, the first antidrug laws of the United States were passed in 1914. The laws were put in effect because of the threat of the Chinese imagrants. In addition, he explains how women were the first to use laudanun, an over the counter drug, as a substitute for drinking; it was unacceptable for women to drink. By explaining this he made the reader feel that society was the cause of women using the substitute, laudanun, for drinking. LeMoult proceeded from there to explain how the money to buy drugs comes from us as society. Since drug addicts turn to crime to get money we become a corrupt society. Due to this we spend unnecessary money protecting inocent citizens by means of law enforcment, jails, and ect. LeMoult says that if we legalize drugs that "Overnight the cost of law enforcement, courts, judges, jails and convict rehabilitation would be cut in half. The savings in tax would be more than $50 billion a year."

This is in his 4th prgh. What's he doing in the first 3 prghs?

I think you've fallen into the interesting detail trap here.

? crime-filled ?

Good use of quote

LeMoult might be correct by saying that our cost of living in society would be cut in half if drugs were legalized, however, he is justifying a wrong to save money. In my opinion legalizing drugs is the easy man's way out. Just because crime is high due to the fact that the cost of drugs is unbeleivable it doesn't make legalizing them right. We all know drugs are dangerous to the body and society without any explanation, therefore, you shouldn't legalize something that is dangerous.

Do we? All drugs? Whose bodies?

How? Legal or illegal?

Cigarettes? alcohol? car racing?

My only and most important argument to LeMoult is the physical harm it would bring by legalizing drugs. People abuse their right to use alcoholic beverages because they are legal. For example, LeMoult himself says the amount of drug addicts is small compared to alcoholics. Why? —of course it is because of the legalization of alcohol. When you make something legal it can and will be done with little hassel. Why allow something to be done with ease when it is wrong? LeMoult's points are good and true but I believe he is approaching the subject in the wrong manner. Drugs are wrong, therefore, should not be legal!

To whom?

All people? This would mean everyone is an alcoholic because alcohol is legal.

Do you mean morally wrong or dangerous?

Nancy,

Your first draft is a good starting point—you clearly understand the structure expected (opening with source info, summarizing the article, responding with your view). Before beginning a second draft, I suggest you do a barebones outline on the article (you're missing a couple of LeMoult's points) and then do one on your response (you seem to have at least two objections instead of one).

What If Drugs Were Legal?
Ben McClelland's Comments

What is it that you want me most to know about your position on LeMoult's article, "Legalize Drugs," Nancy? Try stating that point in a sentence or two. In order to understand your position on LeMoult's article then, just what do I need to know about his article? That is, what specific points do you need to summarize from his article and which ones may you disregard? I ask you to work out these two matters because, as I read your draft, I need a clearer sense of both. Before reading further in my comments, please jot down a list of items on them.

First, with regard to your position, did you say that you were against legalizing drugs because they were physically harmful and, therefore, morally wrong? Those are the points that I gleaned from your last two paragraphs. However, you say, "We all know drugs are dangerous to the body and society *without any explanation* ..." [my emphasis]. Given the nature of LeMoult's radical proposal (which I also have read), I think some further explanation is due us readers. Of course, you do give somewhat of one in the last paragraph, don't you? But your causal linking of illegal drugs and their relatively few addicts and legal alcohol and its relatively many addicts fails to convince me. But perhaps there is something that you could use to your advantage in the behavior of other sorts of addicts: smokers, gamblers, shoppers? What else could you say in favor of your position?

Second, with regard to what you summarize from LeMoult, what main point of his do you want to focus on? In a sentence, what is his major reason for suggesting that we consider legalizing drugs? At two points (paragraph 2 & 3) you indicate that it has to do with crime and the cost of enforcement of drug laws. Why do you include the points on the first antidrug laws and on women's use of laudanum when you don't refer to them later? Do they relate to your argument with LeMoult over legalizing drugs? Moreover, when you say, "LeMoult's points are good and true," to what specific points are you referring? Sometimes it's useful to make a concession to an opponent, but it must be qualified or limited to some specific point that does not detract from your main objection to the opponent's position.

If I were pressed to say what your argument with LeMoult came down to, I would say that you stacked some general point about the harm of drugs against his proposition that legalizing drugs would cut crime and law enforcement costs dramatically. Is that what you attempted? Look again at his data and his logic. Search for ways of composing a more effective argument by 1) calling his conclusions into question and 2) making your case more detailed and convincing.

What If Drugs Were Legal?
Chris Anson's Taped Comments

[Note: Anson creates a scenario where Nancy has handed in, along with her draft, an audio tape on which she has recorded her concerns about the writing. He is responding to both the tape and the writing.]

Hi, Nancy. Uh, thanks for your tape. You know, something just occurred to me as I was, um, listening to it that we haven't really explored or, that hasn't come up in class at all, and that's what happens with speaking in relation to writing. Because here you're talking for about ten minutes on the tape and really coming up with a lot of ideas and, I don't know, it's almost as if, if you'd, uh, if, if you'd done the tape *before* the draft that it would have about twice as much substance! [laughs]. And one of the things that I, uh, that all the small group work does . . . is to give you that chance to talk out everything first. Because on the tape, one of, you mention for example that you're really against the auth–against LeMoult's point, the comparison to drinking, and you talk a little about that in the paper here on, uh, at the end, but you really said a lot more on the tape, there's a lot more detail here, so what I would do now is maybe just *talk* out those ideas, or pull them from your head and make a list of some sort so you can begin elaborating this piece and extending it.

This is a really nicely chosen article–short and sweet, you said–but it's certainly, um, controversial enough and especially current with the crack scene today and Bill Bennett, our drug zzar and all the attention in the media. You know, this has been a controversy for, well, certainly since the sixties but I think it used to be more focused on marijuana so it's maybe even more controversial to talk about legalizing stuff like crack and heroin at such a conservative time.

Um . . . let me, let me make some suggestions here and ask some questions, I guess, so you can think this through as we, um, work over the next week or so. I think the real substance here is the evaluative section because the article is fairly straightforward so your summary seems to capture its gist pretty well for me. You might, you know, something that stood out for me a lot in the article was his point . . . [flipping through pages] . . . here at the end, at the very end, he says here, "I ask only that we give it some thought," and that's a rather clever way to end, you know, he's made a very controversial assertion and now, now he's sort of taking this very balanced position, let's give this some thought. So that if you come down really hard, it's, well, maybe he's forcing your hand, in a way, and if you show too much, um, energy or . . . too much *anger*, I guess, that you'll end up looking just the opposite–not balanced, not "giving it some thought." So you might think about that, and see if there's anything at all in his argument that seems, um, if not reasonable, at least interesting. Another thing I'd do here is to take each of your counter-arguments and see if there's *any* exception to them, and, uh, try to take them and apply them to similar situations. Uh, let me be specific here. If, on page two, one of your main points is this issue of danger to one's health. What if you tried listing as many things you can think of that are legal that are also dangerous, like cigarettes, um, firearms, in a sense, um, certain kinds of recreational—all-terrain vehicles, over-the-counter drugs, and so on. Now what makes these sorts of things different from illegal drugs? You see, then when you find reasons why they're different, your points will seem more carefully thought out and developed. So the all-terrain business, for example, um, these can be safe with the right training and helmets and so on, while it's hard to imagine any doses of crack that could be considered perfectly OK on the human body and people's behavior. And that could be a point for the over-the-counter drugs, about what "abuse" means or how "harm" is defined. Also do a little check on the reasoning behind your statements. For example, I wondered about your last line, "drugs are wrong, therefore, should not be legal." It seems a little circular to me. Or a statement like the one before that, that his points are good and true but also wrong and false. Or maybe here, what you want to think about is whether some are effective and others are not. For example, is it an all-or-none situation? Could, if someone were checking into a rehab center, could they get legally administered drugs and then be weaned from them somehow, so they wouldn't rip off convenience stores to get money for drugs?

Now, I think you've got a good start here, Nancy, and I'd, um, but it's clear that it's just a start, and there are some really good opportunities here to think through the issue and develop this into a strong paper. Um, you'll also, this is a preliminary draft, so you won't be worrying too much at this point about the grammatical and other surface matters, but when you've developed it further you'll, you're gonna want to be tough on yourself about all these little, you know, you shift tenses in the beginning of paragraph two, and you'll want to check for consistency there, and little nagging problems like "and ect." which seems redundant, and spelling like "imagrants" and "laudanun," which has an -m, and commas. Oh, and also, one of the points of this assignment is to chart the changes in your thinking as we go through the process, so don't worry if you start out strongly and modify your position. You know, I wrote a semi-angry letter to one of my colleagues the other day on the computer and went to bed and the next day when I looked at it I'd changed my mind. And I think that's natural.

Ok, Nancy, see you on Friday.

```
┌─────────────────────────────────────────────────────────┐
│              What If Drugs Were Legal?                    │
│              Patricia Stock's Comments                    │
└─────────────────────────────────────────────────────────┘
```

What If Drugs Were Legal?
Patricia Stock's Comments

Dear Nancy,

I turned with interest to reading John LeMoult's "Legalize Drugs" after reading your first draft of "What If Drugs Were Legal?" I read LeMoult's essay four times. I wanted to follow his argument carefully, first, because you reacted to it so strongly as to almost dismiss it out-of-hand ("My only and most important argument to LeMoult is the physical harm it would bring by legalizing drugs."), and second, because LeMoult himself introduced his argument by wondering if it possible, rationally, to consider legalizing drugs. ("Perhaps it is time to think the unthinkable.")

I did not find LeMoult's essay "short and sweet" as you did. I found it detailed and complex. I found his strategy for presenting his ideas sophisticated. He asked me as his reader to bring a lot of what I know about the world to his argument. Perhaps you and I found the argument so different because we have had different life experiences. Let me illustrate what I mean by offering you my reading *[italicized and in brackets]* of the paragraph in LeMoult's essay from which you drew information for your essay:

Drugs have been part of our society for some time. *[Okay, so why do you mention that?]* The first antidrug laws in the United States were passed in 1914. *[I didn't know that. I wonder what the significance of the date is.]* They were really anti-Chinese laws, because people on the West Coast were alarmed at the rise of opium dens among Chinese immigrants. *[Oh, so he's arguing that they were racist laws. Laws were passed because Chinese people were smoking opium. The Chinese people were different; therefore, insecure west coast Americans decided their habits were bad. I think I see where he is going with this. I guess that before the Chinese smoked opium in the United States there were no drug laws. Maybe they were racist laws, but isn't smoking opium something to stop before the custom spread in this country? I see in my mind's eye a vision of the emperor's wife in the film "The Last Emperor." Opium smoking is hideous.]* Before that, there were plenty of opium addicts in the United States *[I didn't know that. What makes him say that? What are his facts?]* but they were mostly white middle-class women who took laudanum (then available over the counter) *[Ah, I didn't know laudanum was opium]* because it was considered unacceptable for women to drink alcohol. *[That is amazing. It was unacceptable for them to drink alcohol, but it was okay for them to take opium. So, opium was acceptable when mostly white middle-class women took it, but not when Chinese immigrants took it. Of course, he doesn't mention much about alcohol here, but his reference to it makes me think of prohibition and what happened then. Not only were people suffering from alcoholism, but they were also getting robbed and killed because of the lucrative business that criminals like Al Capone made of smuggling and selling liquor illegally. LeMoult's allusion makes me think of the failure of prohibition: it failed to stop drinking, and it fostered crime and corruption. I suppose he wanted these ideas to come to my mind when he alluded to alcohol.]*

You can see what was going on in my mind as I read LeMoult, Nancy. I am interested in what was going on in your mind as you read his essay. As I read the second paragraph of your essay, I realized you were reading him very differently from me. Perhaps having grown up as you have at a time when drugs have been used by school children, when so many young people are at-risk because of them, you have read LeMoult with a very different understanding of what he is writing about than I.

It would be good for me to learn how you read him. Let's schedule a conference to talk about your reading of LeMoult and your essay as well.

The Four Seasons
Context

BACKGROUND

This is the final draft of the fourth essay of the course. You have not responded to previous draftings of this paper.

Students have already written a personal narrative, a thesis-support essay, and a comparison-contrast essay. The class has emphasized writing as a process and has worked on those composing strategies and features of discourse that you would typically emphasize in the first half of Freshman Composition.

You may assume that students have the option of rewriting, for a change in grade, one of their course papers by the end of the term.

David is a confident, perhaps even a cocky, student who comes across as someone who thinks he is a better writer than (in your view) he is. However, his confidence is by no means groundless. You have been both taken with and disappointed by aspects of his previous writings, and now you receive this paper.

THE ASSIGNMENT

Most of you are off at school and in a new place, away from the people and settings you have become accustomed to and attached to. Similarly, those of you who are from Tallahassee have likely not had the time or the opportunity to visit some of the old places that are special to you.

Choose some place, atmosphere, or situation that you miss from home—or, if you *are* at home, that you have not had the chance to experience for some time, and miss. Depict this scene, mood, or setting in a way that will allow your reader—someone who does not know about it—to see the significance it has for you.

Remember that because your aim is to give readers a sense of place, you will do well to use specific details.

The Four Seasons
Final Draft

David B.
Final Draft

The Four Seasons

I like Tallahassee very much. The heat and sunshine almost everyday makes each day very pleasant. I intend to spend my next four and one half years here, but I miss my other home, Syracuse, New York. One thing that I truly miss about Syracuse is the four seasons. Each season is distinct and clear in its own way. I will do my best to describe each season to you, but remember that my description cannot compare to experiencing each season for itself.

In the Spring the ground is soft from the melting snow. You can feel the moist ground wanting to seep into your shoes. As the ground begins to dry, the trees begin to blossom and the faint smell of pollen lingers in the air. The flowers work their way out of the ground and bloom for another year. The familiar sound of geese is heard overhead as you look into the sky and see a "V" formation travelling north for the summer. A long winter's nap has ended for the bears, squirrels, rabbits and other hibernating animals. After they awake, their chattering conversations ramble through the forest.

Not only do the animals come out of their shelter in the springtime, but also people. Many people have a tendency to "hole up" in the wintertime. All your neighbors, that you thought had died, open up their houses to allow the spring breeze to come along and carry away that musty air that built up during winter. You can hear voices and

lawnmowers everywhere as people are outside doing their springtime yard work. Wives are planting new flowers while husbands are raking and mowing the lawn. Spring is the season of awakening where everything becomes refreshing.

Following Spring is the season that most people look forward to, that is Summer. Summer is the time of the year when kids are everywhere, because school has been let out. You can hear their voices and giggles fill the atmosphere. People are always outside in the summertime because the sun beats down onto the earth and warms everything up. There are enormous amounts of families going to the beach for the weekend or going on vacation for a week. As you look down the road, you can see heat waves resting on the pavement. The foliage is green and spirits are high. There is a feeling of warmth amongst neighbors, friends, and family.

Fall is my favorite season. I do not care for the way Fall strolls into Tallahassee, the way the leaves and flowers just shrivel away. In Syracuse you can tell when Fall has arrived, because the leaves turn rustic, auburn, garnet, and gold. They fall from the trees onto your lawn, where you spend hours raking the leaves into a pile. After the leaves are sitting neatly in a humongous pile, you may get this crazed feeling. This feeling might just cause you to run and dive into that neat pile. As you are sitting in a natural mattress an aroma of the dried leaves stimulates your olfactories. This aroma gives you a feeling that you are secure.

When you wake up on a typical fall morning you can look out the window and see the ground lightly dusted with frost. So when you get dressed you may put on a sweater. The fall weather is sometimes referred to as

"sweater-weather", because you are able to wear a sweater and be perfectly comfortable. The sweater is just enough to keep the chill off of you. This is a sign that winter is just around the corner.

Winter is the last season of the year. It ranks a close second to Fall in my opinion. Many people complain about snow, but I love it. There is nothing that can compare to the feeling of taking a walk in the winter at night, when the sky is clear and everything is placid. The moon glistens off the snow. While you stroll along, you can hear the soft scrunching of that magical white carpet underneath your feet. You can "feel Jack Frost nipping at your nose" and the rosiness in your cheeks. Yet you stay warm, nestled underneath your winter garb. The atmosphere that surrounds you is serene. It is as though you could disrobe yourself and still stay warm.

After your walk, in the "winter wonderland", you return to the homestead. After hanging up your coat, hat, gloves, and scarf, you shake off the cold and sit by the fire. That burning wood, that has been seasoned since the summer, smells so wonderful and the heat it radiates could lull a person to sleep. Winter nights are great to cuddle up with that special person, by the fire, and listen to the wind blowing outside or watch the snow fall to the ground. That snow gives you a refreshing feeling.

These were my brief descriptions of the four seasons in Syracuse. Of course I only told of the good things about each season. I enjoy the changing seasons and when school is through, I intend to move back up north. The weather down here may be fine for some people, but it was not meant for me. The only real way to understand what I was trying to describe is to experience the four seasons for yourself.

The Four Seasons
Donald Stewart's Comments

David B.
Final Draft

The Four Seasons

I like Tallahassee very much. The heat and sunshine almost everyday makes each day very pleasant. I intend to spend my next four and one half years here, but I miss my other home, Syracuse, New York. One thing that I truly miss about Syracuse is the four seasons. Each season is distinct and clear in its own way. I will do my best to describe each season to you, but remember that my description cannot compare to experiencing each season for itself.

In the Spring the ground is soft from the melting snow. You can feel the moist ground wanting to seep into your shoes. As the ground begins to dry, the trees begin to blossom and the faint smell of pollen lingers in the air. The flowers work their way out of the ground and bloom for another year. The familiar sound of geese is heard overhead as you look into the sky and see a "V" formation travelling north for the summer. A long winter's nap has ended for the bears, squirrels, rabbits and other hibernating animals. After they awake, their chattering conversations ramble through the forest.

Not only do the animals come out of their shelter in the springtime, but also people. Many people have a tendency to "hole up" in the wintertime. All your neighbors, that you thought had died, open up their houses to allow the spring breeze to come along and carry away that musty air that built up during winter. You can hear voices and

lawnmowers everywhere as people are outside doing their springtime yard work. Wives are planting new flowers while husbands are raking and mowing the lawn. Spring is the season of awakening where everything becomes refreshing.

Following Spring is the season that most people look forward to ◯ that is Summer. Summer is the time of the   *;* year when kids are everywhere, because school has been let out. You can hear their voices and giggles fill the atmosphere. People are always outside in the summertime because the sun beats down onto the earth and warms everything up. There are enormous ^ <u>amounts</u> of families   ^ *"number"?* going to the beach for the weekend or going on vacation for a week. As you look down the road, you can see heat waves <u>resting on</u> the pavement. The foliage is green and   *"rising from"?* spirits are high. There is a feeling of warmth amongst neighbors, friends, and family.

Fall is my favorite season. I do not care for the way Fall strolls into Tallahassee, the way the leaves and flowers just shrivel away. In Syracuse you can tell when Fall has arrived, because the leaves turn <u>rustic</u>, auburn, garnet, and   *Sure this is the right word?* gold. They fall from the trees onto your lawn, where you spend hours raking ^ <u>the leaves</u> into a pile. After the leaves   ^ *"them"* are sitting neatly in a humongous pile, you may get this crazed feeling. This feeling might just cause you to run and dive into that neat pile. As you are sitting in a natural mattress an aroma of the dried leaves stimulates your <u>olfactories</u>. This aroma gives you a feeling that you are   *pretentious language* secure.

When you wake up on a typical <u>f</u>all morning you can   *cap.* look out the window and see the ground lightly dusted with frost. So when you get dressed you may put on a sweater. The fall weather is sometimes referred to as

"sweater-weather" ⊙ because you are able to wear a
sweater and be perfectly comfortable. The sweater is just
enough to keep the chill off of you. This is a sign that winter is just around the corner.

commas and periods
always go inside quotes.

Winter is the last season of the year. It ranks a close
second to Fall in my opinion. Many people complain
about snow, but I love it. There is nothing that can compare to the feeling of taking a walk in the winter at night,
when the sky is clear and everything is placid. The moon
glistens off the snow. While you stroll along, you can hear
the soft scrunching of that magical white carpet underneath your feet. You can "feel Jack Frost nipping at your
nose" and the rosiness in your cheeks. Yet you stay warm,
nestled underneath your winter garb. The atmosphere that
surrounds you is serene. It is as though you could disrobe
yourself and still stay warm.

After your walk, in the "winter wonderland" ⊙ you
return to the homestead. After hanging up your coat, hat,
gloves, and scarf, you shake off the cold and sit by the fire.
That burning wood, that has been seasoned since the summer, smells so wonderful and the heat it radiates could lull
a person to sleep. Winter nights are great to cuddle up
with that special person, by the fire, and listen to the wind
blowing outside or watch the snow fall to the ground.
That snow gives you a refreshing feeling.

These ^ were my brief descriptions of the four   *are?*
seasons in Syracuse. Of course ^ I only told of the good
things about each season. I enjoy the changing seasons
and when school is through, I intend to move back up
north. The weather down here may be fine for some   people, but it was not meant for me. The only real way to
understand what I was trying to describe is to experience
the four seasons for yourself.

David—

This is a good topic for a student who's from Syracuse, New York, but going to school in Tallahassee, Florida. Since I'm from a part of the country that has four equally balanced seasons, I don't think I'd like the Sun Belt at all. Like you, I want some change, and I especially like nippy Fall and Winter days. I dislike intense heat and intense cold, but there is no Shangri-La. If I have to choose between summer-like weather most of the time, and the four seasons, I'll take the latter.

Okay. I think you chose a good subject for two reasons: you're in a place where you will not experience the four seasons, and you convince me that you do like that variety.

But now we run into some problems. Have you described the four seasons in Syracuse, or have you described four idealized seasons? I think the latter, and I'll tell you why. In describing Spring, you mention the trees blossoming, flowers working their way out of the ground, geese flying north overhead, and a long winter's nap ending for bears, squirrels, rabbits and other hibernating animals. These are all clichés about Spring. If you must use them, particularize them. Instead of telling us about blossoming trees, tell us how you look forward to the blooming of the redbud tree in your front yard, and of the flowering crab which follows right behind it. Tell us about the particular flowers which blossom in your yard in Syracuse. We'll skip the geese, but let's take a hard look at your list of hibernating animals. How many bears roam the streets of Syracuse? Or do you make frequent trips to the zoo to see them come out of hibernation? If you lived in Yellowstone Park in the winter, mention of hibernating bears would be quite natural. Here, a reader does a double take. What bears are there in Syracuse, or anywhere nearby? Even more to the point, tree squirrels do not hibernate. In winter they are busy digging in places where they buried seeds during the summer. Are you talking about ground squirrels? Do they live in Syracuse? Rabbits don't hibernate, either. The fact that you used these examples suggests to me that you were just tossing off clichéd descriptions of Spring rather than giving us some honest descriptions of Spring in Syracuse. There were, however, a couple of places where you provided some very fine detail. For example, the line, "the faint smell of pollen lingers in the air," is terrific. That's a superb detail. Even the moist ground wanting to seep into one's shoes is pretty good. But the "chattering conversation" of awakening animals rambling through the forest is no good at all.

I won't go into excessive detail, but the same kinds of problems show up in your descriptions of the other seasons.

In Summer, for example, you talk about families going to the beach. In Syracuse? Isn't the nearest beach Lake Ontario, and is it fit to swim in? Perhaps it is. I know Erie was a mess and still may be. At any rate, we need to know what beaches you're talking about. The "going-to-the-beach" detail is a Summer cliché for many parts of the country.

In Fall we get "raking Autumn leaves." Can't you tell us something special about Fall in Syracuse? So, the leaves turn. Fine. Aren't there some particularly spectacular maples in the city? Or other hardwoods whose leaves turn a brilliant red? How about shrubs? In my backyard we have a burning bush which I enjoy tremendously every Fall. It turns a brilliant red and stays that way for some time.

Winter turns out to be a popular song. Why don't you tell us what Syracuse winters are really like? Are they as bad as those in Buffalo, with all that snow? How cold does it get? Any ice skating available?

My larger point is that your descriptions of the seasons are conventional and largely clichéd. Why not give us a detailed picture of the seasons as you experience them in Syracuse?

There's not much to say about the organization of the paper. You go from season to season. I've already commented on aspects of the style of this paper. The good details tell us that you are capable of fresh insights, but, for the most part, you do not provide them or clothe them in language which is distinctive. I wish you would consistently work up to your potential.

The editing is not much of a problem. I've marked a few things which ought to be corrected.

The Four Seasons
Anne Gere's Comments

David B.
Final Draft

The Four Seasons

I like Tallahassee very much. The heat and sunshine almost everyday makes each day very pleasant. I intend to spend my next four and one half years here, but I miss my other home, Syracuse, New York. One thing that I truly miss about Syracuse is the four seasons. Each season is distinct and clear in its own way. I will do my best to describe each season to you, but remember that my description cannot compare to experiencing each season for itself.

In the Spring the ground is soft from the melting snow. You can feel the moist ground wanting to seep into your shoes. As the ground begins to dry, the trees begin to blossom and the faint smell of pollen lingers in the air. The flowers work their way out of the ground and bloom *Good description.* for another year. The familiar sound of geese is heard overhead as you look into the sky and see a "V" formation travelling north for the summer. A long winter's nap has ended for the bears, squirrels, rabbits and other hibernating animals. After they awake, their chattering conversations ramble through the forest. *Do conversations ramble?*

Not only do the animals come out of their shelter in the springtime, but also people. Many people have a tendency to "hole up" in the wintertime. All your neighbors, that you thought had died, open up their houses to allow the spring breeze to come along and carry away that musty air that built up during winter. You can hear voices and

lawnmowers everywhere as people are outside doing their springtime yard work. Wives are planting new flowers while husbands are raking and mowing the lawn. Spring is the season of awakening where everything becomes refreshing.

Can women rake and men plant?

Following Spring is the season that most people look forward to, that is Summer. Summer is the time of the year when kids are everywhere, because school has been let out. You can hear their voices and giggles fill the atmosphere. People are always outside in the summertime because the sun beats down onto the earth and warms everything up. There are enormous amounts of families going to the beach for the weekend or going on vacation for a week. As you look down the road, you can see heat waves resting on the pavement. The foliage is green and spirits are high. There is a feeling of warmth amongst neighbors, friends, and family.

How does this warmth show itself?

Fall is my favorite season. I do not care for the way Fall strolls into Tallahassee, the way the leaves and flowers just shrivel away. In Syracuse you can tell when Fall has arrived, because the leaves turn rustic, auburn, garnet, and gold. They fall from the trees onto your lawn, where you spend hours raking the leaves into a pile. After the leaves are sitting neatly in a humongous pile, you may get this crazed feeling. This feeling might just cause you to run and dive into that neat pile. As you are sitting in a natural mattress an aroma of the dried leaves stimulates your olfactories. This aroma gives you a feeling that you are secure.

How could you combine these sentences?

When you wake up on a typical fall morning you can look out the window and see the ground lightly dusted with frost. So when you get dressed you may put on a sweater. The fall weather is sometimes referred to as

"sweater-weather", because you are able to wear a sweater and be perfectly comfortable. The sweater is just enough to keep the chill off of you. This is a sign that winter is just around the corner.

Winter is the last season of the year. It ranks a close second to Fall in my opinion. Many people complain about snow, but I love it. There is nothing that can compare to the feeling of taking a walk in the winter at night, when the sky is clear and everything is placid. The moon glistens off the snow. While you stroll along, you can hear the soft scrunching of that magical white carpet underneath your feet. You can "feel Jack Frost nipping at your nose" and the rosiness in your cheeks. Yet you stay warm, nestled underneath your winter garb. The atmosphere that surrounds you is serene. It is as though you could disrobe yourself and still stay warm.

After your walk, in the "winter wonderland", you return to the homestead. After hanging up your coat, hat, gloves, and scarf, you shake off the cold and sit by the fire. That burning wood, that has been seasoned since the summer, smells so wonderful and the heat it radiates could lull a person to sleep. Winter nights are great to cuddle up with that special person, by the fire, and listen to the wind blowing outside or watch the snow fall to the ground. That snow gives you a refreshing feeling.

These were my brief descriptions of the four seasons in Syracuse. Of course I only told of the good things about each season. I enjoy the changing seasons and when school is through, I intend to move back up north. The weather down here may be fine for some people, but it was not meant for me. The only real way to understand what I was trying to describe is to experience the four seasons for yourself.

Why is this weather not meant for you?

David—

    This paper is filled with excellent descriptions. You have done a very good job of conveying to your audience the "feel" of the seasons. Phrases like "V formation," "heat waves resting on the pavement," "auburn, garnet and gold," and "soft scrunching" make your descriptions particularly vivid. I come away from this paper with a clear sense of place. Your use of the second person (you) is also effective because it draws the reader into your account. The significance of the four seasons for you remains somewhat vague. Although I understand that you take pleasure in each of the four seasons, I'm still not sure if they have any other meaning for you.

    As noted in the margins, there are several usage problems in this paper. Please check each one and see me if you have questions about any of them.

The Four Seasons
Chris Anson's Comments

[Note: Anson creates a scenario where Dave has handed in, along with his draft, an audio tape on which he has recorded his concerns about the writing. He is responding to both the tape and the writing. Anson also assumes that students have met in a conference group to discuss earlier drafts of their papers.]

Hi, Dave. Well, having grown up in New England, I share a lot of your feelings about the beauty of the different seasons in the northern part of the country. (In fact, I spoke to my mother yesterday and she said they'd gotten nine inches of snow over the weekend!)

First let me talk about structure. A paper with the topic of the four seasons has a real natural structure; it's hard to see an alternative to, uh, to one section on each of the seasons. It's interesting that you chose to start with spring. That's obviously one way to do it because it's the, traditionally the first season of the year when everything comes to life again, and that forces you to end with winter, which has a kind of serenity, not quite the sense of ending and death that fall conveys but certainly not a feeling of life. Now essentially, if you're sticking to one chunk on each season, you've got four alternatives. One possibility would be to begin with summer, then work your way through to spring, which has, um, gives you the advantage of ending on a note of rebirth and rejuvenation. The one you chose is fine, but you didn't say anything about it in your revision plans following the conference group, and we'd really spent some time talking about these various possibilities.

Uh, I guess my strongest reaction has to do with the question of credibility. Because what you're trying to do here is presumably describe something so that people who haven't experienced it can do so through your words. And in this case, if you romanticize too much, and if it's clear that you're romanticizing, um, your reader may question the credi- . . . well, let me put it this way, your reader may be less prone to accepting the case you make for the beauty of the seasons, especially if you're separating yourself from your readers by implying, you know, "you haven't experienced this, so let me tell you how wonderful it is." Part of the problem, for me anyway, stems from two things—a tendency to exaggerate without providing specific, realistic details, and a tendency to interpret the, uh, the phenomenon you're describing very subjectively, so that *your* impressions, *your* sensations and feelings are at the center of the piece.

The exaggeration problem is pretty quickly remedied. Bruce talked about how he was bothered by the image of bears and squirrels and rabbits all carrying on a kind of woodland conversation, and I think I agree, but you really didn't rethink that much. Along those lines, some specific expressions we questioned in the conference group were things like, um, "enormous amounts of families" (by the way, if you're going to say that, it should be "numbers," and we've talked already about that mass vs. count noun business), and "humongous pile," and "stimulating your olfactories," and the cliché about Jack Frost. And Jody also objected to the sex-role stereotyping of wives planting flowers while husbands rake leaves and mow the lawn. Anyway, all this is a matter of a few stylistic revisions which are easily done.

The other problem is harder to describe, but it concerns, um, how much we as readers depend on your feelings to capture the essence of the seasons. Giving impressions and personal responses is perfectly fine to do, but I think it needs to be balanced with some very descriptive details. And, um, what gives me the sense that you haven't really pushed this piece much from the rough draft we talked about comes in your last line, when you say [flipping through paper], when you say here, um, "The only real way to understand what I was trying to describe is to experience the four seasons for yourself." I think we all said to scrap the entire last paragraph because it doesn't do anything, and I even recall that you put a line through it, so what happened? The point of the essay is essentially to give the reader an experience through words, but here it's as if you've told us, "well, you've wasted your time reading this, because I can't capture it in language." And then the whole essay sort of collapses in on itself.

Anyway, I think you get the point here, and I don't want to repeat what we talked about last week. So, what I'd encourage you to do here, Dave, is to spend a lot more time thinking through your drafts before turning them in. Remember that that's where most of the learning comes in; if you, um, if you shortchange yourself at this stage, you'll be giving up that chance to think of alternative strategies, tones, styles, words, and so on.

All in all, this project is about a solid C. OK, Dave, see you in class.

The Four Seasons
Glynda Hull's Comments

David B.
Final Draft

The Four Seasons

I like Tallahassee very much. The heat and sunshine almost everyday makes each day very pleasant. I intend to spend my next four and one half years here, but I miss my other home, Syracuse, New York. One thing that I truly miss about Syracuse is the four seasons. Each season is distinct and clear in its own way. I will do my best to describe each season to you, but remember that my description cannot compare to experiencing each season for itself.

This sentence and its sibling at the end could be seen as an author providing an escape-hatch. Is this tactic okay?

In the Spring the ground is soft from the melting snow. You can feel the moist ground wanting to seep into your shoes. As the ground begins to dry, the trees begin to blossom and the faint smell of pollen lingers in the air. The flowers work their way out of the ground and bloom for another year. The familiar sound of geese is heard overhead as you look into the sky and see a "V" formation travelling north for the summer. A long winter's nap has ended for the bears, squirrels, rabbits and other hibernating animals. After they awake, their chattering conversations ramble through the forest.

A vivid image

Not only do the animals come out of their shelter in the springtime, but also people. Many people have a tendency to "hole up" in the wintertime. All your neighbors, that you thought had died, open up their houses to allow the spring breeze to come along and carry away that musty air that built up during winter. You can hear voices and

I hadn't thought of people hibernating too—this is a neat comparison.

lawnmowers everywhere as people are outside doing their springtime yard work. Wives are planting new flowers while husbands are raking and mowing the lawn. Spring is the season of awakening where everything becomes refreshing.

Following Spring is the season that most people look forward to, that is Summer. Summer is the time of the year when kids are everywhere, because school has been let out. You can hear their voices and giggles fill the atmosphere. People are always outside in the summertime because the sun beats down onto the earth and warms everything up. There are enormous amounts of families going to the beach for the weekend or going on vacation for a week. As you look down the road, you can see heat waves resting on the pavement. The foliage is green and spirits are high. There is a feeling of warmth amongst neighbors, friends, and family.

Fall is my favorite season. I do not care for <u>the way Fall strolls into Tallahassee</u>, the way the leaves and flowers just shrivel away. In Syracuse you can tell when Fall has arrived, because the leaves turn rustic, auburn, garnet, and gold. They fall from the trees onto your lawn, where you spend hours raking the leaves into a pile. After the leaves are sitting neatly in a humongous pile, you may get this crazed feeling. This feeling might just cause you to run and dive into that neat pile. As you are sitting in a natural mattress an aroma of the dried leaves stimulates your olfactories. <u>This aroma gives you a feeling that you are secure</u>.

Another neat image–but I don't get how "strolling" is a way of "shrivelling."

When you wake up on a typical fall morning you can look out the window and see the ground lightly dusted with frost. So when you get dressed you may put on a sweater. The fall weather is sometimes referred to as

Wow–the smell of dried leaves must conjure up powerful associations for you. I bet you could write an interesting paper just about this.

"sweater-weather", because you are able to wear a sweater and be perfectly comfortable. The sweater is just enough to keep the chill off of you. This is a sign that winter is just around the corner.

Winter is the last season of the year. It ranks a close second to Fall in my opinion. Many people complain about snow, but I love it. There is nothing that can compare to the feeling of taking a walk in the winter at night, when the sky is clear and everything is <u>placid</u>. The moon glistens off the snow. While you stroll along, you can hear the soft scrunching of that magical white carpet underneath your feet. You can "feel Jack Frost nipping at your nose" and the rosiness in your cheeks. Yet you stay warm, nestled underneath your winter garb. The atmosphere that surrounds you is serene. It is as though you could disrobe yourself and still stay warm.

This word seems just right.

After your walk, in the "winter wonderland", you return to the homestead. After hanging up your coat, hat, gloves, and scarf, you shake off the cold and sit by the fire. That burning wood, that has been seasoned since the summer, smells so wonderful and the heat it radiates could lull a person to sleep. Winter nights are great to cuddle up with that special person, by the fire, and listen to the wind blowing outside or watch the snow fall to the ground. That snow gives you a refreshing feeling.

These were my brief descriptions of the four seasons in Syracuse. Of course I only told of the good things about each season. I enjoy the changing seasons and when school is through, I intend to move back up north. The weather down here may be fine for some people, but it was not meant for me. The only real way to understand what I was trying to describe is to experience the four seasons for yourself.

David—

You've got an unusual paper here in that some readers will love it and some will feel just as strongly in the opposite direction. What I want you to do is figure out what it is about your paper, and about different readers, that could produce such different reactions. For example,

(1) Your seasonal portraits could have, with a few exceptions, been written by someone who grew up in Tallahassee. What will some readers like about this quality; what will others dislike?

(2) You say at the end of your paper that you've told only the good things about the seasons. Why might this be pleasant to some readers but offensive to others?

(3) You use a lot of phrases that are often used in conjunction with the seasons. Again, what will some readers like about this, others dislike, and why?

Given your consideration of these questions, would you now make any changes in your paper? Why or why not?

The Four Seasons
Rebecca Mark's Comments

David B.
Final Draft

Rather than writing as if some imaginary reader were experiencing this change of seasons, why don't you speak from your own experience. Use "I" and you will avoid the generic sound of the whole essay.

The Four Seasons

I like Tallahassee <u>very much</u>. The heat and sunshine almost everyday makes each day <u>very pleasant</u>. I intend to spend my next four and one half years here, but I miss <u>my other home,</u>^ Syracuse, New York. One thing that I truly miss about Syracuse is the four seasons. Each season is distinct and clear in its own way. I will do my best to describe each season to you, but remember that my description cannot compare to ^ experiencing each season for[itself.] *yourself*

In the Spring the ground is soft from the melting snow. * You can feel the moist ground wanting to seep into your shoes. As the ground begins to dry, the <u>trees begin to blossom</u> and the <u>faint smell of pollen lingers in the air</u>. The flowers work their way out of the ground and bloom for another year. The familiar sound of geese is heard overhead as you look into the sky and see a "V" formation travelling north for the summer. <u>A long winter's nap</u> has ended for the bears, squirrels, rabbits and other hibernating animals. After they awake, their <u>chattering conversations</u> ramble through the forest.

Not only do the animals come out of their shelter in the springtime, but also people. Many people have a tendency to "hole up" in the wintertime. All your neighbors, <u>that you thought</u> ^ <u>had died,</u> ^ <u>open up their houses</u> to allow the spring breeze to come along and carry away that musty air that built up during winter. You can hear voices and

You might think of a more specific and creative title for your next essay.

Sounds boring. You might want to make this sense of boredom a conscious choice by emphasizing how nice and pleasant everything is.

Might want to combine sentences using subordinate construction.

^ *Nice touch*
^ *"to you experiencing"*

These are clichés. You can avoid clichés by letting us know exactly where you are, what trees you are looking at, who is with you, is it only pollen that you smell?

Sounds like Disney. Could be anywhere USA, not specifically Syracuse.

^ *Nice touch—your voice.*
^ *How? Be specific.*

MARK

lawnmowers everywhere as people are outside doing their springtime yard work. <u>Wives are planting new flowers while husbands are raking and mowing the lawn</u>. Spring is the season of awakening where everything becomes refreshing.

Stereotypical gender roles. Do your mother and father and all their friends actually divide the labor in this fashion, and if they do what do you think about this?

Following Spring is the season that ^ <u>most people</u> look forward to, that is Summer. Summer is the time of the year when kids are everywhere, because school has been let out. You can hear their voices and giggles fill the atmosphere. People are always outside in the summertime because the sun beats down onto the earth and warms everything up. There are enormous amounts of families going to ^ <u>the beach</u> for the weekend or going <u>on vacation</u> for a week. As you look down the road, you can see heat waves resting on the pavement. The <u>foliage is green</u> and spirits are high. There is a feeling of warmth amongst neighbors, friends, and family.

^ Do you? Let us hear your voice.

Name specific children.

^ What beach?

Where?

What land?

How do people in your community express this "feeling"?

Fall is my favorite season. I do not care for the way Fall strolls into Tallahassee, the way the leaves and flowers just shrivel away. In Syracuse you can tell when Fall has arrived, because the leaves turn rustic, auburn, garnet, and gold. They fall from the trees onto your lawn, where ^ <u>you</u> spend hours raking the leaves into a pile. After the leaves are sitting neatly in a ^ <u>humongous</u> pile, you may get this crazed feeling. This feeling might just cause you to run and dive into that neat pile. As you are sitting in a natural mattress an aroma of the dried leaves stimulates your olfactories. This aroma gives you a feeling that you are secure.

Yes. Excellent. This is the kind of personal involvement you need throughout the essay.

^ "J"

^ Good—your voice.

Too "safe." What other feelings does this experience give you? J remember the wild feeling of being buried alive by my brothers in a pile of musty leaves.

When you wake up on a typical fall morning you can look out the window and see the ground ^ <u>lightly dusted</u> with frost. So when you get dressed you may put on a sweater. The fall weather is sometimes referred to as

^ Cliché

"sweater-weather", because you are able to wear a sweater and be perfectly comfortable. The sweater is just enough to keep the chill off of you. This is a sign that winter is just around the corner.

Winter is the last season of the year. It ranks a close second to Fall in my opinion. Many people complain about snow, but I love it. There is nothing that can compare to the feeling of taking a walk in the winter at night, when the sky is clear and everything is placid. ^ The moon glistens off the snow. While you stroll along, you can hear the soft scrunching of that magical white carpet underneath your feet. You can "feel Jack Frost nipping at your nose" and the rosiness in your cheeks. Yet you stay warm, nestled underneath your winter garb. The atmosphere that surrounds you is serene. It is as though you could disrobe yourself and still stay warm.

^ *Cliché*

Let us hear a story, a narrative, of what you or you and some of your friends did in the snow. Also, Syracuse snow isn't just any snow. It is some of the deepest snow in the country. Let us see, feel, hear, smell, taste that snow.

After your walk, in the "winter wonderland", you return to the homestead. After hanging up your coat, hat, gloves, and scarf, you shake off the cold and sit by the fire. That burning wood, that has been seasoned since the summer, smells so wonderful and the heat it radiates could lull a person to sleep. Winter nights are great to cuddle up with that special person, by the fire, and listen to the wind blowing outside or watch the snow fall to the ground. That snow gives you a refreshing feeling.

These were my brief descriptions of the four seasons in Syracuse. Of course I only told of the good things about each season. I enjoy the changing seasons and when school is through, I intend to move back up north. The weather down here may be fine for some people, but it was not meant for me. The only real way to understand what I was trying to describe is to experience the four seasons for yourself.

Yes but why? We perhaps could appreciate them more fully in their rich complexity.

MARK

David,

    While this is a good idea for an essay, you don't ever let us feel what it is about the seasons you really miss. Because you write from a generic position, we don't hear about Syracuse, your life, your memories. Instead you describe a northern town which could be anywhere USA and the people could be anyone. I know it is often difficult to use the first person "I" and to let people in on your real feelings about home, but try it once anyway. You will write an essay you will truly enjoy writing and anyone who reads it will learn about you and Syracuse. The best writers and journalists are the ones who write down the most specific details and images. If you would like to rewrite this I would love to read it.

Tribute
Context

BACKGROUND

This essay is written in response to the second assignment in the course. It is handed in as a final draft with no previously required drafts. Up to this point, the class has focused on invention and on substantive content in writing.

You may assume that students have the option of rewriting any of their course papers for a change in grade.

In these first two weeks of the course, you have come to sense that Jennifer, the writer of this paper, is a quiet, sensitive person and a student writer who values both her writing and her teachers' responses to her writing.

THE ASSIGNMENT

Think of a person who has made a strong impression on who you are or on what you think or believe. Describe the impression and explain how he or she made this imprint on you.

Tribute
Final Draft

Jennifer S.
Final Draft

Tribute

It's a shame how it takes a tragic slap in the face to wake us from our sheltered dreams of life. We travel through life with an umbrella and while life falls in torrents, we hide until like a bolt of lightning something shatters to make us understand. I know now not to judge a person by the obvious but to look deep into the heart, where the true person lies. For him I learned too late, for it was with the permanent closing of his eyes that mine were opened for the first time to see him, the real him, as well as everyone, everything else, as if the sun had risen for the first time.

Daddy was a smart man, smarter than I'll ever be. I can't remember asking him a question that went unanswered long. If he didn't know the answer (which seemed rare), he knew how to find it. And if a math problem could be solved, he could solve it.

He had a love and a talent for music. He used to say that he had missed his calling, that he should have been a musician. He played the guitar to relax. I find myself humming those familiar tunes that I grew up hearing day after day, though never tiring of.

Daddy was the one I came to with the splinters and loose teeth because they were a little more than mom and a little Bactine could handle. I used to wonder why he didn't become a surgeon. Other times, when he had me laughing so hard that I was crying, I wondered why he

he didn't become a comedian. At times like that, no one could have asked for a better father.

But alcoholism is a disease that captures and imprisons its victim and offers no escape. It toys with the personality and eventually physically destroys its victim. Daddy was no exception. He was too weak to overcome his opponent, so as time unfolded Daddy became weaker and more addicted. His personality was so different from day to day that we never knew whether it would be "Daddy" or "not." The horrors I experienced through these years turned me almost completely against that wonderful, helpless person who, at that point, needed support probably more than he ever needed it before. How could I have been so blind? Deep down, I knew he didn't mean to act so cruel, but I was too young and too weak myself to cope, to put up with the horrible atmosphere and relentless fear I was trapped in. So I quietly turned against him, left him out in the cold, and slammed the door right in his face.

Then, on a warm summer night, July 20, 1976, we were downstairs when we heard him collapse upstairs, a noise that could have been most anything, but we knew instantly the sound of death. The remainder of the night is rather vague. The siren, the neighbors, the tears, the fear, all centered around a man lying in the floor, his lungs weak and begging for air. Seeing him suffering is still a recurring nightmare. The ambulance came and rushed him to the hospital. But it was too late. He died of a massive heart attack before he ever reached the hospital. The doctor said his heart literally exploded into a million lifeless fragments in his body.

I walked outside the emergency room away from the commotion, the aroma of medicine the presence of death.

The night was warm, but the chill of death was more dominant. I wanted to cry, but the tears would not come. Perhaps they just wouldn't have done my feeling justice. I thought back to when I was a little girl sitting on my Daddy's knee. What happened to those times? Where did it all go wrong? I remember looking up at the sky and wondering if he was looking down at me. "Did you know I loved you, Daddy?", I whispered to the vast, star-lit night, "Did you know that?"

Then came the tears. I couldn't stop them. They rolled down my face onto my chin, then into the night, gone forever. I had to get it out, cry away my sorrow, my regret, but not that a man had died, but that I had let him slip away without giving him the love and respect he needed and deserved.

At that moment, on that muggy summer night in July, I learned something. Like a bolt of lightning it struck, and the truth, like rain, flooded. I learned not to judge people on the outside, but to look deep, beyond the surface, to the heart, where the true person really lives. I can't bring my Daddy back, but I can treat his memory with enough respect not to let it happen again. Daddy is gone now, but not completely. A part of him will live on forever within the hearts and minds of those who believe in him. I am one of those.

Tribute
Frank O'Hare's Comments

Jennifer,

This is a stunning accomplishment, a real tribute to the memory of your father, whose qualities shine through—musician, tender healer for his little daughter, problem solver, comedian. I am sure that your father knew that you loved him, that you believe in him.

But it is difficult to treat an affliction like alcoholism as a disease. The horrors you experienced over those many years, the horrible atmosphere, the fear can become intolerable. I wish you could see that you probably didn't "let him slip away," that you are being too harsh when you say that you "slammed the door right in his face." Alcoholism corrodes the personality and brutalizes the alcoholic's relatives too. You are both victims of this dread disease.

This paper is an impressive blending of all five elements of PACES.* Your overall purpose was clear, and you crafted this essay for your audience with great skill. You have skillfully selected specific incidents from your life with your father to give your readers a sense of his qualities. You also showed respect for your audience (and for your father's memory) by avoiding specific details about the years of suffering.

Paragraphs six through eight are dramatic, effective, convincing. You showed admirable skill in shaping and organizing the story of his death and your reaction to it after you left the emergency room. The self you have projected convinces us of your sincerity and love.

There are, of course, one or two spots where I'd like to see you tighten up your sentence structure, but, quite frankly, I don't want to deal with them now. I want to enjoy this essay—its skillful organization, its powerful details, its maturity, its love.

When I began to bracket in the left-hand margin passages that were especially effective, I thought I might be bracketing too many!** As you know, a double bracket (and I rarely double bracket!) means you have produced a real gem.

This paper vibrates with honesty. Well done! Thanks for sharing this memory.

[* "PACES" is an anagram for Purpose, Audience, Code (or language), Experience, and Style.]

[** In the text, O'Hare brackets something in every paragraph. He double brackets paragraph 1, the first half of paragraph 6, the second half of paragraph 7, paragraph 8, and the end.]

Tribute
Cheryl Nims' Comments

Jennifer S.
Final Draft

Tribute

It's a shame how it takes a tragic slap in the face to wake us from our sheltered dreams of life. [We travel through life with an umbrella and while life falls in torrents, we hide until like a bolt of lightning something shatters to make us understand.] I know now not to judge a person by the obvious ^ but to look deep into the heart, where the true person lies. For him I learned too late, for it was with the permanent closing of his eyes that mine were opened for the first time to see him, the real him, as well as everyone, everything else, as if the sun had risen for the first time.

Daddy was a smart man, smarter than I'll ever be. I can't remember asking him a question that went unanswered long. If he didn't know the answer (which seemed rare), he knew how to find it. And if a math problem could be solved, he could solve it.

He had a love and a talent for music. He used to say that he had missed his calling, that he should have been a musician. He played the guitar to relax. I find myself humming those familiar tunes that I grew up hearing day after day, though never tiring of.

Daddy was the one I came to with the splinters and loose teeth because they were a little more than mom and a little Bactine could handle. I used to wonder why he didn't become a surgeon. Other times, when he had me laughing so hard that I was crying, I wondered why he

How right you are. Good opening.

* *This is such a powerful sentence! See what you can do with punctuation here—to help your reader follow.*

^ *"outward physical appearance"? "what we think we see"? Help me out here.*

It's very comforting to feel that our fathers know everything, isn't it?

Great detail!

he didn't become a comedian. At times like that, no one could have asked for a better father.

But alcoholism is a disease that captures and imprisons its victim and offers no escape. It toys with the personality and eventually physically destroys its victim. Daddy was no exception. He was too weak to overcome his opponent, so as time unfolded Daddy became weaker and more addicted. His personality was so different from day to day that we never knew whether it would be "Daddy" or "not." The horrors I experienced through these years turned me almost completely against that wonderful, helpless person who, at that point, needed support probably more than he ever needed it before. How could I have been so blind? Deep down, I knew he didn't mean to act so cruel, but I was too young and too weak myself to cope, to put up with the horrible atmosphere and relentless fear I was trapped in. So I quietly turned against him, left him out in the cold, and slammed the door right in his face.

Then, on a warm summer night, July 20, 1976, we were downstairs when we hard him collapse upstairs, a noise that could have been most anything, but we knew instantly the sound of death. The remainder of the _night is rather vague_. The siren, the neighbors, the tears, the fear, all centered around a man lying in the floor, his lungs weak and begging for air. Seeing him suffering is still a recurring nightmare. The ambulance came and rushed him to the hospital. But it was too late. He died of a massive heart attack before he ever reached the hospital. The doctor said his heart literally exploded into a million lifeless fragments in his body.

I walked outside the emergency room away from the commotion, the aroma of medicine ^the presence of death.

Nice move into this prgh. Sets up startling contrast.

Jennifer, I can only imagine how hard this must have been.

Good transition into remainder of prgh.

I know it must be.

* Use punctuation here to make reader stop and pause.

The night was warm, but the chill of death was more dom-   *Good contrast. I can*
inant. I wanted to cry, but the tears would not come.   *"feel" the chill.*
Perhaps they just wouldn't have done my feeling ^ justice.   ^ *"feelings"?*
I thought back to when I was a little girl sitting on my
Daddy's knee. What happened to those times? Where did
it all go wrong? I remember looking up at the sky and
wondering if he was looking down at me. "Did you know
I loved you, Daddy?", I whispered to the vast, star-lit
night, "Did you know that?"

Then came the tears. I couldn't stop them. They
rolled down my face onto my chin, then into the night,
gone forever. I had to get it out, cry away my sorrow, my
regret, ~~but~~ not that a man had died, but that I had let him
slip away without giving him the love and respect he needed and deserved.

At that moment, on that muggy summer night in
July, I learned something. Like a bolt of lightning it
struck, and the truth, like rain, flooded. I learned not to
judge people on the outside, but to look deep, beyond the
surface, to the heart, where the true person really lives. I
can't bring my Daddy back, but I can treat his memory
with enough respect not to let it ^ happen again. Daddy is   ^ *What?*
gone now, but not completely. A part of him will live on
forever within the hearts and minds of those who believe
in him. I am one of those.

Jennifer,

*Thank you for sharing your father with me. I hope writing helped you con-
tinue sorting through your own feelings. I think your father was lucky to have
a daughter like you. And I'll bet he knew how much you loved him.*

*Watch sentence structure and punctuation—particularly in the areas marked
with *. Remember that our readers depend on punctuation signals to help
them read with understanding.*

Very Powerful! Good Job!

Tribute
Tilly Warnock's Comments

Jennifer S.
Final Draft

Tribute

It's a shame how it takes a tragic slap in the face to wake us from our sheltered dreams of life. We travel through life with an umbrella and while life falls in torrents, we hide until like a bolt of lightning something shatters to make us understand. I know now not to judge a person by the obvious but to look deep into the heart, where the true person lies. For him I learned too late, for it was with the permanent closing of his eyes that mine were opened for the first time to see him, the real him, as well as everyone, everything else, as if the sun had risen for the first time.

Try reading this aloud to hear what you've written.

Your last sentence here brings together previous ideas and sets up reader expectations.

Daddy was a smart man, smarter than I'll ever be.   I can't remember asking him a question that went unanswered long. If he didn't know the answer (which seemed rare), he knew how to find it. And if a math problem could be solved, he could solve it.

He had a love and a talent for music. He used to say that he had missed his calling, that he should have been a musician. He played the guitar to relax. I find myself humming those familiar tunes that I grew up hearing day after day, though never tiring of.

You bring him and your relationship to him alive.

Daddy was the one I came to with the splinters and loose teeth because they were a little more than mom and a little Bactine could handle. I used to wonder why he didn't become a surgeon. Other times, when he had me laughing so hard that I was crying, I wondered why he

he didn't become a comedian. At times like that, no one could have asked for a better father.

But alcoholism is a disease that captures and impris- *The shift here works well, I think. Your voice is con-vincing.* ons its victim and offers no escape. It toys with the personality and eventually physically destroys its victim. Daddy was no exception. He was too weak to overcome his opponent, so as time unfolded Daddy became weaker and more addicted. His personality was so different from day to day that we never knew whether it would be "Daddy" or "not." The horrors I experienced through *You mention the horrors but don't show your reader. Is this when you felt you weren't looking beyond the surface? Look at your final para-graph.* these years turned me almost completely against that won-derful, helpless person who, at that point, needed support probably more than he ever needed it before. How could I have been so blind? Deep down, I knew he didn't mean to act so cruel, but I was too young and too weak myself to cope, to put up with the horrible atmosphere and relent-less fear I was trapped in. So I quietly turned against him, left him out in the cold, and slammed the door right in his face.

Then, on a warm summer night, July 20, 1976, we were downstairs when we hard him collapse upstairs, a noise that could have been most anything, but we knew instantly the sound of death. The remainder of the night is rather vague. The siren, the neighbors, the tears, the fear, all centered around a man lying in the floor, his lungs weak and begging for air. Seeing him suffering is still a recurring nightmare. The ambulance came and rushed him to the hospital. But it was too late. He died of a massive heart attack before he ever reached the hospital. The doc-tor said his heart literally exploded into a million lifeless fragments in his body.

I walked outside the emergency room away from the commotion, the aroma of medicine the presence of death.

The night was warm, but the chill of death was more dominant. I wanted to cry, but the tears would not come.
Perhaps they just wouldn't have done my feeling justice.
I thought back to when I was a little girl sitting on my
Daddy's knee. What happened to those times? Where did
it all go wrong? I remember looking up at the sky and
wondering if he was looking down at me. "Did you know
I loved you, Daddy?", I whispered to the vast, star-lit
night, "Did you know that?"

Then came the tears. I couldn't stop them. They
rolled down my face onto my chin, then into the night,
gone forever. I had to get it out, cry away my sorrow, my
regret, but not that a man had died, but that I had let him
slip away without giving him the love and respect he needed and deserved.

At that moment, on that muggy summer night in
July, I learned something. Like a bolt of lightning it
struck, and the truth, like rain, flooded. I learned not to
judge people on the outside, but to look deep, beyond the
surface, to the heart, where the true person really lives. I
can't bring my Daddy back, but I can treat his memory
with enough respect not to let it happen again. Daddy is
gone now, but not completely. A part of him will live on
forever within the hearts and minds of those who believe
in him. I am one of those.

*I'm not sure I under-
stand this last para-
graph. Are you saying
that you didn't see your
father's heart. Your first
page suggests that you
did.*

Jennifer—

*You bring together many ideas and feelings about your father and make clear
how he influenced what you think and believe. In your conclusion, you say you
didn't see your father beyond the surface, although you suggest earlier, for
example on pages 1 and 2, that you did. I hope you will continue to work with
this. Have you shown it to your family? Can you imagine writing this for
strangers who might benefit from your experience and understanding? What do
you want to do with this now?*

Tribute
Richard Larson's Comments

Jennifer S.
Final Draft

Tribute

It's a shame how it takes a tragic slap in the face to wake us from our sheltered dreams of life. We travel through life with an umbrella and while life falls in torrents, we hide until like a bolt of lightning something shatters to make us understand. I know now not to judge a person by the obvious but to look deep into the heart, where the true person lies. For him I learned too late, for it was with the permanent closing of his eyes that mine were opened for the first time to see him, the real him, as well as everyone, everything else, as if the sun had risen for the first time.

See comment at end.

Daddy was a smart man, smarter than I'll ever be. I can't remember asking him a question that went unanswered long. If he didn't know the answer (which seemed rare), he knew how to find it. And if a math problem could be solved, he could solve it.

He had a love and a talent for music. He used to say that he had missed his calling, that he should have been a musician. He played the guitar to relax. I find myself humming those familiar tunes that I grew up hearing day after day, though never tiring of.

Daddy was the one I came to with the splinters and loose teeth because they were a little more than mom and a little Bactine could handle. I used to wonder why he didn't become a surgeon. Other times, when he had me laughing so hard that I was crying, I wondered why he

he didn't become a comedian. At times like that, no one could have asked for a better father.

But alcoholism is a disease that captures and imprisons its victim and offers no escape. It toys with the personality and eventually physically destroys its victim. Daddy was no exception. He was too weak to overcome his opponent, so as time unfolded Daddy became weaker and more addicted. His personality was so different from day to day that we never knew whether it would be "Daddy" or "not." The horrors I experienced through these years turned me almost completely against that wonderful, helpless person who, at that point, needed support probably more than he ever needed it before. How could I have been so blind? Deep down, I knew he didn't mean to act so cruel, but I was too young and too weak myself to cope, to put up with the horrible atmosphere and relentless fear I was trapped in. So I quietly turned against him, left him out in the cold, and slammed the door right in his face.

Which years were these? How many years were good years, before alcoholism struck him? How old were you when it did?

Then, on a warm summer night, July 20, 1976, we were downstairs when we hard him collapse upstairs, a noise that could have been most anything, but we knew instantly the sound of death. The remainder of the night is rather vague. The siren, the neighbors, the tears, the fear, all centered around a man lying in the floor, his lungs weak and begging for air. Seeing him suffering is still a recurring nightmare. The ambulance came and rushed him to the hospital. But it was too late. He died of a massive heart attack before he ever reached the hospital. The doctor said his heart literally exploded into a million lifeless fragments in his body.

How old were you?

I walked outside the emergency room away from the commotion, the aroma of medicine the presence of death.

LARSON

The night was warm, but the chill of death was more dominant. I wanted to cry, but the tears would not come.
Perhaps they just wouldn't have done my feeling justice.
I thought back to when I was a little girl sitting on my
Daddy's knee. What happened to those times? Where did
it all go wrong? I remember looking up at the sky and
wondering if he was looking down at me. "Did you know
I loved you, Daddy?", I whispered to the vast, star-lit
night, "Did you know that?"

Then came the tears. I couldn't stop them. They
rolled down my face onto my chin, then into the night,
gone forever. I had to get it out, cry away my sorrow, my
regret, but not that a man had died, but that I had let him
slip away <u>without giving him</u> the love and respect he needed and deserved.

Not even as a child? You sounded earlier as if you did love him then.

At that moment, on that muggy summer night in
July, I learned something. Like a bolt of lightning it
struck, and the truth, like rain, flooded. I learned not to
judge people on the outside, but to look deep, beyond the
surface, to the heart, where the true person really lives. I
can't bring my Daddy back, but I can treat his memory
with enough respect not to let it happen again ^. Daddy is
gone now, but not completely. A part of him will live on
forever within the hearts and minds of those who believe
in him. I am one of those.

See end comment.

^ With whom?

See attached comment.

Jennifer--

This paper is an earnest remembrance of your father, as well as a reflection by you on some of your behavior (not very fully detailed) toward him. But the focus is on your feelings of guilt, and of discovery of how much you loved your father, after he had died. The paper does not tell much of the *impression* your father made on you, except so far as his death has affected you. Could you tell us more of your father's impact or influence on you, and tell us how you came to feel that influence? How did he help you to become what you are? How did he, while he was alive, help you to learn? Or did he? That is, adjust the "focus" of your piece a little--away from you to some extent, to your father and what he was or did.

You give us a little information about the positive qualities of your father, but you lead us to think that there may have been more such qualities, and that the qualities may have shaped you more than you tell us about. The reader would like to know more about who your father was and what he did.

You might reconsider your first and final paragraphs. Do you think that might be too heavy with metaphoric characterizations of your feelings? I think you might soften the first and last paragraphs, making clear your feelings of regret about not appreciating your father but doing so more economically than you now do.

I'd urge you to do another draft of this piece with the suggestions I just made in your mind as you work. If you'd like to discuss the paper before you revise, please do come in.

The John Cougar Concert
Context

BACKGROUND

This selection presents two rough drafts and the final draft of a concert review. **Respond to the final draft.**

This assignment is the fourth of five multiple-draft assignments based on various aims of discourse. The final draft is the third draft the student has handed in. You have read and perhaps commented on these earlier drafts.

You may assume that students have the option of rewriting one of their course papers for a change in grade.

THE ASSIGNMENT

Choose a book, movie, album, a product, or anything else about which we tend to make judgments, and write an essay evaluating this subject. Base your evaluations on appropriate criteria and support them with reasons and evidence. Design the essay for publication in the school newspaper.

The John Cougar Concert
First Draft

The John Cougar Concert

Stated as being one of the best rock shows on the road by <u>Rolling Stone Magazine</u>, John Cougar took his fans and me, on what I call a roller coaster ride of emotion. And what a ride it was.

Before the show even started, the most noticeable thing was the stage. There it stood, quite bare with only a white backdrop. This plain setting pointed to John Cougar's no-nonsense approach to rock and roll. Although it was a plain setting, the crowd knew it was going to be a great show.

Refering back to what I said earlier about roller coaster of emotion, the ride was about to start. Starting with "Grandma's Theme", and "Smalltown" from the "<u>Scarecrow</u>" album, John Cougar got the emotions rolling. After those semi-fast songs, John Cougar really got the crowd on their feet with "Authority Song", "Serious Business", and "Crumblin Down". Once John Cougar had the audience at a emotional high, he went into an extended version of "Play Guitar" in which he had the whole audience singing to it. Then came kind of a reflective mood for lovers when he sang "Jack and Diane", and "Everyone needs a Hand to Hold on to." Then the emotions turned to a more somber mood when John Cougar talked about the plight of the American farmer. This is a political stance he is very well known for. He also talked briefly about Farm Aid which was a concert that he and other rock stars were organizing to help the American farmers. After talking briefly about those issues, John Cougar quickly went into one of his more popular songs that tell of many typical farmers–"Rain on the Scarecrow." This song typifies what happens when a farmer runs out of money and the consequences he must face.

John Cougar knew that these issues were very important to him, but he didn't want to dwell on them for too long. That is why he got the crowd started on a climb towards another emotional peak. He sang "R.O.C.K. in the U.S.A." which is a salute to 1960's rock and roll. It is a very upbeat song about how some famous rockers such as James Brown, Frankie Lyman, and Mitch Ryder finally made it in the music business. Right after that, Cougar went into a 60's medley with classic songs such as "Proud Mary", "Under the Boardwalk", and "Cold Sweat." These songs topped off an incredible variety of emotions.

John Cougar, in my opinion, did a very good job at presenting his concert in a roller coaster form. I believe he knew that by starting off slowly, then picking up momentum, then slowing things down with his songs for lovers, then almost putting a mood of saddness with his stance on the situation of American farmers, and getting the crowd on it's feet again with a classic 60's medley, would leave a very satisfied crowd. It was a very interesting form, but effective in every sense of the word.

The John Cougar Concert
Second Draft

The John Cougar Concert

On December 13, 1985, at the Ohio Center, John Cougar took his fans and me on what I call a roller coaster ride of emotion. And what a ride it was. Rolling Stone Magazine even stated, "Forget the Springsteen comparison, this is simply one of the best rock shows on the road."

Before the show even started, the most noticeable thing was the stage. At most concerts you would expect fancy equipment and garish decor, but Cougar's stage was practically bare with only a white backdrop. This plain setting pointed to John Cougar's no-nonsense approach to rock and roll.

It was nearing 8:00 pm (the scheduled time to begin) and the crowd was starting to get excited. People were chanting, "We want Cougar, we want Cougar!" Suddenly the lights went out and the roller coaster of emotions was about to start.

A roar of elation went through the crowd when Cougar appeared on stage. There he stood dressed only in a white t-shirt, worn out Levis, and cowboy boots. Again, pointing to his no-nonsense approach to rock and roll.

Immediately he started into one of his newest hits, "Small Town" from the "Scarecrow" album. The emotions really started rolling with that song. People were jumping up and down and standing on their chairs. After that "warm up" song, Cougar got the whole crowd on their feet with "I want all of you to get up off your seat and get into it!" With that, Cougar went into his more energetic songs such as "Authority Song", "Serious Business", and "Crumblin Down". The whole audience must have listened to Cougar's command because everyone was singing along, dancing, and having a great time. John Cougar knew he had the audience at an emotional high because he went into an extended version of "Play Guitar." The crowd was in a frenzy during that song. People were releasing so much energy by cheering and dancing.

After all his high powered songs, John Cougar slowed the emotions by singing a couple of songs for lovers. Songs such as "Jack and Diane", and "Everyone Needs

Needs a Hand to Hold on to" had a few couples embracing each other. After that, Cougar paced across the stage in a very serious manner. He started to talk about an issue that is very important to him–that of the American farmer and the problems that they are facing. It is an issue he is very well known for. He also talked briefly about Farm Aid which was a benefit concert that he and other rock stars were organizing to help American farmers. With that, Cougar went into a very emotional song, "Rain on the Scarecrow" off of the "Scarecrow" album. This song typifies what happens when a farmer runs out of money and the consequences he must face. (Add lines in song.) You could actually feel the emotions of saddness and despair by the incredible way John Cougar projected this song. (Explain why people like songs. Plus quote.)

John Cougar knew that these issues were very important to him, but he didn't want to dwell on them for too long. That is why he got the crowd started on a climb towards another emotional peak. He sang "R.O.C.K. in the U.S.A." which is a salute to 1960's rock and roll. It is a very upbeat song about how some famous rockers such as James Brown, Frankie Lyman, and Mitch Ryder finally made it in the music business. You could tell Cougar was really working hard because you could see sweat drip off his face. Cougar again urged the crowd to join in. He quickly went into a 60's medly with classic songs such as "Proud Mary", "Under the Boardwalk", and "Cold Sweat." These songs topped off an incredible variety of emotions.

John Cougar, in my opinion, did a very good job at presenting his concert in a roller coaster form. I believe he knew that by starting off slow, then fast, then slow, and then fast again would leave a very satisfied crowd. I could tell it was a very satisfied crowd because instead of rushing for the exit, everyone sat back down for a few minutes to relax after the show was over. It was a very interesting form, but effective in every sense of the word.

The John Cougar Concert
Final Draft

Frank C.
Final Draft

The John Cougar Concert

On a cold and blustery evening on December 13, 1985, at the Ohio Center, John Cougar took his fans and me on what I call a roller coaster ride of emotion. And what a ride it was. <u>Rolling Stone Magazine</u> even stated, "Forget the Springsteen comparison, this is simply one of the best rock shows on the road."

Before the show even started, the most noticeable thing was the stage. At most concerts you would expect fancy equipment and flashy decor, but Cougar's stage was practically bare with only a white backdrop and basic instruments. This plain setting pointed to John Cougar's no-nonsense approach to rock and roll.

It was nearing 8:00 P.M. (the scheduled time to begin) and the crowd was starting to get excited. People were chanting, "We want Cougar, we want Cougar!" My old high school friends and I were also joining in the chanting. We, like all the others, wanted to see this man from a small town in Indiana perform. Suddenly the lights went out and the roller coaster of emotions was about to start.

A roar of elation went through the crowd when Cougar appeared on stage. There he stood with his shoulder length black hair and intent eyes. There was no fancy costume either, just a white t-shirt, worn out Levis, and cowboy boots. Again, pointing to his no-nonsense approach to rock and roll.

Immediately he belted into one of his newest hits,

"Small Town" from the Scarecrow album. The emotions really started rolling with that song. People were jumping up and down and standing on their chairs. After that "warm up" song, Cougar yelled at the crowd in a very urging voice, "I want all of you to get up off your seat and get into it!" With that, Cougar roared into his more energetic songs such as "Authority Song", "Serious Business", and "Crumblin Down". The whole audience must have listened to Cougar's command because everyone was singing along, dancing, and having a great time. John Cougar knew he had the audience at an emotional high because he went into an extended version of "Play Guitar". People released so much energy by cheering and singing during this song. I even found myself to be out of breath.

After all his high powered songs, John Cougar slowed the emotions by singing a couple of songs for lovers. Songs such as "Jack and Diane" and "Everyone Needs A Hand To Hold On To" had a few couples embracing each other. After that, Cougar paced across the stage in a very serious manner. He started to talk about an issue that is very important to him - that of the American farmer and the problems that they are facing. It is an issue he is very well known for. He also talked briefly about Farm Aid which was a benefit concert that he and other rock stars were organizing to help American farmers. With that, Cougar went into a very emotional song, "Rain on the Scarecrow". This song typifies what happens when a farmer runs out of money and the consequences he must face. Lines like "Called my old friend Schepman up to auction off the land, he said, John it's just my job and I hope you understand", really makes you feel discouraged, the way you would feel if you had to ask your friend to sell something very dear to you. You could actually feel the emotions of sadness and despair by the incredible way John Cougar projected this song.

John Cougar knew that these issues were very important to him, but he didn't want to dwell on them for too long. That is why he got the crowd started on a climb towards another emotional peak. He sang "R.O.C.K. in the U.S.A." which is a salute to 1960's rock and roll. It is a very upbeat song about how some famous rockers such as James Brown, Frankie Lyman, and Mitch Ryder finally made it in the music business. I could tell Cougar was really working hard because I could see sweat drip off his face. Cougar again urged the crowd to join in. He rocketed into a 60's medley with classic songs such as "Proud Mary", "Under the Boardwalk", and "Cold Sweat". These songs topped off an incredible variety of emotions.

John Cougar, in my opinion, did a very good job at presenting his concert in a roller coaster of emotion. For three hours, he and his band members, including Larry Crane, and Mike Wanchic: guitar, Kenny Aronoff: drums, and Toby Myers: bass played non-stop with no intermissions. Even though there was no opening band, I believe John Cougar knew that by starting slow, then fast, then slow, and then fast again would leave a very satisfied crowd. Satisfying it was, because instead of rushing for the exit, everyone, including myself, had to sit back down to relax. For $16.00, this concert was definitely worth every penny.

The John Cougar Concert
Glynda Hull's Comments

Frank C.
Final Draft

Frank—you've done a fine job with the revisions. With a little fine tuning, this piece will be ready for publication. See what you think about the sentence-level suggestions I've made below.

The John Cougar Concert

On a cold and blustery evening on December 13, 1985, at the Ohio Center, John Cougar took his fans and me on what I call a roller coaster ride of emotion. And what a ride it was. ^ <u>Rolling Stone Magazine</u> ~~even~~ stated, "Forget the Springsteen comparison, this is simply one of the best rock shows on the road."

> ^ *"Even Rolling Stone"— How does this sound to you, the <u>even</u> being put at the front?*

<u>Before the show even started, the most noticeable thing was the stage.</u> At most concerts you would expect fancy equipment and flashy decor, but Cougar's stage was practically bare with only a white backdrop and basic instruments. This plain setting pointed to John Cougar's no-nonsense approach to rock and roll.

> *I'd work on this sentence a little. It might confuse some readers, this idea that the stage is visible <u>before</u> the show.*

It was nearing 8:00 P.M. (the scheduled time to begin) and the crowd was starting to get excited. People were chanting, "We want Cougar, we want Cougar!" [My old high school friends and I were also joining in the chanting. We, like all the others, wanted to see this man from a small town in Indiana perform.] Suddenly the lights went out ^ and the roller coaster of emotions was about to start.

> *I like your addition here. You give the flavor of both the crowd and the singer and suggest a connection between them.*
>
> ,

A roar of elation went through the crowd when Cougar appeared on stage. There he stood with his shoulder length black hair and intent eyes. There was no fancy costume either, ▼ just a white t-shirt, worn out Levis, and cowboy boots. [Again, pointing to his no-nonsense approach to rock and roll.]

> ▼ *Try a dash (–) here instead of a comma.*
>
> *I wonder if there's a way to suggest this rather than say it explicitly. Maybe omit this phrase.*

Immediately he ^ <u>belted</u> into one of his newest hits,

> ^ *I like this word here.*

"Small Town" from the <u>Scarecrow</u> album. The emotions really started rolling with that song. People were jumping up and down and standing on their chairs. After that "warm up" song, Cougar yelled at the crowd in a very urging voice, "I want all of you to get up off your seat and get into it!" With that, Cougar roared into his more energetic songs such as "Authority Song", "Serious Business", and "Crumblin Down". The whole audience must have listened to Cougar's command because everyone was singing along, dancing, and having a great time. <u>John Cougar knew he had the audience at an emotional high because he went into an extended version of "Play Guitar"</u>. People released so much energy by cheering and singing during this song. I even found myself to be out of breath.

Why is this an indication that he knew? Does he usually do this song at such a moment?

After all his high powered songs, John Cougar slowed the emotions by singing a couple of songs for lovers. Songs such as "Jack and Diane" and "Everyone Needs A Hand To Hold On To" had a few couples embracing each other. After that, Cougar paced across the stage in a very serious manner. He started to talk about an issue that is very important to him - ~~that of~~ the American farmer and the problems that they are facing. [It is an issue he is very well known for]. He also talked briefly about Farm Aid which was a benefit concert that he and other rock stars were organizing to help American farmers. With that, Cougar went into a very emotional song, "Rain on the Scarecrow". This song typifies ^ ~~what happens when a farmer~~ runs out of money ~~and the consequences he must face~~. Lines like "Called my old friend Schepman up to auction off the land, he said, John it's just my job and I hope you understand", really makes you feel discouraged the way you would feel if you had to ask your friend to sell something very dear to you. You could actually feel the

See if you think this reads better.

Maybe omit? Do you see why?

^ "the consequences for a farmer when he" — I don't know—your version may be better.

Maybe use the symbol for a line break (I) where appropriate.

This doesn't sound quite right broken apart by the lyrics. Can you re-arrange?

emotions of sadness and despair by the incredible way
John Cougar projected this song.

^ ~~John Cougar knew that~~ these issues were very impor-   ^ *Although*
tant to ^ ~~him, but~~ he didn't want to dwell on them for too   ^ *John Cougar*
long. That is why he got the crowd started on a climb   *-Listen to both versions,*
towards another emotional peak. He sang "R.O.C.K. in   *and see what the differ-*
the U.S.A." which is a salute to 1960's rock and roll. It is   *ence is.*
a very upbeat song about how some famous rockers such
as James Brown, Frankie Lyman, and Mitch Ryder finally
made it in the music business. I could tell Cougar was
really working hard because I could see sweat drip off his
face. Cougar again urged the crowd to join in. He rocketed into a 60's medley with classic songs such as "Proud
Mary", "Under the Boardwalk", and "Cold Sweat". These
songs topped off an incredible variety of emotions.

John Cougar, in my opinion, did a very good job at
presenting his concert in a roller coaster of emotion. For
three hours, he and his band members ^ including Larry   —
Crane, and Mike Wanchic; ^ guitar, ^ Kenny Aronoff^;   , ; ,
drums, ^ and Toby Myers; ^ bass ^ played non-stop with no   ; , —
intermissions. Even though there was no opening band, I   *See if you understand*
believe John Cougar knew that by starting slow, then fast,   *how I've used semi-*
then slow, and then fast again would leave a very satisfied   *colons (;) and commas*
crowd. Satisfying it was, because instead of rushing for   *here, and why.*
the exit, everyone, including myself, had to sit back down
to relax. For $16.00, this concert was definitely worth
every penny.

The John Cougar Concert
Peter Elbow's Comments

Dear Frank,

I could wrestle you some more if I wanted to–about the fact that you decided to keep pushing the rollercoaster image when I said in my comment on your draft that I thought you over-used it. I persist in my feeling–feels kind of overdone or even corny to me–but in fact I'm glad to see you making up your own mind, deciding to use it, making your own choice. I'm curious whether that decision was one you made on your own, or whether it was based on group members saying they liked your stressing the rollercoaster image. (And after all, I'm not the typical or main reader of the student paper.)

You've made your final draft much stronger and tighter. In almost every case it seems to me as though what you add is more detail, more specifics. (Even down to naming the names of the co-musicians–and I like that. I like hearing people's names even when they don't mean anything to me. Makes it all sound more real.) These details help sharpen the piece; help us see or hear. What's interesting to me also, is that such details (his hair, you running out of breath) make it more like a *story* and less like a standard review. Where it was mostly, "what he did," it's become a bit more, "what it was like for me going to the concert." It's true that you sort of tried to make earlier versions about what happened to you, but they weren't so convincing. So here too, where I suggested that you break out of narrative more (some reflections on the nature of the music in one of the pieces or some other reflection), you chose to go *more* in the direction of narrative. And in this case I no longer have any impulse to fight you–you persuade me it's good your way.

A stray thought: by calling the banker "Schepman," do you think he was trying to imply he was Jewish? It bothered me; feels like stereotyping. But he calls him "my friend." Did the song make it sound like they were real friends?

I marked places where I felt most life. The wiggly lines were not disaster places but sentences which somehow felt odd or awkward: made me pause or read them twice–or they didn't sound comfortably in my ear.

Best,

Peter

The John Cougar Concert
Ben McClelland's Comments

You have succeeded in placing us with you and the crowd at the Cougar concert, Frank. You establish us in time and place. And you proceed in an orderly chronology. As a reader, I can vicariously experience just about everything there—except, that is, for the music. I'm having trouble hearing the main event: Cougar's music. And since you are my eyes and ears, I'm counting on you to define and evaluate it for me. To be sure, you do explain some basic things—it's energetic, fast, slow, sad, or upbeat. But, Frank, a concert review *evaluates* the music. Suppose I've never heard about Cougar? Help me decide from your characterization of his music whether to buy an album of his.

To do this you need to assess the songs' lyrics (some of which you already do). But also you need to define and rate the musicality of his work—both the composing and the performing. If you're uncertain about how to do this, take a look at some reviews in *Rolling Stone* to get an idea of published reviewers' style and vocabulary. Let me quote a sample from a copy of *RS* that I just picked up from a pile on the floor:

> Heavy hitters on the U.K. independent scene and darlings of the fickle British music press, The Woodentops make hyperactive pop with an appealing esprit de group. Almost every track begins at raveup intensity and stays there; with chirpy lead vocals and warbling keyboards, their records often sound like the Doors' *L.A. Woman* played at 45 rpm speed . . . . Somewhere between an elf and a satyr, diminutive lead singer and songwriter Rolo McGinty is the individual for whom they invented the word fey, and his breathy charisma pervades every track. Skiffly rhythms form the backdrop for sounds that echo everything from rockabilly to hip-hop. On "Wheels Turning" (the first single), guitars shiver and wail, Bo Diddley style, above a sturdy bass and drum thump. [Michael Azerrad, "Review of The Woodentops' 'Wooden Foot Cops on the Highway,'" *Rolling Stone* (May 5, 1988: 75.)]

Coincidentally, the mailman delivered yesterday a published review of a rock band that my son plays in. These few lines illustrate how this reviewer describes "Plan 9" and its music with a combination of "in-group" coinages and standard musical vocabulary:

> They're the ever-changing neo-psych, boffo-grunge unit, the Rhode Island band that has most consistently made dents in the national indie tour . . . Sea Hunt isn't a bad little record, especially the 13-minute title track, the most circular, lilting and swing-oriented of all the extended instrumentals the band has become known for . . . . The blues tinges that have cropped up in the last few years are apparent in the phrasing and riffling of the band's oozy swells. And traces of improvisation remain a tad in the form of McClelland's string work. [Jim Macnie, "Back to the Future," *The Newpaper*, Providence, RI, Section Two, September 15, 1988: 7.]

I hope you'll consider this essay for revision and resubmission. I'd like to hear more about Cougar's music, especially what you think about it.

The John Cougar Concert
Richard Larson's Comments

Frank C.
Final Draft

The John Cougar Concert

On a cold and blustery evening on December 13, 1985, at the Ohio Center, John Cougar took his fans and me on what I call a roller coaster ride of emotion. And what a ride it was. Rolling Stone Magazine even stated, "Forget the Springsteen comparison, this is simply one of the best rock shows on the road."

Before the show even started, the most noticeable thing was the stage. At most concerts you would expect fancy equipment and flashy decor, but Cougar's stage was practically bare with only a white backdrop and basic instruments. This plain setting pointed to John Cougar's no-nonsense approach to rock and roll.

How do you mean "no-nonsense"? How does a bare stage contrast with other performers' approaches?

It was nearing 8:00 P.M. (the scheduled time to begin) and the crowd was starting to get excited. People were chanting, "We want Cougar, we want Cougar!" My old high school friends and I were also joining in the chanting. We, like all the others, wanted to see this man from a small town in Indiana perform. Suddenly the lights went out and the roller coaster of emotions was about to start.

A roar of elation went through the crowd when Cougar appeared on stage. There he stood with his shoulder length black hair and intent eyes. There was no fancy costume either, just a white t-shirt, worn out Levis, and cowboy boots. Again, pointing to his no-nonsense approach to rock and roll.

How do you mean? This, by the way, isn't a sentence.

Immediately he belted into one of his newest hits,

"Small Town" from the <u>Scarecrow</u> album. The emotions really started rolling with that song. People were jumping up and down and standing on their chairs. After that "warm up" song, Cougar yelled at the crowd in a very urging voice, "I want all of you to get up off your seat and get into it!" With that, Cougar roared into his more energetic songs such as "Authority Song", "Serious Business", and "Crumblin Down". The whole audience must have listened to Cougar's command because everyone was singing along, dancing, and having a great time. John Cougar knew he had the audience at an emotional high because he went into an extended version of "Play Guitar". People released so much energy by cheering and singing during this song. I even found myself to be out of breath.

After all his high powered songs, John Cougar slowed the emotions by singing a couple of songs for lovers. Songs such as "Jack and Diane" and "Everyone Needs A Hand To Hold On To" had a few couples embracing each other. After that, Cougar paced across the stage in a very serious manner. He started to talk about an issue that is very important to him - that of the American farmer and *'farmers'?* the problems that they are facing. It is an issue he is very *What exactly is the* well known for. He also talked briefly about ^ <u>Farm Aid</u> *'issue' here? How to help* <u>which</u> was a benefit concert that he and other rock stars *them solve their prob-* were organizing to help American farmers. With that, *lems?* Cougar went into a very emotional song, "Rain on the *^ Punctuate?* Scarecrow". This song typifies what happens when a farmer runs out of money and the consequences he must face. Lines like "Called my old friend Schepman up to auction off the land, he said, John it's just my job and I hope you understand", really makes you feel discouraged, *^ Word form?* the way you would feel if you had to ask your friend to sell something very dear to you. You could actually feel the emotions of sadness and despair by the incredible way John Cougar projected this song.

John Cougar knew that these issues were very important to him, but he didn't want to dwell on them for too long. That is why he got the crowd started on a climb towards another emotional peak. He sang "R.O.C.K. in the ^ U.S.A." which is a salute to 1960's rock and roll. It is a very upbeat song about how some famous rockers such as James Brown, Frankie Lyman, and Mitch Ryder finally made it in the music business. I could tell Cougar was really working hard because I could see sweat drip off his face. Cougar again urged the crowd to join in. He rocketed into a 60's medley with classic songs such as "Proud Mary", "Under the Boardwalk", and "Cold Sweat". These songs topped off an incredible variety of emotions.

^ Punctuate? Maybe omit "which"?

John Cougar, in my opinion, did a very good job at presenting his concert in a roller coaster of emotion. For three hours, he and his band members, including Larry Crane, and Mike Wanchic: guitar, Kenny Aronoff: drums, and Toby Myers: bass played non-stop with no intermissions. Even though there was no opening band, I believe John Cougar knew that by starting slow, then ^ fast, then slow, and then fast again would leave a very satisfied crowd. Satisfying it was, because instead of rushing for the exit, everyone, including myself, had to sit back down to relax. For $16.00, this concert was definitely worth every penny.

"to create"? "in" isn't quite strong enough.

^ "going"?

Frank—

This essay, which seems to me to have changed little since the second draft, is a vivid, engaged, and specific report of Cougar's concert. I value your enthusiasm for the concert and your evident pleasure in it; it's good that you expressed those reactions.

But the paper remains essentially a report of the concert and your personal responses. The assignment, however, asked for an "evaluation" based upon criteria and supported by reasons. To some extent you've given criteria (the emotional "roller coaster") and other standards (the audience's responses), but you do less with these bases for judgment than the assignment meant to elicit. To put the point differently: Is any concert that could be said to create an "emotional roller coaster" good? Is any concert good that has the audience involved? Are these the only, or the principal, bases for judgment? Why? Does the quality of the music played matter? The eloquence of the words as a kind of poetry? The sentiments expressed in the songs? I don't mean to imply that all these matters need to be touched in an essay such as you are writing. But I think that the bases of judgment should be formulated a little more explicitly than you have done here, and that the narrative of the concert might be at least somewhat subordinated to a discussion of features that make the concert, in your view, praiseworthy. That discussion requires *some* detachment.

Writing such a review is, of course, a matter of balance. One *wants* the details; one wants the experience. But, even in a school newspaper, one probably wants a bit more: signs of a detached reflection on whether, overall, the concert was an artistically satisfying experience—and why.

I'd like to see you rewrite this piece with the goal of striking the balance I've just described, somewhat more than the present essay does.

```
┌─────────────────────────────────────────────────────┐
│                                                       │
│            The John Cougar Concert                    │
│            Ronald Lunsford's Comments                 │
│                                                       │
└─────────────────────────────────────────────────────┘
```

The John Cougar Concert
Ronald Lunsford's Comments

[Lunsford presents no comments on the pages of the student's writing. Instead, he identifies places he wants to respond to in the text with a number and writes out his comments on a separate page. (The brackets indicate where he inserts these numbers in the text.) Then he types a letter to the student.]

1. [Prgh 1] I like the roller coaster imagery in your paper.

2. [Prgh 1] Will your readers know what is being referred to with the "Springsteen comparison"? I wonder if it would be more effective to shorten your quote to: "this is simply one of the best shows on the road."

3. [Prgh 1] This is the second use of "even" in two sentences. I think I know what it means in the first sentence, but I am not so sure what it means here? Can you find a better way to say what you mean?

4. [Prgh 4, last line] This is a sentence fragment.

5. [Prgh 5, last line] You use this word "even" again here in a way that makes me wonder exactly what you mean. Do you mean to imply that this is a behavior that you do not usually exhibit, or that your excitement here produced something that it does not often produce—your being out of breath—or something else?

6. [Prgh 6, sentence 8] Somehow, I don't think "typifies" works the way you want it to. Look it up in a good dictionary and see if you agree.

7. [Prgh 6, last line] "Projected" doesn't seem to capture what it is that makes this song so effective in producing this feeling in listeners. Can you help me see how Cougar does this? Is it the tone of his voice, the power of the lines themselves—I don't quite see that in what you've quoted—or what?

8. [Prgh 8, sentence 3] What do the two parts of this sentence—the lack of an opening band and Cougar's pacing of his show—have to do with each other? You imply a connection, but I don't see it. And, look at the structure of this sentence. Your phrase, "starting slow, then fast, then slow, and then fast again," seems like conversational shorthand. I think you mean something like: "by starting with a slow number, then moving to a fast-paced song, offering another slow number, and, finally moving to a second very fast song . . . ." Or, could you simply say, "by moving back and forth between slow and fast songs." . . . At any rate, the way you have your sentence structured now makes it very hard to see what the subject is for the verb "would leave."

Frank,

You have put a good deal of work into this essay, and it is well on its way to being a good evaluation. You convince me that this topic is interesting to you—and that's the first step in engaging your reader. I like the way you have added detail from draft to draft, giving substance to the claims you are making about the concert. And, I like the roller-coaster motif.

If you are still engaged in writing about this topic, I would suggest that you revise this paper for your portfolio. If you do so, consider some of the following suggestions:

1) Make the criteria by which you evaluate this event clearer. If you look back at the assignment, you will see that I am asking for a criterion-based evaluation. In order to write one of these, you need to begin by asking yourself what makes a concert good. I do not mean to suggest that you will turn your paper into a list, but you should have a list in your mind. That will help you decide what materials to keep, and what to drop—and what you might want to add. For example, you tell us in the second paragraph that Cougar's stage was practically bare and you compare it to other stages which are filled with fancy equipment. So, are you suggesting that good concerts have bare stages and not-so-good ones have stages with fancy equipment? I suspect not. But if not, then how does this detail further your purpose of showing that this was a good concert? At this point, your essay is structured by narrative—that is, you seem to be telling us what happened at this concert. In your revision, you may still want to tell the story of this concert, but your sense of what makes a concert good should be the real structuring principle by which you decide what to tell us about it.

2) In places you can do a better job of finding the right words to convey what you mean. In my "marginal" comments, I have drawn attention to your use of certain words—for example, "even" and "typifies." See if you agree with me that you don't quite say what you mean in these, and other, places.

3) Editing. Study the use of periods and commas in quotation marks as explained in your handbook and see if you can correct some of the errors you have in this paper. Also look up the use of the colon in listing, and correct problems in your last paragraph.

I hope these suggestions help. In our next conference, we'll discuss whether you want to revise this essay for your portfolio; if so, be prepared to tell me how (and if) these suggestions might help you in the next draft.

Part Two

An Anthology of Readings on Response

Post-Structural Literary Criticism and the Response to Student Writing

Edward M. White

Responding to texts, whether they are artistic or naive, whether they are sonnets by Milton or diagnostic essays by our freshman composition students, is the business that unites us as teachers of literature and of writing. Theories of reading lie behind the ways we respond to all texts, even though we tend, because of the nature of our training, to be much more aware of these theories when we read literature than when we grade papers. Recent developments in literary theory are bound to be of particular interest to teachers of writing for a number of reasons: they not only make strong statements about the nature of the interaction between reader and writer, but they have seized the imaginations of so many of our new Ph.D.'s and teaching assistants that there is no way to avoid the implications of these theories for our writing programs.

Although writing teachers are a rather conservative lot, they seem to have responded to post-structural literary theory with a surprising calm. I want to suggest in this paper that the general hospitality writing teachers and researchers have shown toward post-structural literary theory is the result of a basic correspondence between these theories and the practice of the best writing teachers.

Despite the forbidding jargon which decorates literary theory these days, at least in part because of its origins in French philosophy, writing teachers have good reason to read and understand the major texts. Post-structural criticism espouses a theory of reading that justifies viewing student writing as part of a larger process. It also has a fundamental ground of practical good sense that helps us understand why the best of us teach the way we do, and why we have so much trouble communicating writing theory to colleagues for whom the New Criticism is still new.

Before we turn to the issues raised by the post-structuralists, it is important to remind ourselves of some of the certainties which we used to be able to rely upon and which recent theories have put in question. Much of structuralist or formalist criticism rested on the supposition that the reader's task was essentially to submit herself to the text, in order to discern the meaning that resided there, quite independent of either the author or the reader. A good location of that idea is Mark Schorer's essay, "Technique as Discovery," first printed in the *Hudson Review* in 1948:

When we speak of technique, then, we speak of nearly everything. For technique is the means by which the writer's experience, which is his subject matter, compels him to attend to it; technique is the only means he has of discovering, exploring, developing his subject, of conveying its meaning, and, finally, of evaluating it. And surely it follows that certain techniques are sharper tools than others, and will discover more; that the writer capable of the most exacting technical scrutiny of his subject matter will produce works with the most satisfying content, works with thickness and resonance, works which reverberate with maximum meaning.

For Schorer, the work reverberates with this meaning on its own, if the technique is sufficient; the work itself has content, thickness, and resonance, independent of author and reader. Our task as readers is to understand so much about technique that we can obtain entry into the achieved content of the work, and hence come to understand the "maximum meaning" it has to offer.

The implications of this theory of reading for the teaching of writing were profound and wide-ranging. On the positive side, it urged readers of student writing to attend to the texts that the student produced, rather than to the student's social class, appearance, or moral predispositions. Since, as Vygotsky taught us, language and thought were virtually the same, the theory provided the teacher with a certain valuable scepticism for the student who claimed, "I know what I mean but I just don't know how to say it": if you don't know how to say it, we could self-righteously reply, then you don't know what you mean! Most important, it focused both students' and teachers' attention on the craftsmanship of prose, what Schorer calls "technique," and on the way that that craftsmanship conveys meaning. In so doing, this theory provided a useful if limited framework for the teaching of writing, since craftsmanship is always teachable, if not always learnable, in a way that inspiration, say, is not.

However, the belief that meaning resided in the text itself caused a series of theoretical and practical problems for writing teachers. Even though every sensible teacher knew we must respond differently to a student text than to a finished piece of literature, the theory gave no good basis for such a different response and suggested few practical ways of coping with the weakest of our students. Most damaging of all, the theory urged us to consider student writing as a product to be analyzed, as if every student composition were a failed Shakespeare sonnet.

Now, despite the popular slogan "writing is a process, not a product," we make ourselves foolish if we ignore the fact that writing is a product as well as a process. Every student turning in a paper to be graded, every scholar producing a paper for delivery or publication or promotion, knows perfectly well that writing is an important and measurable product. But the theory of reading, and hence of writing, that defines writing as only or principally a product distorts the teaching of writing severely. It turns the writing teacher into only a judge of texts, and limits the teacher's intervention (and hence its value) to the end of the writing process, where such intervention is not likely to do very much good.

It thus strikes me as no accident that the proponents of writing as process began articulating their views and pursuing their valuable research at about the same time that post-structural literary critics began arguing that reading was a process, a creative (rather than passive) interaction between reader and text. The constricting theories of the formalists and the structuralists were no more satisfying for the teaching of writing than they were for the reading of literature. Rhetoric, that basic reader-response discipline, began to reassert its claims, and a group of modern rhetoricians began examining how writers, using classical and modern forms of invention, could identify ideas appropriate to the audiences they were addressing. Edward Corbett's *Classical Rhetoric for the Modern Student* came out in 1965, the same year Ross Winterowd published *Rhetoric and Writing*; and Young, Becker, and Pike published their influential *Rhetoric: Discovery and Change* in 1970. Professor Young and many others began to focus the attention of composition teachers upon the sequential and recursive stages of the writing process and upon the many possible locations of useful teacher intervention. Research into the writing process has been flourishing on many fronts in recent years, from the detailed charts and elaborate equipment of Linda Flower and Sondra Perl, to the theoretical and practical work on children's language learning by such diverse investigators as James Britton (whose work reflects the approaches of Piaget and other learning theorists) and Steven Krashen (whose work grows out of linguistics and foreign language learning).

At the same time this burst of activity in the field of composition was going on, structural literary theory was taking root in many of the graduate schools. Jacques Derrida's *Of Grammatology* appeared in 1967, as good a date as any for the beginning of the movement. The 1970s saw major articles and books by Wolfgang Iser (*The Implied Reader*, 1974), and Stanley Fish, whose *Is There a Text in This Class?* (1980) compiles his major articles from the previous decade. In addition, of course, we have an outpouring of books and articles from the familiar catalogue of reader-response and deconstructionist critics, and a covey of new journals such as *Diacritics* and *New Literary Criticism*.

None of the issues raised by post-structural literary criticism are easy or without elaborate complexity. In many ways, the differences among these critics are large, and arguments about those differences have created a lively, if minor, new industry. Nonetheless, it remains possible to speak of these theorists as a group in certain restricted contexts, as I propose to do. They unite in their opposition to the belief that meaning resides in a text, and it is this opposition in particular that I want to pursue here. In *Five Readers Reading* (1975), for example, Norman Holland comes perilously close to presenting a text as a Rorschach blot, open to whatever the reader may discern. Another school of theorists, the "deconstructionists," who have their roots in French philosophy rather than in psychology, disavow this form of psychological subjectivism, but nonetheless argue that, at best, the text offers only a guide to the reader, as if it were a musical score which must be performed or (to use a favorite term of these theorists) "played" in order to become real. A convenient and inclusive summary of many of the attitudes expressed in these books and articles was published in the Fall 1982 issue of *Critical Texts*. Vincent Leitch nicely captures the destabilization of the concept of the text, the peculiar language of the theorists, and the relocation of the reader from outside the reading process (where his job was to discern the meaning in the text) to the center of the process (where he joins with or even replaces the author as creator of meaning):

> In the era of post-structuralism, literature becomes textuality and tradition turns into intertextuality. Authors die so that readers may come into prominence. Selves, whether of critic, poet or reader, appear as language constructions—texts. What are texts? Strings of differential traces. Sequences of floating signifiers. Sets of infiltrated signs, dragging along numerous intertextual elements. Sites for the free play of grammar, rhetoric and illusory reference, as Paul de Man puts it. What about the "meaning" or "truth" of the text? The random flights of signifiers across the textual surface, the dissemination of meaning, offers "truth" under one condition: that the chaotic processes of textuality be willfully regulated, controlled or stopped. Truth comes forth in the reifications of reading. It is not an entity or property of the text. No text utters its truth; the truth lies elsewhere—in a reading. Constitutionally, reading is misreading. Post-structuralism wishes to deregulate controlled dissemination and celebrate misreading.

As with much post-structural theory, once we strip away the jargon, this statement has an almost eerily familiar sound. Where have we seen writing that is evidently a "chaotic process of textuality" which only makes sense to a peculiarly sensitive reader, who must "misread" in order to understand? Where in our experience do we regularly see texts which can at best charitably be called "sequences of floating signifiers"? Whatever one may say about literary texts in this regard (and I do not mean to trivialize the elaborate concepts Leitch alludes to), we can surely agree that this is a most apt description of most of our freshman themes, indeed of student writing in general. I do not say this in mockery. The simple fact is that the definition of textuality and the reader's role in developing the meaning of a text that we find in recent literary theory happens to describe with uncanny accuracy our experience of responding with professional care to the writing our students produce for us.

It is important to distinguish the kind of "misreading" that Leitch describes from the misreading inherent in the New Criticism, where all meaning was assumed to lie in the text. If we are limited to what the student put on the paper, we tend to be literalists, putting aside our intuitions of what the student meant to say or our predictions of what the student could say if he followed the best insights of the text. This formalistic misreading of student writing, which pretends to be objective, demands that the student believe that our concept of what was written is what is "really" there. By comparing the student text with what Nancy Sommers calls our "ideal text," we appropriate the student's text, deny the creative impulse that must drive writing, and turn revision into editing.

Once we accept the necessity of "misreading," as the post-structuralists use the term, we tend to be less sure of the objectivity of our reading and more ready to grant to the student possible intentions or insights not yet present on the page. Even more important, we respond with questions rather than with judgment (or invective!), since our aim is to urge the student back into "the chaotic process of textuality" (that is, the flux of ideas behind the writing), where revision occurs.

Post-structural theory differs most sharply from the old New Criticism in its underlying assumption that meaning is not necessarily identical with expression. This assumption allows us to spend time, as we should in our writing classes, on both invention and revision. We know from our practice as teachers and as writers that the act of invention, the discovery of what we have to say, goes on throughout the writing process; we learn as we write, and successive drafts bring us closer and closer, not to some predetermined coding of the known, but to an understanding of the previously unknown. As teachers of writing, we seek in the texts our students produce that sense of original vision, that unique perception of new combinations of experiences and ideas that Derrida tends to call "différence." Our creative misreading of the drafts we receive, our perception of possibilities as well as product, our awareness that we see on the page only a "trace" of a mind in action, then allow us to ask our students to pursue and refine these traces in revision. This theory of reading brings reading and writing together as parallel acts, both of them consisting of the making of meaning: the writer seeks to make meaning out of experience, while the reader seeks to make meaning out of a text. The best composition teachers help their students improve their writing by making them conscious of readers and of the ways readers interact with their texts.

It is for these reasons, I think, that the most effective teachers of writing are traditionally those who are the most human and the most demanding with their students. Whatever their curriculum, they establish themselves, or other defined audiences, as live and sympathetic readers, willing to participate in the quest for meaning that is writing. The research that Nancy Sommers and others have recently published on teacher response to writing tends to confirm these impressions. They point out that the writing class, to be effective, needs to decenter authority, to model the fact that every writer needs to be—and in fact is—an authority on what he or she is writing. Readers can recognize that authority in the writer without necessarily granting it to the text at hand, and therefore they can urge revision without taking "ownership" of the paper from the writer. (Surely the most irritating question we can hear from our students about their revisions is, "Is that what you wanted?" Revisions should take them closer to what *they* want.) Sommers rightly deplores the confusion she has found in routine paper marking, which almost universally treats the student text as simultaneously a finished product with editing faults and an unfinished part of the writing and thinking process. As this research becomes better known, as it should, writing teachers will find themselves thinking more clearly about their relationship to particular student texts, considering their reading as part of the whole writing process, and hence making more useful and constructive the endless hours of work on student papers.

I have been suggesting that one reason composition teachers have not been, and need not be, taken aback by the new critical theories of the post-structuralists is that, despite the elaborate jargon, many of the new ideas have a very familiar ring to them. The final example I want to use to support this idea is Stanley Fish's concept of "the interpretive community," his ingenious means of rescuing his theory of reading from the anarchy of pure subjectivism. Fish defines an interpretive community as made up of those whose common agreements about how to read texts becomes an agreement about how they will in fact write for themselves those texts: "Interpretive communities are made up of those who share interpretive strategies not for reading (in the conventional sense) but for writing texts, for constituting their properties and assigning their intentions. In other words, these strategies exist prior to the act of reading and therefore determine the shape of what is read rather than, as is usually assumed, the other way around" (171). The concept, according to Fish, serves a number of purposes: "This, then, is the explanation both for the stability of interpretation among different readers (they belong to the same community) and for the regularity with which a single reader will employ different interpretive strategies and thus make different texts (he belongs to different communities)." Fish also argues that literature may be defined as whatever a particular interpretive community decides is literature, since readers for him, in his most recent theoretical phase, actually make texts.

This useful concept helps us, for example, to see why we as composition teachers tend to respond to student writing the way we do: our interpretive community has a set of coherent and powerful assumptions and strategies for approaching (Fish would say writing) student texts. Such texts exist in general in order to be criticized, and Nancy Sommers has found a grim sameness in most of the teacher commentary she and her fellow researchers have collected: "There seems to be among teachers an accepted, albeit unwritten canon for commenting on student texts. This uniform code of commands, requests, and pleadings demonstrates that the teacher holds a license for vagueness while the student is commanded to be specific" (152-53). As Sommers lists the standard comments we tend to write on student papers, whatever they have to say, it becomes apparent that the leaders of composition research have been seeking, in one sense, to shake up an out-of-date interpretive community, to revise what we ask for—and thus what we get—from student writing.

Fish's concept is thus creative, powerful, and useful in many different contexts. But revolutionary? Not in the least. Composition teachers—and English teachers who have participated over the years in holistic essay readings to ensure fairness in the scoring of writing tests—will see the interpretive community as a very familiar innovation indeed. It takes nothing away from these theorists to say that sensible writing teachers were implementing some aspects of their theories in the classroom before the theories were well (or badly) articulated. We need theories to support as well as to generate good practice, and it is all to the good that in recent years these theories have been appearing in great abundance. Besides, we are in a profession (like most professions) where nothing is known unless the "right" people know it, so the whole enterprise of reading and writing profits when literary scholars discover and promote theories that happen to support good composition teaching.

Finally, the teaching of writing goes on, carrying the rest of our scholarship and teaching on its back, with little glory for its theories and small renown even for the stars of its research. Sheridan Blau speaks for the laborers in these classrooms and their practical cast of mind when he writes, "Ultimately the sufficiency of a composition teacher is a function of his capacity to respond to what is in front of him, not by rules but with intelligence." Writing teachers who combine this practical intelligence with respect for the traces of insight to be found as they read student papers will read and profit from post-structural literary criticism without outrage or astonishment at its discoveries.

Works Cited

Blau, Sheridan. *The Center Magazine* 14 (1981): 39.

Corbett, Edward P.J. *Classical Rhetoric for the Modern Student.* New York: Oxford UP, 1965.

Derrida, Jacques. *Of Grammatology.* Trans. G.C. Spivak. Baltimore: Johns Hopkins UP, 1976.

Fish, Stanley. *Is There a Text in This Class? The Authority of Interpretive Communities.* Cambridge: Harvard UP, 1980.

Holland, Norman. *Five Readers Reading.* New Haven: Yale UP, 1975.

Iser, Wolfgang. *The Implied Reader: Patterns of Communication in Prose Fiction from Bunyan to Beckett.* Baltimore: Johns Hopkins UP, 1974.

Leitch, Vincent. " ." *Critical Inquiry* __ (Fall 1982): pp.

Schorer, Mark. "Technique as Discovery." *Hudson Review* 1 (1948): 67-87.

Sommers, Nancy. "Responding to Student Writing." *College Composition and Communication* 33 (May 1982): 148-56.

Winterowd, W. Ross. *Rhetoric and Writing.* Boston: Heath, 1965.

Young, Richard, Alton Becker, and Kenneth Pike. *Rhetoric: Discovery and Change.* New York: Harcourt, Brace and World, 1970.

Responding to Student Writing

Nancy Sommers

More than any other enterprise in the teaching of writing, responding to and commenting on student writing consumes the largest proportion of our time. Most teachers estimate that it takes them at least 20 to 40 minutes to comment on an individual student paper, and those 20 to 40 minutes times 20 students per class, times 8 papers, more or less, during the course of a semester add up to an enormous amount of time. With so much time and energy directed to a single activity, it is important for us to understand the nature of the enterprise. For it seems, paradoxically enough, that although commenting on student writing is the most widely used method for responding to student writing, it is the least understood. We do not know in any definitive way what constitutes thoughtful commentary or what effect, if any, our comments have on helping our students become more effective writers.

Theoretically, at least, we know that we comment on our students' writing for the same reasons professional editors comment on the work of professional writers or for the same reasons we ask our colleagues to read and respond to our own writing. As writers we need and want thoughtful commentary to show us when we have communicated our ideas and when not, raising questions from a reader's point of view that may not have occurred to us as writers. We want to know if our writing has communicated our intended meaning and, if not, what questions or discrepancies our reader sees that we, as writers, are blind to.

In commenting on our students' writing, however, we have an additional pedagogical purpose. As teachers, we know that most students find it difficult to imagine a reader's response in advance, and to use such responses as a guide in composing. Thus, we comment on student writing to dramatize the presence of a reader, to help our students to become that questioning reader themselves, because, ultimately, we believe that becoming such a reader will help them to evaluate what they have written and develop control over their writing (Knoblauch and Brannon).

Even more specifically, however, we comment on student writing because we believe that it is necessary for us to offer assistance to student writers when they are in the process of composing a text, rather than after the text has been completed. Comments create the motive for doing something different in the next draft; thoughtful comments create the motive for revising. Without comments from their teachers or from their peers, student writers will revise in a consistently narrow and predictable way. Without comments from readers, students assume that their writing has communicated their meaning and perceive no need for revising the substance of their text.[1]

Yet as much as we as informed professionals believe in the soundness of this approach to responding to student writing, we also realize that we don't know how our theory squares with teachers' actual practice—do teachers comment and students revise as the theory predicts they should? For the past year my colleagues, Lil Brannon, Cyril Knoblauch, and I have been researching this problem, attempting to discover not only what messages teachers give their students through their comments, but also what determines which of these comments the students choose to use or to ignore when revising. Our research has been entirely focused on comments teachers write to motivate revisions. We have studied the commenting styles of thirty-five teachers at New York University and the University of Oklahoma, studying the comments these teachers wrote on first and second drafts, and interviewing a representative number of these teachers and their students. All teachers also commented on the same set of three student essays. As an additional reference point, one of the student essays was typed into the computer that had been programmed with the "Writer's Workbench," a package of twenty-three programs developed by Bell Laboratories to help computers and writers work together to improve a text rapidly. Within a few minutes, the computer delivered editorial comments on the student's text, identifying all spelling and punctuation errors, isolating problems with wordy or misused phrases, and suggesting alternatives, offering a stylistic analysis of sentence types, sentence beginnings, and sentence lengths, and finally, giving our freshman essay a Kincaid readability score of 8th grade which, as the computer program informed us, "is a low score for this type of document." The sharp contrast between the teachers' comments and those of the computer highlighted how arbitrary and idiosyncratic most of our teachers' comments are. Besides, the calm, reasonable language of the computer provided quite a contrast to the hostility and mean-spiritedness of most of the teachers' comments.

The first finding from our research on styles of commenting is that *teachers' comments can take students' attention away from their own purposes in writing a particular text and focus that attention on the teachers' purpose in commenting*. The teacher appropriates the text from the student by confusing the student's purpose in writing the text with her own purpose in commenting. Students make the changes the teacher wants rather than those that the student perceives are necessary, since the teachers' concerns imposed on the text create the reasons for the subsequent changes.

We have all heard our perplexed students say to us when confused by our comments: "I don't understand how you want me to change this" or 'Tell me what you want me to do." In the beginning of the process there was the writer, her words, and her desire to communicate her ideas. But after the comments of the teacher are imposed on the first or second draft, the student's attention dramatically shifts from "This is what I want to say," to "This is what you the teacher are asking me to do."

This appropriation of the text by the teacher happens particularly when teachers identify errors in usage, diction, and style in a first draft and ask students to correct these errors when they revise; such comments give the student an impression of the importance of these errors that is all out of proportion to how they should view these errors at this point in the process. The comments create the concern that these "accidents of discourse" need to be attended to before the meaning of the text is attended to.

It would not be so bad if students were only commanded to correct errors, but, more often than not, students are given contradictory messages; they are commanded to edit a sentence to avoid an error or to condense a sentence to achieve greater brevity of style, and then told in the margins that the particular paragraph needs to be more specific or to be developed more. An example of this problem can be seen in the following student paragraph:

wordy — be precise   *which Sunday?*   *comma needed*
Every year [on one Sunday in the middle of January] tens of

word choice   ^
millions of people <u>cancel</u> all events, plans or work to watch

the Super Bowl. This audience includes [little boys and

wordy   *Be specific — what reasons?*
girls, old people, and housewives and men.] <u>Many reasons</u>

You need
to do
more   have been given to explain why the Super Bowl has become   *This*
research.   *passage*
            and why   *what spots?*   *needs to*
            so popular~~that~~ commercial <u>spots</u> cost up to $100,000.00.   *be*
                                                                           expanded
            awkward   *in order*
            <u>One explanation is that people</u> like to take sides and root for   *to be more*
                                                                           interesting
            another what?   *spelling*   *to a*
            a team. <u>Another</u> is that some people like the pageantry and   *reader*

            excitement of the event. These reasons alone, however, do

                too colloquial
            not explain <u>a happening</u> as big as the Super Bowl.

In commenting on this draft, the teacher has shown the student how to edit the sentences, but then commands the student to expand the paragraph in order to make it more interesting to a reader. The interlinear comments and the marginal comments represent two separate tasks for this student; the interlinear comments encourage the student to see the text as a fixed piece, frozen in time, that just needs some editing. The marginal comments, however, suggest that the meaning of the text is not fixed, but rather that the student still needs to develop the meaning by doing some more research. Students are commanded to edit and develop at the same time; the remarkable contradiction of developing a paragraph after editing the sentences in it represents the confusion we encountered in our teachers' commenting styles. These different signals given to students, to edit and develop, to condense and elaborate, represent also the failure of teachers' comments to direct genuine revision of the text as a whole.

Moreover, the comments are worded in such a way that it is difficult for students to know what is the most important problem in the text and what problems are of lesser importance. No scale of concerns is offered to a student, with the result that a comment about spelling or a comment about an awkward sentence is given weight equal to a comment about organization or logic. The comment that seemed to represent this problem best was one teacher's command to his student: "Check your commas and semicolons and think more about what you are thinking about." The language of the comments makes it difficult for a student to sort out and decide what is most important and what is least important.

When the teacher appropriates the text for the student in this way, students are encouraged to see their writing as a series of parts—words, sentences, paragraphs—and not as a whole discourse. The comments encourage students to believe that their first drafts are finished drafts, not invention drafts, and that all they need to do is patch and polish their writing. That is, teachers' comments do not provide their students with an inherent reason for revising the structure and meaning of their texts, since the comments suggest to students that the meaning of their text is already there, finished, produced, and all that is necessary is a better word or phrase. The processes of revising, editing, and proofreading are collapsed and reduced to a single trivial activity, and the students' misunderstanding of the revision process as a rewording activity is reinforced by their teachers' comments.

It is possible, and it quite often happens, that students follow every comment and fix their texts appropriately as requested, but their texts are not improved substantially, or, even worse, their revised drafts are inferior to their previous drafts. Since the teachers' comments take the students' attention away from their own original purposes, students concentrate more, as I have noted, on what the teachers commanded them to do than on what they are trying to say. Sometimes students do not understand the purpose behind their teachers' comments and take those comments very literally. At other times students understand the comments, but the teacher has misread the text and the comments, unfortunately, are not applicable. For instance, we repeatedly saw comments in which teachers commanded students to reduce and condense what was written, when in fact what the text really needed at this stage was to be expanded in conception and scope.

The process of revising always involves a risk. But, too often revision becomes a balancing act for students in which they make the changes that are requested but do not take the risk of changing anything that was not commented on, even if the students sense that other changes are needed. A more effective text does not often evolve from such changes alone, yet the student does not want to take the chance of reducing a finished, albeit inadequate, paragraph to chaos–to fragments–in order to rebuild it, if such changes have not been requested by the teacher.

The second finding from our study is that *most teachers' comments are not text-specific and could be interchanged, rubber-stamped, from text to text.* The comments are not anchored in the particulars of the students' texts, but rather are a series of vague directives that are not text-specific. Students are commanded to "Think more about [their] audience, avoid colloquial language, avoid the passive, avoid prepositions at the end of sentences or conjunctions at the beginning of sentences, be clear, be specific, be precise, but above all, think more about what [they] are thinking about." The comments on the following student paragraph illustrate this problem.

Begin by telling your reader
what you are going to write about

In the sixties it was drugs, in the seventies it was rock and

avoid "one of the"

roll. Now in the eighties, <u>one of the</u> most controversial sub-

elaborate

jects is nuclear power. The United States <u>is in great need of</u>

its own source of power. Because of environmentalists,

coal is not an acceptable source of energy. [Solar and wind

be
specific   power have not yet received the technology necessary to

avoid "it seems"
use them.] It seems that nuclear power is the only feasible   *Think*
more
about
means right now for obtaining self-sufficient power.   *your*
reader.

However, too large a percentage of the population are

be precise
against nuclear power claiming it is unsafe. With as many

problems as the United States is having concerning energy,

it seems a shame that the public is so quick to "can" a very

Thesis
sentence   feasible means of power. Nuclear energy should not be
needed

given up on, but rather, more nuclear plants should be built.

One could easily remove all the comments from this paragraph and rubber-stamp them on another student text, and they would make as much or as little sense on the second text as they do here.

We have observed an overwhelming similarity in the generalities and abstract commands given to students. There seems to be among teachers an accepted, albeit unwritten canon for commenting on student texts. This uniform code of commands, requests, and pleadings demonstrates that the teacher holds a license for vagueness while the student is commanded to be specific. The students we interviewed admitted to having great difficulty with these vague directives. The students stated that when a teacher writes in the margins or as an end comment, "choose precise language," or "think more about your audience," revising becomes a guessing game. In effect, the teacher is saying to the student, "Somewhere in this paper is imprecise language or lack of awareness of an audience and you must find it." The problem presented by these vague commands is compounded for the students when they are not offered any strategies for carrying out these commands. Students are told that they have done something wrong and that there is something in their text that needs to be fixed before the text is acceptable. But to tell students that they have done something wrong is not to tell them what to do about it. In order to offer a useful revision strategy to a student, the teacher must anchor that strategy in the specifics of the student's text. For instance, to tell our student, the author of the above paragraph, "to be specific," or "to elaborate," does not show our student what questions the reader has about the meaning of the text, or what breaks in logic exist, that could be resolved if the writer supplied specific information; nor is the student shown how to achieve the desired specificity.

Instead of offering strategies, the teachers offer what is interpreted by students as rules for composing; the comments suggest to students that writing is just a matter of following the rules. Indeed, the teachers seem to impose a series of abstract rules about written products even when some of them are not appropriate for the specific text the student is creating (Sommers and Schleifer). For instance, the student author of our sample paragraph presented above is commanded to follow the conventional rules for writing a five paragraph essay to begin the introductory paragraph by telling his reader what he is going to say and to end the paragraph with a thesis sentence. Somehow these abstract rules about what five-paragraph products should look like do not seem applicable to the problems this student must confront when revising, nor are the rules specific strategies he could use when revising. There are many inchoate ideas ready to be exploited in this paragraph, but the rules do not help the student to take stock of his (or her) ideas and use the opportunity he has, during revision, to develop those ideas.

The problem here is a confusion of process and product; what one has to say about the process is different from what one has to say about the product. Teachers who use this method of commenting are formulating their comments as if these drafts were finished drafts and were not going to be revised. Their commenting vocabularies have not been adapted to revision and they comment on first drafts as if they were justifying a grade or as if the first draft were the final draft.

Our summary finding, therefore, from this research on styles of commenting is that the news from the classroom is not good. For the most part, teachers do not respond to student writing with the kind of thoughtful commentary which will help them think about their purposes and goals in writing a specific text. In defense of our teachers, however, they told us that responding to student writing was rarely stressed in their teacher-training or in writing workshops; they had been trained in various prewriting techniques, in constructing assignments, and in evaluating papers for grades, but rarely in the process of reading a student text for meaning or in offering commentary to motivate revision. The problem is that most of us as teachers of writing have been trained to read and interpret literary texts for meaning, but, unfortunately, we have not been trained to act upon the same set of assumptions in reading student texts as we follow in reading literary texts (Emig and Parker). Thus, we read student texts with biases about what the writer should have said or about what he or she should have written, and our biases determine how we will comprehend the text. We read with our preconceptions and preoccupations, expecting to find errors, and the result is that we find errors and misread our students' texts.[2] We find what we look for; instead of reading and responding to the meaning of a text, we correct our students' writing. We need to reverse this approach. Instead of finding errors or showing students how to patch up parts of their texts, we need to sabotage our students' conviction that the drafts they have written are complete and coherent. Our comments need to offer students revision tasks of a different order of complexity and sophistication from the ones that they themselves identify, by forcing students back into the chaos, back to the point where they are shaping and restructuring their meaning (Berthoff).

For if the content of a student text is lacking in substance and meaning, if the order of the parts must be rearranged significantly in the next draft, if paragraphs must be restructured for logic and clarity, then many sentences are likely to be changed or deleted anyway. There seems to be no point in having students correct usage errors or condense sentences that are likely to disappear before the next draft is completed. In fact, to identify such problems in a text at this early first draft stage, when such problems are likely to abound, can give a student a disproportionate sense of their importance at this stage in the writing process (McDonald). In responding to our students' writing, we should be guided by the recognition that it is not spelling or usage problems that we as writers first worry about when drafting and revising our texts.

We need to develop an appropriate level of response for commenting on a first draft, and to differentiate that from the level suitable to a second or third draft. Our comments need to be suited to the draft we are reading. In a first or second draft, we need to respond as any reader would, registering questions, reflecting befuddlement, and noting places where we are puzzled about the meaning of the text. Comments should point to breaks in logic, disruptions in meaning, or missing information. Our goal in commenting on early drafts should be to engage students with the issues they are considering and help them clarify their purposes and reasons in writing their specific text.

For instance, the major rhetorical problem of the essay written by the student who wrote the first paragraph (the paragraph on nuclear power) quoted above was that the student had two principal arguments running through his text, each of which brought the other into question. On the one hand, he argued that we must use nuclear power, unpleasant as it is, because we have nothing else to use; though nuclear energy is a problematic source of energy, it is the best of a bad lot. On the other hand, he also argued that nuclear energy is really quite safe and therefore should be our primary resource. Comments on this student's first draft need to point out this break in logic and show the student that if we accept his first argument, then his second argument sounds fishy. But if we accept his second argument, his first argument sounds contradictory. The teacher's comments need to engage this student writer with this basic rhetorical and conceptual problem in his first draft rather than impose a series of abstract commands and rules upon his text.

Written comments need to be viewed not as an end in themselves— a way for teachers to satisfy themselves that they have done their jobs— but rather as a means for helping students to become more effective writers. As a means for helping students, they have limitations; they are, in fact, disembodied remarks—one absent writer responding to another absent writer. The key to successful commenting is to have what is said in the comments and what is done in the classroom mutually reinforce and enrich each other. Commenting on papers assists the writing course in achieving its purpose; classroom activities and the comments we write to our students need to be connected. Written comments need to be an extension of the teacher's voice—an extension of the teacher as reader. Exercises in such activities as revising a whole text or individual paragraphs together in class, noting how the sense of the whole dictates the smaller changes, looking at options, evaluating actual choices, and then discussing the effect of these changes on revised drafts—such exercises need to be designed to take students through the cycles of revising and to help them overcome their anxiety about revising: that anxiety we all feel at reducing what looks like a finished draft into fragments and chaos.

The challenge we face as teachers is to develop comments which will provide an inherent reason for students to revise; it is a sense of revision as discovery, as a repeated process of beginning again, as starting out new, that our students have not learned. We need to show our students how to seek, in the possibility of revision, the dissonances of discovery— to show them through our comments why new choices would positively change their texts, and thus to show them the potential for development implicit in their own writing.

Notes

1.   For an extended discussion of revision strategies of student writers see Nancy Sommers, "Revision Strategies of Student Writers and Experienced Adult Writers," *College Composition and Communication* 31 (December 1980): 378-388.

2.   For an extended discussion of this problem see Joseph Williams' "The Phenomenology of Error."

Works Cited

Berthoff, Ann. *The Making of Meaning*. Montclair, NJ: Boynton/Cook Publishers, 1981.

Emig, Janet, and Robert P. Parker, Jr. "Responding to Student Writing: Building a Theory of the Evaluating Process." Unpublished papers, Rutgers University.

Knoblauch, C.H., and Lil Brannon. "Teacher Commentary on Student Writing: The State of the Art." *Freshman English News* 10 (Fall 1981): 1-3.

McDonald, W.U. "The Revising Process and the Marking of Student Papers." *College Composition and Communication* 24 (May 1978): 167-170.

Sommers, Nancy. "Revision Strategies of Student Writers and Experienced Adult Writers." *College Composition and Communication* 31 (December 1980): 378-388.

Sommers, Nancy, and Ronald Schleifer. "Means and Ends: Some Assumptions of Student Writers." *Composition and Teaching* 2 (December 1980): 69-76.

Williams, Joseph. "The Phenomenology of Error." *College Composition and Communication* 32 (May 1981): 152-168.

On Students' Rights to Their Own Texts: A Model of Teacher Response

Lil Brannon and C. H. Knoblauch

I.A. Richards has said that we begin reading any text with an implicit faith in its coherence, an assumption that its author intended to convey some meaning and made the choices most likely to convey the meaning effectively.[1] As readers, therefore, we tolerate the writer's manipulation of the way we see the subject that is being addressed. Our tolerance derives from a tacit acceptance of the writer's "authority" to make the statements we are reading.[2] When reading a textbook, for instance, we assume that its writer knows at least as much about the book's subject as we do, and ideally even more. When we read a newspaper article, we take for granted that the writer has collected all the relevant facts and presented them honestly. In either case, "authority" derives partly from what we know about the writer (for instance, professional credentials or public recognition) and partly from what we see in the writer's discourse (the probity of its reasoning, the skill of its construction, its use of references that we may recognize). The sources of writers' authority may be quite various. But whatever the reason for our granting authority, what we are conceding is the author's right to make statements in exactly the way they are made in order to say exactly what the writer wishes to say.

The more we know about a writer's skill, the more we have read of that individual's work or heard of his or her reputation, the greater the claim to authority. This claim can be so powerful that we will tolerate writing from that author which appears to be unusually difficult, even obscure or downright confusing. For instance, our having read Dylan Thomas' "Fern Hill" with pleasure may lead us to work harder at reading "Altarwise by Owlight," although we may not understand it readily and may not derive the same pleasure from reading it. As readers, we see this harder material as a problem of interpretation, not a shortcoming of the composer. Writers may, of course, compromise their authority through evident or repeated lapses, but, in general, readers will assume that problematic texts demand greater effort from them, not rewriting from the author. Writers in fact depend on readers' willingness to stay with a text, even a difficult one, without judging it prematurely on the basis of its apparent violation of their own perspectives or impressions of some subject. The incentive to write derives from an assumption that people will listen respectfully and either assent to or earnestly consider the ideas expressed. And ordinarily readers will make an honest effort to understand a writer's text provided that its ideas matter to them and provided that the writer's authority is sufficient to compel their attention.[3] When we consider how writing is taught, however, this normal and dynamic connection between a writer's authority and the quality of a reader's attention is altered because of the peculiar relationship between teacher and student. The teacher-reader assumes, often correctly, that student writers have not yet earned the authority that ordinarily compels readers to listen seriously to what writers have to say. Indeed, teachers view themselves as authorities, intellectually maturer, rhetorically more experienced, technically more expert than their apprentice writers. Oddly, therefore, in classroom writing situations, the reader assumes primary control of the choices that writers make, feeling perfectly free to "correct" those choices any time an apprentice deviates from the teacher-reader's conception of what the developing text "ought" to look like or "ought" to be doing.[4] Hence, the teacher more often than the student determines what the writing will be about, the form it will take, and the criteria that will determine its success. Student writers, then, are put into the awkward position of having to accommodate not only the personal intentions that guide their choice-making, but also the teacher-reader's expectations about how the assignment should be completed. The teacher's role, it is supposed, is to tell the writers how to do a better job than they could do alone, thereby in effect appropriating the writers' texts. In reading those texts and commenting on them, the teacher-evaluator "fixes" the writing in ways that appear to approximate the Platonic Discourse, the Ultimate Propriety, that any given student text may have suggested but not achieved. Of course, that Platonic Discourse exists only in the teacher's mind (where it often resides secretly as a guide to judging) and may have little to do with what individual writers initially tried to accomplish.

When teachers appropriate their students' texts, they do so with what appear to be the best of motives. By making elaborate corrections on student writing, teachers appear to be showing the discrepancy between what the writing has actually achieved and what ideal writing ought to look like, perhaps with the conviction that any student who perceives the difference can also narrow it. But this correcting also tends to show students that the teacher's agenda is more important than their own, that what they wanted to say is less relevant than the teacher's impression of what they should have said. The writer wants to talk about how she got her first job while the teacher wants an exercise in comparison and contrast.

Once students perceive this shift of agenda, their motives for writing also shift: the task is now to match the writing to expectations that lie beyond their own sense of their intention and method. Therefore, far from controlling the responses of an intended reader, they are forced to concede the reader's authority and to make guesses about what they can and cannot say. One consequence is often a diminishing of students' commitment to communicate ideas that they value and even a diminishing of the incentive to write.

We are not suggesting that students texts are, in fact, authoritative. But we do argue that incentive is vital to improvement and also that it is linked crucially to the belief that one's writing will be read earnestly. Since teachers do not grant student writers the authority that ordinarily justifies serious reading, they tend to undervalue student efforts to communicate what they have to say in the way they wish to say it. Yet it is precisely the chance to accomplish one's own purposes by controlling one's own choices that creates incentive to write. Denying students control of what they want to say must surely reduce incentive and also, presumably, the likelihood of improvement. Regardless of what we may know about students' authority, therefore, we lose more than we gain by preempting their control and allowing our own Ideal Texts to dictate choices that properly belong to the writers.

When we pay more attention to our Ideal Texts than to the writers' purposes and choices, we compromise both our ability to help students say effectively what they truly want to say and our ability to recognize legitimately diverse ways of saying it. Teaching from the vantage point of the Ideal Text is paternalistic: the teacher "knows best," knows what the writer should do and how it should be done, and feels protective because his or her competence is superior to that of the writer. This paternalism is sometimes liberal and sometimes conservative. The conservative teacher is prone to underestimate the writer's competence, using the Ideal Text to measure degrees of failure. Conversely, the liberal teacher is prone to exaggerate the writer's competence, assuming that, although the writer has not matched the Ideal Text, some quality in the writing nonetheless excuses the lapse. For instance, a teacher might sympathize with a student's sincerity or effort despite misgivings about perceived errors. The trouble with both types of paternalism is the teachers' assumption that they always and necessarily know what writers mean to say and are therefore always reliable judges of how well writers actually say it. There is little suspicion that the Ideal Text may simply be irrelevant in terms of what a writer attempted to do. Hence, teachers are distracted from offering the best kind of assistance—that is, helping writers achieve their own

purposes—while insisting on ideas, strategies, or formal constraints that
are often not pertinent to a writer's own goals.

An example from our recent research demonstrates the extent to
which adherence to an Ideal Text interferes with the ability to read student writing in ways that can best help writers to achieve their goals. We
asked students to write an essay on the Lindbergh kidnapping trial, stating a purpose and an intended audience.[5] One student, John, decided to
write out a version of the prosecution's closing oral argument. Here is an
excerpt:

> Ladies and gentlemen of the jury. I wholeheartedly believe
> that the evidence which has been presented before you has
> clearly shown that the man who is on trial here today is beyond
> a doubt guilty of murder of the darling little, innocent
> Lindbergh baby.
>
> Sure, the defendant has stated his innocence. But who are we
> to believe? Do we believe the testimony of a man who has been
> previously convicted; in fact convicted to holding up innocent
> women wheeling baby, carriages? Or do we believe the testimo-
> ny of one of our nation's greatest heroes, Charles A. Lindbergh.
> Mr. Lindbergh believes the defendant is guilty. So do I.
>
> All I ask, ladies and gentlemen of the jury, is that you look
> at the evidence. First we have the evidence that the defendant
> suddenly became $44,486 richer since April 2. Is it only a coinci-
> dence that the ransom was paid the same night?
>
> Don't forget the testimony of Mr. Whited and Mr. Rossitor
> both of whom said they saw the accused on or around Feb. 27 in
> New Jersey even though the accused lives in the Bronx. The kid-
> napping occurred on March 1.

We asked forty teachers to assess the quality of this writing in light of
what the writer was trying to do. They all responded in one of two ways,
neither of which recognized the writer's control over choices. One group,
the conservatives, felt that John was taking on the persona of the prose-
cuting attorney seriously addressing the jury at the time of the trial.
However, this group concluded that John's argument was not convincing
because of his blatant use of emotional appeal. These readers felt that no
self-respecting member of the jury would be convinced by such senti-
mentalized language as "darling little, innocent Lindbergh baby."
According to them, John tended to depend too much on emotions and too
little on logic. The second group, the liberals, concluded, on the contrary,
that John had adopted the persona of a "mock" attorney and that his

writing was intentionally satirical. They too pointed to the use of emotional language but saw it as consistent with a satiric purpose. Each group, in other words, referred to exactly the same textual evidence to bolster its argument, even though the two arguments were diametrically opposed.

In both cases, the teachers were reading John's text from the perspective of their own shared Ideal Text, one in which straightforward logic, freed from patronizing emotional appeal, was sufficient for persuasion. The conservative group denied John the possibility that his writing could have been competent because they measured the limits of competence with reference to a model that ruled out John's overtly emotional appeal. The liberal teachers accepted precisely the same Ideal Text, but they credited John with more, rather than less, sophistication. They assumed that John must surely be writing satire because he could not possibly mean what he appeared to be saying on the page. Hence they granted him a competence that he may not have had while ignoring the competence that he actually manifested in his essay. Both groups were surprised when we showed them the actual transcript of the prosecution's summation in Hauptmann's trial. They discovered that its strategy and language were in fact very similar to those in John's essay:

> Why, men and women, if that little baby, if that little, curly-haired youngster were out in the grass in the jungle, breathing, just so long as it was breathing, any tiger, any lion, the most venomous snake would have passed that child without hurting a hair of its head.

The point is not that John's choice of language, or even the original prosecutor's choice, was "right" in some absolute sense. Rather, John's choice was simply not wrong; yet the teachers' Ideal Text interfered with their acceptance of John's perfectly plausible option.

What this example suggests is the value of consulting a student writer about what he or she wanted to say before suggesting how he or she ought to say it. In other words, it shows why we ought to relinquish our control of student writing and return it to the writers: doing so will not only improve student incentive to write, but will also make our responses to the writing more pertinent. But how and to what extent can we relinquish control? The question is attitudinal more than methodological. Teachers need to alter their traditional emphasis on a relationship between student texts and their own Ideal Text in favor of the relationship between what the writer meant to say and what the discourse actually manifests of that intention. This shift entails our recognizing that even inexperienced writers operate with a sense of logic and purpose that may not appear on the page but that nonetheless guides their choices.[6] We must replace our professional but still idiosyncratic models of how writing ought to appear, and put in their place a less authoritarian concern for how student texts make us respond as readers and whether those responses are congruent with the writers' intentions or not. The focus then will be not on the distance between text and some teacher's personal notion of its most ideal version, but rather on the disparity between what the writer wanted to communicate and what the choices residing in the text actually cause readers to understand. Necessarily, the emphasis on form that mainly preoccupies us when we think in terms of an ideal model will change to an emphasis on the writer's ideas and communicative goals. And this changed emphasis will allow the writer to sense both a real control over the discourse and also the reader's real interest in what is being said. The consequence can be a reinforcement of the writer's incentive to keep writing and therefore an enriched environment in which to improve skills.

This change in teacher attitude and teacher-student relationship does, of course, demand some changes in pedagogy. Because students are largely unaccustomed to having their writing taken seriously, teachers may well have to dramatize the transfer of control they wish their students to perceive. Single-draft writing assignments, for instance, do not allow writers to assert control because they offer only one chance to write. Students, therefore, must accept a teacher's pronouncements without the opportunity to reassert their points of view or to explain what they were trying to do. Multiple-draft assignments, on the other hand, provide an opportunity for dialogue about how effectively the writer's choices have enabled the communication of intentions. Multiple-draft assignments also place emphasis on revision, on the progressively more complete achievement of communicative effect, so that what might be regarded as "errors" on a single-draft assignment may be seen as opportunities to clarify or refine relationships between intention and effect. By focusing on error, the teacher is the authority, a judge of the writing. But if revision is the focus, the writer retains control, assuming responsibility to create a discourse that conveys intended meanings in a way that enables a reader to perceive them.

It is not sufficient, however, simply to have students rewrite their statements. The way we talk to them about their successive drafts is just as important as offering them a chance to revise.[7] It would be easy to point out errors, just as on single-draft assignments, and to require copyediting on the next draft. But the concern is not merely to ask for editing in order to make discourse look superficially better; rather, it is to work with the writer in examining the effectiveness of some intended communication and to initiate improvement where possible. Nor is the concern merely to test the writer's ability to follow directions in order to approximate the teacher-evaluator's Ideal Text. Instead, it is to pursue writers' real intentions until they are satisfactorily conveyed. In other words, the teacher's proper role is not to tell the student explicitly what to do but rather to serve as a sounding-board enabling the writer to see confusions in the text and encouraging the writer to explore alternatives that he or she may not have considered. The teacher's role is to attract a writer's attention to the relationship between intention and effect, enabling a recognition of discrepancies between them, even suggesting ways to eliminate the discrepancies, but finally leaving decisions about alternative choices to the writer, not the teacher.

At the start, students and teachers need to share their different perceptions as makers and readers of a discourse. Writers know what they *intended* to communicate. Readers know what a text has *actually* said to them. If writers and readers can exchange information about intention and effect, they can negotiate ways to bring actual effect as closely in line with a desired intention as possible. Answering some general questions can help in the sharing of this information. If both teachers and students answer the questions separately, and then compare their answers, the differences in their answers can generate discussion and elicit other, more specific questions leading toward revision. The general questions include "What did the writer intend to do?" "What has the writing actually said?" and "How has the writing done what it is supposed to do?" The first one concerns the anticipated effect of a discourse; the second concerns its literal statements; and the third pertains to the writer's and reader's estimate of how or in what way the content, shape, and sequence of those statements achieve the desired effect. In the case of John's essay, a portion of which appeared earlier, an answer to the first question might be, "the writing should show that the prosecution is convinced of Hauptmann's guilt." An answer to the second question might be, "the writing says that Hauptmann had a previous criminal record, etc." and an answer to the third question might be, "the use of sentimental language in describing the Lindbergh baby works on the jury's emotions and makes them unsympathetic to Hauptmann."

We can ask and answer the questions using several different teaching formats, including one-to-one conferences, peer-group collaborations, and even certain kinds of comments on student essays. Again, attitudes are more important than methods. The questions initiate a process of negotiation, where writer and peers or writer and teacher (or tutor) work together to consider, and if possible to enhance, the relationship between intention and effect. First, do the writer's and the teacher's responses agree or differ? If they differ, what evidence does each reader have to support the reading? Answering this question will lead both teacher and student into the text in order to discuss the reasons for variant perceptions. If the responses agree, does every part of the text contribute helpfully to sustaining the writer's intentions? And, finally, do the parts need clarifying or elaborating in order to improve their effectiveness? The teacher's principal concern in asking and cooperatively answering these questions is to make the writer think about what has been said, not to tell the writer what to do. The point is to return control of choice-making as soon as possible to the writer, while also creating a motive for making changes. Negotiation assumes, of course, that neither teacher nor writer stays relentlessly with an initial position. The teacher resists the temptation to say, "Do it this way," which reduces the writer's role to a trivial one of following directions. Meanwhile, the student, faced with the reality of a reader's misunderstanding, can no longer say, "But what I really meant was . . . ." Of course, the process of negotiation does not move the writing toward the teacher's Ideal Text; in fact, it does not even guarantee a more successful next draft. But what it does is to force the writer to reassert control and thereby gain experience in revising. Since the impulse to revise arises out of a sense of not having fully communicated some intended message, the rewriting is not merely formulaic but is, in fact, inventive, a reconstituting of the meanings that the writer is concerned to convey.

Ideally, readers should respond to writers face to face. But to the extent that this is inconvenient, there is a way for teachers to simulate the conference model without having the student actually present. Students may compose drafts in which they also write out their intentions in a large column to the right of the text itself. After composing, the writers go back through their drafts and explain, paragraph by paragraph, what they were trying to say or do and how they expected the reader to react to it. Students will improve as estimators of their own intentions as they practice writing them out; but it is important to add that teachers remain free to raise questions about intentions that the writers may not have explained in the margin. Especially in the beginning, teachers may need to encourage their students to estimate intent at as many points in the draft as they can, sometimes even sentence by sentence, because, the more commentary the writers can provide, the more certain the teacher is about what the writers want to do and the more help the teacher can offer in doing it effectively.

Notice how John describes his intentions on the first draft of his simulated address to the jury:

Ladies and gentlemen of the jury. I wholeheartedly believe that the evidence which has been presented before you has clearly shown that the man who is on trial here today is beyond a doubt guilty of murder of the darling little, innocent Lindbergh baby.	Informal, putting the jury at ease. Telling my (prosecution's) belief of guilt confidently. Touching at human spirit.
Sure, the defendant has stated his innocence. But, who are we to believe? Do we believe testimony of a man who has been previously convicted; in fact convicted of holding up innocent women wheeling baby carriages? Or do we believe the testimony of one of our nation's greatest heroes, Charles A. Lindbergh. Mr. Lindbergh believes the defendant is guilty. So do I.	Showing the *negative* side of defendant and connecting his past with similarity of crime he is accused of now. Showing the *integrity* of the father of the victim of the murder. Overall a very *biased* view.
All I ask, ladies and gentlemen of the jury is that you look at the evidence. First we have the evidence that the defendant suddenly became $44,486 richer since April 2. Is it only a coincidence that the ransom was paid the same night? Don't forget the testimony of Mr. Whited and Mr. Rossiter both of whom said they saw the accused on or around Feb. 27 in New Jersey even though the accused lives in the Bronx. The kidnapping occurred on Mar. 1.	List of evidence, all against accused. Not too much detail is given, but if I leave the jury with a series of factual pieces of evidence against the defendent, the jury will say to themselves, "Wow, there is so much going against him, he's guilty."

Potentially, a comparison of John's stated intentions and the actual effects of the writing might give rise to various points of negotiation. Consider the third and fourth paragraphs. Although John has indicated what he wanted to accomplish ("List of evidence, all against accused. Not too much detail is given"), he may not yet have done what he thinks he has done ("if I leave the jury with a series of factual pieces of evidence against the defendant, the jury will say to themselves, 'Wow, there is so much going against him, he's guilty.'"). The teacher (or peer or tutor) might raise questions here ("Did the defense counter any of this testimony and thereby discredit it? If so, would the jury be convinced by John's listing of 'facts'?"). John's teacher did raise these questions, and John's response to them demonstrated his control of the writing. He agreed that his first idea, that all he needed to do was list the facts, would not create the effect that he desired. Later he extensively rewrote this portion of the text, noting the defense's inability to counter convincingly each piece of evidence submitted by the prosecution. The result of the dialogue between John and his teacher was to give John a chance to re-examine his initial choices and come up with a new strategy for creating the impact he wished to have on the jury. John remained in control of the choices, although it took the questions of a reader to help him see that he had not yet done what he thought he had done.

It may be that other teaching strategies beyond those suggested here work equally to promote the transfer of responsibility from teacher to student that we have been advocating. Our concern has been only secondarily to show how it can be done, and primarily to argue that it should be done. Although student texts are not, in fact, authoritative, we must nonetheless accept a student writer's authority to the extent that we grant the writer control over the process of making choices: that is, we tentatively acknowledge the composer's right to make statements in the way they are made in order to say what he or she intended to say. Often, to be sure, we will see deficiencies in the resulting discourse, but if we preempt the writer's control by ignoring intended meanings in favor of formal and technical flaws, we also remove the incentive to write and the motivation to improve skills. Conversely, granting students control of their own writing can create a rich ground for nurturing skills because the writer's motive for developing them lies in the realization that an intended reader is willing to take the writer's meaning seriously. If the writer is allowed to have something to say, then the saying of it is more likely to matter. The methods we have described allow the teacher to return control of a discourse to the writer as soon as possible by encouraging multiple drafts, each stimulated by the responses of a reader. Subsequent drafts are not always closer to a teacher's sense of formal, technical, or intellectual propriety, but they invariably show writers responding to the issues raised in their own texts, attempting to close perceived gaps between what was intended and what earlier drafts actually said. As these gaps are successfully narrowed, one draft at a time, the motive to solve technical problems is strengthened, in a context in which the writer's intentions matter more than teachers' Ideal Texts.

Eventually, of course, teachers judge student writing, and they invoke standards in the process. Preferably, in multiple-draft assignments, evaluation occurs only (1) after writers have had the opportunity to receive peer and teacher responses to their writing; (2) after they have had a chance to revise as they wish; and (3) after they have decided that their writing is finished and ready to be evaluated. And when evaluation is undertaken, as a last step in the process we propose, the standards invoked do not have to do with fixed preconceptions about form or content as stipulated by some Ideal Text. Instead, they relate to communicative effectiveness as an experienced reader assesses it in a particular writing situation. The standards of communicative effectiveness are how well the writer's choices achieve stated or implied purposes given the needs and expectations of an intended audience. If the evaluator finds the writer's choices to be *plausible* (as opposed to "correct") all of the time, the grade for that writing is higher than if the choices occasionally or frequently create uncertainties that cause failures in communication.

Evaluation, then, is the natural conclusion of the process of response and negotiation, carried through successive drafts. By responding, a teacher creates incentive in the writer to make meaningful changes. By negotiating those changes rather than dictating them, the teacher returns control of the writing to the student. And by evaluating, the teacher gives the student writer an estimate of how well the teacher thinks the student's revisions have brought actual effects into line with stated intentions. By looking first to those intentions, both in responding and in evaluating, we show students that we take their writing seriously and that we assume that they are responsible for communicating what they wish to say. The sense of genuine responsibility kindled in inexperienced writers can be a powerful first step in the development of mature competence.

Notes

1. See I. A. Richards, *Practical Criticism* (New York: Harcourt, Brace, 1929), especially Part III, passim.

2. The concept of authority or *ethos* is, of course, an ancient one. For definition and elaboration see Aristotle, *Rhetoric* (1356a2).

3. Reader-response criticism, as practiced by Wolfgang Iser, Norman Holland, Stanley Fish, Georges Poulet, and others, considers these issues in extensive scholarly detail. For a survey of this work, see *Reader-Response Criticism: From Formalism to Post-Structuralism*, edited by Jane P. Tompkins.

4. For the prevalence of this style of commenting and some arguments about its insufficiency, see C.H. Knoblauch and Lil Brannon, "Teacher Commentary on Student Writing: The State of the Art." See also Dennis Searle and David Dillon, "The Message of Marking: Teacher Written Responses to Student Writing at Intermediate Grade Levels."

5. We adapted this exercise from W. Edgar Mooer's *Instructor's Manual to Creative and Critical Thinking*.

6. For more on this assumption see David Bartholomae, "The Study of Error."

7.   Nancy Sommers has noted the radical unfamiliarity of unskilled writers with revision strategies that experienced writers take for granted. See her "Revision Strategies of Student Writers and Experienced Adult Writers."

Works Cited

Bartholomae, David. "The Study of Error." *College Composition and Communication* 31 (October 1980): 253-69.

Knoblauch, C.H., and Lil Brannon. "Teacher Commentary on Student Writing: The State of the Art." *Freshman English News* 10 (Fall 1981): 14.

Mooer, W. Edgar. *Instructor's Manual to Creative and Critical Thinking.* Boston: Houghton Mifflin, 1967.

Richards, I.A. *Practical Criticism.* New York: Harcourt, Brace, 1929.

Searle, Dennis, and David Dillon. "The Message of Marking: Teacher Written Responses to Student Writing at Intermediate Grade Levels." *Research in the Teaching of English* 14 (October 1980): 233-42.

Sommers, Nancy. "Revision Strategies of Student Writers and Experienced Adult Writers." *College Composition and Communication* 31 (December 1980): 378-88.

Tompkins, Jane, ed. *Reader-Response Criticism: From Formalism to Post-Structuralism.* Baltimore: Johns Hopkins UP, 1980.

The Concept of Control in Teacher Response: Defining the Varieties of "Directive" and "Facilitative" Response

Richard Straub

In two pioneering articles in 1982, "Responding to Student Writing" and "On Students' Rights to Their Own Texts," Nancy Sommers, Lil Brannon, and C.H. Knoblauch gave shape to a set of principles that brought process theory and poststructural concepts of knowledge and authority to bear on the ways teachers respond to student writing. Beyond calling on us to write out our comments in full statements, make them "text-specific," and focus on different concerns at different stages of drafting, they urged us to be careful about the amount of control we exert over students when we read and comment on their writing. We should not impose our "idealized texts" on students' writing. We should not "appropriate" student texts by overlooking their purposes for writing and emphasizing our purposes for commenting. Instead of being "directive," we should be "facilitative," providing feedback and support but not dictating the path of revision.[1]

A decade and a-half later, our professional talk about teacher response is still dominated by the concept of control—largely, I think, because it goes to the heart of our teaching and our identity as teachers: How much are we to assert our vision of what makes writing good and direct students' work as writers? How much are we to allow students to find their own ways as learning writers? How much do we teach to the written product? How much do we try to help students develop their attitudes toward writing, their composing processes, and their understanding of writing as a social action? With a remarkable consistency, the recent scholarship on response has urged us to reject styles that take control over student texts and encouraged us instead to adopt styles that allow students to retain greater responsibility over their writing.

Yet even as we have expanded the scope of our inquiry and deepened our discussion, we have continued to look at response in dualistic ways. Teacher commentary is either directive or facilitative, authoritative or collaborative, teacher-based or student-based. One is encouraging and good, the other critical and bad. Jeffrey Sommers asserts that teachers must become "collaborators rather than judges" (177). Robert Probst calls on teachers to take on the role of "common reader" and abandon the roles of "hostile reader," "proofreader," "gatekeeper," and "authority figure" (73). He advises us to write comments that place responsibility on the student instead of making "pronouncements from on high" that "encourage submission and discipleship" (76). Joseph Moxley advises teachers to "avoid 'appropriating' students' texts and simplifying students' roles to that of army privates following orders." The teacher's proper role, he explains, "is not to tell the student explicitly what to do but rather to serve as a sounding board enabling the writer to see confusions in the text and encouraging the writer to explore alternatives that he or she may not have considered" (3). Similarly, Elizabeth Flynn sets a "feminine" style of response against the traditional directive style, which she sees as "masculine." A masculine style puts the teacher in the role of an evaluator, a "judge"; a feminine style, by contrast, creates the teacher as "a sympathetic reader" and "a friendly adviser" (50). In her review of literature on response, Brooke Horvath notes how scholars have come to eschew the "negative, excessively judgmental response" of the "critic" and to extol commentary written by teachers in the role of "motivator" or "friend" (273). David Fuller explains how he has moved from commenting as a "detached critic" to commenting as an "interested reader":

> I have reconsidered my role as a responder and no longer approach a paper as a "teller" but as a "shower." I show by reacting as a reader to the writing—asking questions, reacting to the "student purpose," agreeing, disagreeing, noting my problems, understanding. I do not, now, tell the student "what to do"; I let the student see the effect the text had on me and make decisions based on that. (314)

Rebecca Rule, explaining her rationale for making responses that keep control in the hands of the student, notes:

> As [a] teacher, I must be careful not to take over—because the minute I do, the success (if there is one) becomes mine, not his— and the learning is diminished. I can contribute; I can guide; I can brainstorm with him; I can suggest exercises; I can offer models; I can tell him where the comma goes; I can support him wholeheartedly. But I must not take over. (50)

All of these authors echo Sommers and Brannon and Knoblauch in calling on teachers—rightly, I believe—to resist taking over student texts and instead to make comments that share responsibility with the writer. But they also reinforce the dichotomy between directive and facilitative response and perpetuate, however unintentionally, the notion that some comments control student writing and others do not and the notion that there is a particular level of control—and a particular style—that is optimal in teacher response.

Although the issue of control in teacher commentary is still very much alive and well, it remains curiously undefined and is not well understood. We have come to see directive, teacher-based response, monolithically and simplistically, as authoritarian response. And we have come to pack an expanding number of roles and strategies into our concept of facilitative response, without adequately defining these methods or mapping the relationships among them. A teacher who responds as a facilitator, we are told, can respond as a teacher reader, a guide, a friendly adviser, a diagnostician, a coach, a motivator, a collaborator, a fellow explorer, an inquirer, a confidant, a questioning reader, a representative reader, a common reader (or average reader or real reader), a sounding board, a subjective reader, an idiosyncratic reader, a sympathetic reader, a trusted adult, and a friend. She can support, advise, explore, engage, question, motivate, encourage, nurture, receive, interpret, and provide reader reactions—and so on. All these forms of response share the basic trait of somehow engaging students in an exchange about their writing, but they remain undifferentiated, each one presumably functioning in more or less the same way as the others. Following the lead of Brannon and Knoblauch, we have turned away from trying to define various types of commentary in terms of specific textual features and have discussed them instead more figuratively in terms of general attitudes, responding roles, and social action.[2] Such diverse, undifferentiated ways of talking about response, not surprisingly, have created a tangle of issues, misunderstandings, and questions about authority and control in teacher response: How do different kinds of response create different images of the responder and establish various relationships with the student? What kinds of comments distinguish a directive responder from a facilitative one? What specific strategies mark the commentary of an editor? A critic? Or a gatekeeper? What strategies distinguish a "reader" from a "guide"? A "coach" from a "fellow explorer"? A "common reader" from a "trusted adult reader"? How do different comments exert control over the writer's choices? Is there a way for a teacher to offer help or guidance—or even play back his reading of a text—and *not* assume control over student writing? If we are to build on the recent study of teacher response and turn this theory more productively into practice, we need a way to distinguish the varieties of directive and facilitative response, tie different types of commentary to specific textual strategies, examine their likely effects, and consider how these response styles fit in with different teaching approaches and classroom goals. As Charles Bazerman puts it:

"When I know what I want to do, I know how to read, whether with a proofreader's eye, a textual analyst's structural vision, an editor's helpful hand, a professorial challenge, a marker's red bludgeon, or a companionly ease. Each of these stances invokes separate reading processes. In each way of reading I look for and respond to different things" (144). The question is, how can we link various types of commentary to different stances or roles—and thereby gain greater control over the ways we respond to student writing? By examining several sets of teacher comments, I hope to demonstrate the difficulties we have run into by talking about teacher commentary in terms of the broad categories of directive and facilitative response and point to a more productive way to describe various types of commentary.

Directive commentary—the commentary of the critic and the judge—is identified easily enough. It is highly critical and sets out for the student in no uncertain terms what is not working in the paper and what needs to be done, as in the following comments, made in response to a rough draft written by a college freshman in the middle of the semester.

Can
What if drugs were legal? ~~Could~~ you imagine what it would do to

20
our society? ~~Well according to~~ John E. LeMoult, a lawyer with ~~twenty~~
what?
years of experience on the subject, feels we should at least consider it.
Keep yourself in the background.
I would like to comment on his article "Legalize Drugs" in the June 15,
Just state your position.
1984, issue of the *New York Times*. I disagree with LeMoult's idea of

legalizing drugs to cut the cost of crime.

is   cliché
LeMoult's article ~~was~~ short and sweet. He gives the background of

the legalization of drugs. For example, the first antidrug laws of the

United States were passed in 1914. ~~The laws were put in effect~~ because

of the threat of the Chinese imagrants. In addition, he explains how

women were the first to use laudanun, an over the counter drug, as a
            ^ *because*
substitute for drinking; it was unacceptable for women to drink. By
wordy
explaining this he made the reader feel that society was the cause of

women's using the substitute, laudanun, for drinking. LeMoult proceeds

~~ed~~ from there to explain how the money to buy drugs comes from us as
                                                for
society. Since drug addicts turn to crime to get money, we become a cor-

rupt society. *Good material—needs to be tightened up.*

Clearly, these comments are highly controlling. The teacher, like an editor, freely marks up the writing—circling errors, underlining problem areas, and inserting corrections on the student's text. She concentrates on formal propriety, using terse, sometimes elliptical, comments that tell the student, Nancy, in no uncertain terms what is wrong and what must be changed. She even makes a smattering of editorial changes herself. She has a definite and rather narrow agenda for the writing, and she clearly imposes this agenda on the student writer. She does this in spite of the fact—or because of the fact—that she gives little attention to the content of the writing. Her goal is not untypical of many another writing teacher: to get the student to produce clean, formally correct prose. It is a clear instance of a teacher's imposing an idealized text on the student, her own model of what counts in a piece of writing and how that writing ought to appear, especially formally and structurally, without any real concern for the writer's purposes and meanings.

But what about the comments written on the same piece of student writing by Edward White and Jane Peterson? Here is a sampling of their comments to Nancy (for the full responses see 32-35).

White's Comments

Now that you are clear on what you have to say (see your last prgh), revise the opening to begin your argument.

Select the parts of LeMoult's article that are appropriate for your paper and omit the rest. Be sure to quote accurately.

[End note:] The paper is a good discovery draft that could become a good paper. As you revise, be sure you focus each prgh on its central idea. I enjoy the energy of your style.

Peterson's Comments

This is in his 4th prgh. What's he doing in the first 3 prghs?

Do we? All drugs?

Cigarettes? alcohol? car racing?

Do you mean morally wrong or dangerous?

[End note:] Your first draft is a good starting point—you clearly understand the structure expected (opening with source info, summarizing the article, responding with your view). Before beginning a second draft, I suggest you do a barebones outline on the article (you're missing a couple of LeMoult's points) and then do one on your response (you seem to have at least two objections instead of one).

Are these comments directive? If so, what makes them directive? Are
they directive in the same way as the first set of comments presented
above? Are they directive but in different ways? Is one set more or less
directive than the other? Can either set of comments be seen as facilitative? How can we tell? The current scholarship might lead us to form one
impression or another, but it doesn't provide a way of making such distinctions. In order to address these questions and get a better way of
describing response styles, we need to look beyond the general labels of
"directive" and "facilitative" and look more carefully at the specific
comments these teachers make.

A Method for Analyzing Teacher Comments

The most effective way to take up an examination of teacher response is
to study individual comments, in detail, and describe the *focuses* and
modes of these comments. What areas of writing do the comments focus
on? Do they deal with local concerns—matters of wording, sentence
structure, and correctness? Do they deal with global matters of content,
focus, and organization? With the larger contexts of writing instruction—
for instance, the rhetorical situation, the assignment, the student's composing processes, or the student's ongoing work as a writer? How are the
comments presented? How do the structure, voice, and content of the
comments affect the way they create the teacher as a responder on the
page? Is a given comment presented as a criticism of the writing? Is it a
command? A piece of advice? A question? By charting a teacher's predominant focuses and modes of commentary—in a set of comments or,
better yet, across a series of his responses—we can get a good impression
of his responding style.

    In the following analyses, I will look at each set of comments, indi-
vidually and collectively, and identify the focuses and modes of those
comments. I will study comments as they appear on the page, independent of the larger classroom setting but seen amid the conventions that
typically go along with such teacher-student interactions. I will try to
determine how the comments themselves create an image of the teacher
on the page, implicitly establish some relationship with the student, and
exert varying degrees of control over the student's writing choices.

    Generally speaking, the more comments a teacher makes on a piece
of writing, the more controlling he will likely be. The more a teacher
attends to the text, especially local matters, and tries to lead the student
to produce a more complete written product, the more likely he is to
point to specific changes and the more control he is likely to exert over

the student's writing. The more a teacher attends to the student's writing processes and the larger contexts of writing, and gears his comments to the student behind the text and her ongoing work as a writer, the less likely he is to point to specific changes and the less control he is likely to assume over the student's writing. The following comments, for example, all offer advice to the student, but they deal with different focuses and assume varying degrees of control:

- Try to rearrange these sentences. (local structure)
- Try to explain how these drugs are dangerous. (development)
- Try to go back and do some brainstorming about the threat that illegal drugs pose to society. (student's writing processes)

Thus, a teacher who does a lot of work with sentence structure and correctness will tend to be more directive than, say, a teacher who frequently asks the student to consider the rhetorical situation or to try some technique of revision.

The extent to which a teacher assumes control over student writing is also determined to a great extent by the way he frames his comments—by the *modes* of commentary he employs. For instance, comments framed as **corrections** tend to exert greater control over the student than **criticisms** of the writing or calls for revision that are stated as **commands**:

- [The teacher adds "recreational" before the word "drugs" in the student's sentence in order to clarify the meaning.] (correction)
- Circular reasoning. (evaluation)
- Stick with the third person—don't get into your own experience. (command)

Criticisms and commands, in turn, assume greater control than **qualified evaluations** or **advice**, respectively:

- It seems to me you don't go far enough into this point. (qualified evaluation)
- I'd consider starting the essay here. (advice)
- Maybe it'd help to just talk out those ideas or make some sort of list. (advice)

Praise is a special case. **Praise comments** are less controlling than criticism or commands because they place the teacher in the role of an appreciative reader or satisfied critic and obviate the need for revision.

Nevertheless, they underscore the teacher's values and agendas and exert a certain degree of control over the way the student views the text before her and the way she likely looks at subsequent writing.

These authoritative modes of commentary, to varying degrees, are more controlling than questions and nonevaluative statements—or what might be called interactive comments, because they tend to initiate a more active response from the student and place greater responsibility on her to come up with her own ideas and revisions.[3] Some interactive comments, of course, assume greater control than others. Closed questions usually imply an evaluation or indirectly call on the student to add certain information or consider certain text-based revisions:

- Which drugs did you have in mind?
- Have you proved the "wrongness" of drugs just by saying that they are?

Open questions allow the student more room to figure out things on her own:

- If danger is the issue, how would you respond to the idea that cigarettes, motorcycles, and hang gliding are dangerous?
- What other things would you consider dangerous to society? Should they be illegal?

The least controlling types of commentary are reflective comments, which provide lessons, offer explanations of other comments, present reader responses, or simply make interpretations of the writing:

- Your first argument deals with the financial reasons for legalizing drugs. (interpretive)
- In academic writing, the trick is to express your opinion with authority. (instructional)
- [I'd delete "without any explanation."] Some people would want it explained. (explanatory)
- I think I'm following your point, but I'm having to do a lot of filling in. (reader response)

Used as a predominant strategy in a set of comments, different modes of response enact different roles for the teacher and exert different degrees of control over the student's writing.[4] As Margie Krest notes, "The way we phrase our responses to students is just as important as what we actually tell them" (27).

I am assuming, of course, that the way comments are framed has a direct influence on the meaning of the comments. I am assuming, further, that the words written on a student's paper inscribe certain social relationships between the teacher and the student and that these words come with their own adequate context. My goal is not to determine how the teacher actually intends a given comment or to predict how the student would likely understand it. As Knoblauch and Brannon point out, such determinations cannot reliably be made without access to the actual context in which the comment was made:

> A single comment on a single essay is too local and contingent a phenomenon to yield general conclusions about the quality of the conversation of which it is a part. Any remark on a student essay, whatever its form, finally owes its meaning and impact to the governing dialogue that influences some student's reaction to it. Remarks taken out of this context can appear more restrictive or open-ended, more facilitative or judgmental, than they really are in light of a teacher's overall communicative habits. ("Teacher Commentary" 287)

But although the meaning of a set of comments is no doubt influenced by the teacher's actual persona and the larger classroom setting, it is no less the case that this meaning is largely determined by the way the comments are presented on the page. In fact, it is arguable that, during the time the student reads a set of comments, the image of the teacher that comes off the page *becomes* the teacher for that student and has an immediate impact on how those comments come to mean. Instead of the actual or intended meaning, I am attempting to interpret the immediate sense of the comment—the conventional meaning derivable from the words on the page—and define the typical ways that teacher comments inscribe certain implicit relationships with students.

Having outlined this method of analyzing teacher comments, I'd like to return to White's and Peterson's comments, analyze their focuses and modes of commentary, and describe the images they create and the kind of control they exert over Nancy's writing.

Analyzing the Focuses and Modes of Teacher Responses

Let's begin by taking a closer look at White's commentary, considering first the case that his comments are directive. White seems clearly to assume a rather authoritative stance about this student's revision. He has certain ideas about what needs to be done to the draft to make it into a "good paper." He knows where its main idea lies, and he does not hesitate to tell the student precisely where she should develop her arguments. Many of his comments are presented in the form of imperatives and tell the student what to do by way of revision, creating him in the image of an editor or critic:

> [R]evise the opening to begin your argument.
>
> Select the parts of LeMoult's article that are appropriate for your paper and omit the rest.
>
> Focus this prgh on this argument and develop your case.
>
> Now develop this one.
>
> Make this into a full closing prgh.
>
> Be sure you focus each prgh on its central idea.

His comments assert his authority over the student. In this sense, he is directive.

Yet on several counts White's comments are clearly different from the first set of responses presented above. First of all, White does not cover the page with markings about surface features. Almost all of his comments focus on large conceptual matters of content and organization. He is also careful to communicate his ideas clearly to the student, writing his comments out in full statements, not in terse, editorial marks and phrases. Although he lays out ways the writing can be improved, he works with the student's ideas and intentions and even offers some comments that play back his understanding of the text:

> Now that you are clear on what you have to say . . . .
>
> Your first argument here: the financial reasons are not good enough for legalization.
>
> Second argument.

If White appropriates the student's choices here and there by deciding where she should make changes, he does not emphasize his own agenda so much that he takes control out of the student's hands. If he doesn't hesitate to tell the student what the writing needs, he does not tell her how the writing "ought to look," as the first responder does when, for example, she dictates surface changes in the first two paragraphs, telling Nancy to delete the opening phrase of sentence 2, to condense the first three sentences of paragraph 2, and to tighten up the rest of the paragraph. He also imposes no particular content on the student's writing.

Instead, he works with the student's ideas, trying to lead her to develop and organize her arguments against legalizing drugs. Even if he makes certain choices for the student, it can hardly be said that he is trying, in Brannon and Knoblauch's words, to "define restrictively what a student would (or will) have to do in order to perfect it in the teacher's eyes" (*Rhetorical Traditions* 123). He is trying to lead the student to make certain gains in the next draft, not dictate how the writing should look. If White's comments are authoritative, they are not authoritarian.

Looked at against the first two sets of responses, Peterson's comments seem more student-friendly and less directive. But are they directive or facilitative? How much control do they assert over the writer? By examining her comments in terms of their focuses and modes, we can see the ways in which Peterson assumes a definite control over the student's writing even as she encourages Nancy's own work at revision. The dominant strategy in Peterson's response is the spattering of questions she presents in her marginal comments. The questions indicate areas where she is unsure about what the writer is getting at and look to prompt Nancy to consider how she might make changes in the text so that her audience will better understand what she has to say. Notably, they deal with specific content concerns that come up moment-by-moment as she reads the text. Nine of the 10 questions are closed. Three of them ask the writer to add information to clarify a point:

> [This is in his 4th prgh–] what's he doing in the first 3 prghs?
>
> Whose bodies?
>
> To whom?

Six of them prompt the writer to reconsider specific statements:

> Do we? All drugs?
>
> Cigarettes? alcohol? car racing?
>
> Legal or illegal?
>
> All people?
>
> Do you mean morally wrong or dangerous?

These short, staccato-like comments create Peterson in the role of a questioning and somewhat demanding reader who dramatizes the difficulties she has with the text and who is willing to call for what she needs to know. They are designed to elicit particular changes in the text, but they do so in a way that allows the student to retain a certain amount of control over the writing—but only a certain amount. Although they are not as controlling as criticism or commands ("This is an overstatement," "Explain how drugs are dangerous to society"), these closed questions regulate what the student attends to in her revision and assert a rather firm control over her choices as a writer.

In her end note, Peterson takes on a more open and encouraging posture and deals with the larger content of the writing. She praises the writer's efforts and then suggests, in two open-ended advisory comments, in a general way, how Nancy might go about her revision:

> Before beginning a second draft, I suggest you do a barebones outline on the article (you're missing a couple of LeMoult's points) and then do one on your response (you seem to have at least 2 objections instead of one).

She presents two criticisms of the draft here, but tellingly they are embedded as asides within her suggestions, keeping her tone positive, keeping her emphasis on what is working and what could be made to work better. Notably, her advice does not call for specific revisions of the text, but suggests how Nancy might go about taking up the task of revision. If Peterson's questions and criticism create her as an interested and even an expectant reader, her praise and advice create her as a collaborator or supportive guide. Her comments both direct Nancy to make particular changes in the text and look to engage her in her own choices and revisions as a writer. She employs the strategies, one might say, of both directive and facilitative response. Ultimately, her response style, as I read it, lies somewhere between White's moderately directive style and the following responses by Anne Gere, which are clearly facilitative:

Gere's Marginal Comments

What about starting with this point? (end of prgh 1)

How does this advance LeMoult's argument for legalizing drugs? (first half of prgh 2)

How can you be sure we all know "without any explanation"? (end of prgh 3)

Can you develop this argument? (prgh 4, re: drugs and alcohol)

Gere's End Comments

You have done a good job of summarizing much of LeMoult's article. I think you have overlooked a couple of important points, however. Reread the section where he traces the history of drugs in this country, and look again at his distinction between drugs and alcohol.

I find your argument against legalizing drugs the most convincing when you compare the number of alcoholics with the number of drug addicts. Perhaps you can develop this idea further. In contrast, I find the statements that we all know drugs are wrong less than convincing. Just exactly why is legalizing drugs the easy way out? If danger is the issue, how do you respond to the idea that cars are dangerous? (Think about how many people are killed and maimed in automobile accidents every year.) In your next draft try to focus on developing more convincing arguments against legalized drugs.

When you have completed your next draft, try reading it aloud before you turn it in. I think you will find a number of places where your ears will help you express your ideas more effectively.

Like Peterson, Gere establishes a positive, easygoing atmosphere and creates herself as a supportive teacher-reader. Yet there is a clear difference between her comments and Peterson's. Gere makes only a few marginal comments, all of them dealing with matters of content that go beyond the level of the sentence. The comments take the form of questions and are designed to lead the student to consider reshaping and developing what she has said. They allow her to decide on what specific changes she makes and how she makes those changes. Rather than telling Nancy to cut the first three sentences of the introduction, she suggests it through a question: "What about starting with this point?" Rather than telling her authoritatively to develop the argument in her last paragraph in a command, she frames the comment as a question and only indirectly suggests such a change: "Can you develop this argument?" Both comments refrain from directly telling Nancy what to do. Her other questions are more open-ended. One poses a problem for her to consider: "How does this advance LeMoult's argument for legalizing drugs?" Another challenges her with a question, "How can you be sure we all know 'without any explanation'?" Both questions, especially the first, are to be distinguished from the type of questions Peterson presents in her comments. Peterson's questions present a series of prompts intended to lead the writer to make specific changes in the text. They provide a clear direction for the writer's revision and are somewhat controlling. Gere's questions call on the writer to reexamine a position she has taken, but do not indicate any particular revision. They provide less overt help and direction, and give Nancy greater control over her writing choices.

Gere's end comments adopt a mixture of authoritative and interactive postures. While some of her comments present judgments about the writing and indicate what the writer would do well to work on by way of revision, others go back over this ground and help the writer better understand the issues at stake and how to address them in the next draft. The foundation of Gere's end note is built on evaluative comments. Four of her 13 comments are presented as evaluations of the writing—half of them positive, half of them critical. Notably, both of the critical comments are framed as qualified evaluations. She doesn't say, "You have overlooked a number of crucial points"; she says, "*I think* you have overlooked *a couple* of important points." She doesn't say, "Your argument that drugs are wrong is ineffective"; she underscores the subjective nature of her evaluation and tempers the weight of the judgment by saying: "*I find* the statements that we all know drugs are wrong *less than convincing*" (emphasis mine). Moreover, rather than presenting her evaluations by themselves or adding other authoritative comments after them, Gere follows each of these evaluations with more moderate forms of response—advice and questions—that offer additional guidance and information that the student would likely see as help:

> I think you have overlooked a couple of important points, however. Reread the section where he traces the history of drugs in this country, and look again at his distinction between drugs and alcohol.

> I find your argument against legalizing drugs the most convincing when you compare the number of alcoholics with the number of drug addicts. Perhaps you can develop this idea further.

> I find the statement that we all know drugs are wrong less than convincing. Just exactly why is legalizing drugs the easy way out? If danger is the issue, how do you respond to the idea that cars are dangerous? . . . In your next draft try to focus on developing more convincing arguments against legalizing drugs.

The kinds of advice Gere offers also affects her control as a responder. While some of her advisory comments suggest particular changes in the text–

> Perhaps you can develop this idea further.

> In your next draft try to focus on developing more convincing arguments against legalized drugs

others offer advice about taking up certain reading and writing activities:

Reread the section where he traces the history of drugs in this
country, and look again at his distinction between drugs and
alcohol.

When you have completed your next draft, try reading it aloud
before you turn it in.

These process-based advisory comments provide a direction for the
writer, but they do not specify particular textual changes. They leave the
student room to make her own decisions and place greater responsibility
on her as a writer than text-based advice.

Gere's response alternately shifts, then, from comments that point to
concerns, to comments that indicate possible ways of addressing those
concerns, to comments that try to help the writer better understand the
issues at stake. By juggling these various strategies of response and generally making use of moderate modes, she offers some, but not much,
direction to the student. Her comments look to guide the student to come
up with a better written product, but they also help her get more practice
in her writing processes and more comfortable making decisions as a
writer. Ultimately, Gere is a fairly nondirective responder.

Gere's style of response, however, is only one of the many ways that
a teacher can be "facilitative." Consider, as a final example, the following
set of responses, which are also facilitative but employ strategies and
offer a style that is facilitative in a very different way. The comments,
written by Peter Elbow, are not presented on the student's text but in a
separate letter to the student.

Dear Nancy,

It's fine not to worry about mechanics or correctness or nice
sentences on a rough draft (I don't either); a way to put all attention on your train of thought; but remember that you'll need to
get mechanics up to snuff for the final draft.

Seems like you've tried to build yourself a good framework
and foundation—to build on for future drafts. You do an OK job
of introducing the article. You don't give a full summary, but
weren't asked to. And it strikes me that you move fairly quickly
to one of your best arguments: alcohol. The widespread abuse is
so undeniable.

My reactions. I don't disagree with your position, but somehow I find myself fighting you as I read. I'm trying to figure out
why. I don't want to legalize drugs, but somehow I want to listen more to that writer. After all, he has a delicate thesis: not that

we should do it but think about doing it. There's nothing wrong with you picking on part of his argument (legalizing) and ignoring the other part ("let's just think about it")—but the effect is somehow to make it seem as though you are having a closed mind and saying "Let's not even think about it." I guess I feel that the drug situation is so terrible that we have to let ourselves think about more things; I'm feeling stuck. So I think (self-centeredly) that the question for your next draft is this: what can you do to get a reader like me not to fight you so much? Try thinking about that; see what you can come up with.

I'd be happy to talk more about this in a conference.

Best,

Peter

Elbow offers some instruction, advice, and praise at the beginning and end of his response, but for the most part he acts as a sounding board for the writing. He describes how he experiences the words on the page and offers his reactions to what he reads, leaving it up to the writer, given this reading, to decide on a course for revision. Instead of prompting the student to address certain areas of the text, like White and Peterson, he gives his reading of the overall content of the writing and notes the effect it has on him. Instead of asking a series of focused questions or presenting direct evaluations of the writing, like Peterson and Gere, he writes most of his comments as reader responses, or what he himself might call "movies of the reader's mind" (*Sharing and Responding* 43-52). Significantly, these reader responses take two forms. In one, Elbow plays back his reading of the text or offers his own views on the subject without making overt evaluations. In the other, he plays back his reading of the text and indirectly presents in this reading his moment-to-moment judgments about the writing. The two forms of reader response are played off each other throughout the heart of his response in paragraph three—his interpretations and remarks (in regular type) leading into, and preparing the ground for, his more judgmental reader reactions (in italics):

> My reactions. I don't disagree with your <u>position</u>, *but somehow I find myself fighting you as I read.* I'm trying to figure out why. I don't want to legalize drugs, *but somehow I want to <u>listen</u> more to that writer.* . . . There's nothing wrong with you picking on part of his argument (legalizing) and ignoring the other part ("let's just think about it")—*but the effect is somehow to make it seem as though you are having a closed mind and saying "Let's not even think*

about it." I guess I feel that the drug situation is so terrible that
we have to let ourselves think about more things; *I'm feeling
stuck.* (emphasis mine)

Half of these comments give a kind of summary transcript of Elbow's
reading of the writing as an everyday reader, one who is reading for the
meaning and interest it holds for him. They are among the least controlling modes of response since they do little more than dramatize how the
words are being understood by an individual reader, not by someone in
charge of judging, criticizing, or improving the writing. The other half of
the comments move beyond this function of a reader playing back the
text and inject some evaluation into the reading. These reader reactions
mute the sharpness of conventional evaluations and temper the authority of the responder. In fact, Elbow goes out of his way to qualify his judgments. Instead of saying "I am fighting you as I read," he says: "*somehow
I find myself* fighting you as I read." Instead of saying "you come across
as being closed minded," he says, "*the effect is somehow to make it seem as
though* you are having a closed mind and saying 'Let's not even think
about it'" (emphasis mine). Nevertheless, these reader reactions present
certain judgments about the writing and, however indirectly, invoke a
certain degree of control over the writer's way of looking back on the text.
Significantly, they also provide some direction for the student's revision.

Although Elbow makes no overt evaluations about what is wrong
with the writing and no calls for specific changes, he still provides the
dissonance that is necessary to initiate revision. He is not a critic. He is a
guide only in a very general sense of the term. And he is not a common
reader who reads the writing almost exclusively for its content and information without making judgments about how it can be improved; his
reader-response comments frequently go beyond simply playing back
the text and offer critical judgments about the writing. He is a sounding
board with a teacher's purpose, reading first for the meaning and interest the writing holds for him and then, along the way, inserting his
teacherly sense of what he likes and what rubs him the wrong way. His
comments do not direct or even overtly guide the writer about changes
to be made in the writing. But they do provide some implicit direction for
the writer's subsequent work. Elbow is content to allow the student to
infer, on the basis of his reading, what might be done by way of revision.

If Elbow provides little direct assistance for making specific changes
in the next draft and assumes only modest control over the writer's choices, it may be because he is as concerned with encouraging students to
engage in the practice of revision as he is with leading them to produce a
better subsequent draft. He lets Nancy know through his reading that he

is not persuaded by her argument, but he does not, on the basis of this reading, lead her to make any specific changes that might make the writing more persuasive. He leaves it up to the student to decide what to do, perhaps because he thinks there is more to be gained from allowing the student to come up with her own changes. It would make sense then that his responses do not offer as much direction—or exert as much control— over the student's writing. If White and Peterson provide more direction and are more controlling in their responses, it may be because they are intent on helping Nancy revise her text into a better written product and because they see such work with completed texts as central to the student's development as a writer.

*   *   *

In the analyses above, I have been distinguishing among different styles of commentary by describing, individually and collectively, five teacher's predominant methods of commentary. I have been looking beyond general attitudes and styles and into the particular language and strategies these teachers adopt, examining what they say to the student and how they say it. In effect, I have been employing a grammar of teacher control, looking to determine the implicit control that teachers establish through how many comments they make, what they focus on, and how they frame their comments. Through these analyses, we can see how, while White and Peterson look to offer direct assistance with the revision of the text, they employ different strategies in offering this help and direction, with slightly different goals. White is more willing to tell the student what she would do best to work on, through directive comments. Peterson is more willing to prompt the student through pointed questions. White takes on the role of an editor who has definite views about how the writing would best be revised. Peterson takes on the role of a trouble-shooting reader who looks to help the writer see the need for revision. We can also see that Gere is reluctant to provide specific ways of revision. She offers more explicit criticism and advice than Peterson, but she refrains from prompting the writer to make specific changes in the writing, preferring instead to offer broad advice and open-ended questions. Gere takes on the role of a helpful mentor, pointing to areas to consider and more quietly guiding the writer to take up revision activities. She provides some direction for revision, but seems more intent on leading the student to take up issues on her own and gain experience in making her own choices as a learning writer. Elbow's style is the least controlling of the group—and provides the least direct guidance for revision—largely because his reader-response comments do not point directly to particular changes to be made in the writing. More than anything else, he tries to be a sounding board for the writing, one who plays back his reading of the text and subtly injects his evaluations and advice for revision within these reader responses. Whatever questions or advice he provides is minimal, since his main purpose as a responder seems to be to show the writer how the writing acted on him as an individual reader and provide only enough ideas to think about that will nudge the writer to initiate certain lines of revision on her own. To a large extent, his comments are geared to the student behind the text. They are designed to engage her in making her own writing choices and developing her experiences as a writer.

None of the last four responders is directive in the authoritarian sense that Brannon and Knoblauch have in mind—that is, in the sense that most of the scholarship has in mind when they talk about "directive" responses. They all resist taking over the text or dictating particular changes, and they try to engage the student in looking back on her writing and allow her to maintain control over her own writing choices. Significantly, all four responders also make some use of directive strategies of response—comments that point to some problems or concerns in the writing or that call on the writer to take up certain tasks or revisions. But they all enact different strategies, construct different roles, assume different degrees of control, and offer different kinds of help to the student. White's responses are clearly directive, but they are not so directive as to usurp the student's control over the writing. Both Elbow's and Gere's responses are clearly facilitative, but each of them emphasizes rather different facilitative strategies, invokes different degrees of control over the student's text, and enacts a distinctive style of commentary. Peterson's responses lie somewhere in between, leaning at times toward a more directive stance, at times toward a more facilitative one. How effective each response style will be depends in part on the larger goals of the class, the teacher's style, and the individual student. But each, it seems to me, is made effective first of all by the way the teacher constructs his or her comments on the page, opening a line of communication with the student, offering text-specific responses, and providing direction to the student even as they leave the real work of revision up to her.

Conclusion

More than the general principles we voice or the theoretical approach we take into class, it is what we value in student writing, how we communicate those values, and what we say individually on student texts that carry the most weight in writing instruction. It is how we receive and respond to the words students put on the page that speaks loudest in our teaching. Yet although we have given a good deal of thought to our relationship to our students, we have not, as Charles Bazerman points out, "confronted this relationship in its most central form in the writing classroom—what transpires between teacher and student across the written page" (141). So it is important, as he goes on to say, "to consider how we construct ourselves as readers, what influences that construction, and how that construction acts as a variable in student writing" (143).

This study works against the rather established idea that there are essentially only two ways of commenting on student writing—one helpful, encouraging, and effective, the other controlling and ineffective. It suggests that we should not reject all directive styles of response any more than we should all adopt some standard facilitative style. Instead, the study offers a more detailed and open-ended way of analyzing teacher commentary, one that is based on a close reading of comments as they appear on the page. By understanding the great variety of ways teachers can create themselves in their comments—the many ways teachers may be directive and facilitative—we will be more able to describe, reflect on, and develop our own responding practices and shape our comments to better fit our teaching styles, our classroom goals, and the needs of our individual students.

The main question of teacher response, this study suggests, is not a question of whether or not to impose our views on students and somehow control their writing choices. Given the power relations that adhere in the classroom, all teacher comments in some way are evaluative and directive. In all comments, a teacher intervenes in the writing and, however directly or indirectly, indicates that something needs to be attended to. The question is, when and to what extent we as individual teachers should exert control over student writing through our comments: How much should I make decisions for the writer? How much should I leave the student to figure out on her own? How much can I productively allow the student to explore her own writing choices? What is the best style for me, given my propensities as a teacher, given what I have to accomplish in the class, given what I think is going to help students learn to write better? What kind of comments will be best for this student, with this paper, at this time?

Of course, the optimum style of response for any teacher is going to be a function of her personality and teaching style. Some teachers will be inclined to be more directive in their teaching and responding. Others will be more open and interactive. Others still will seek some middle ground. The more a teacher's comments tap into her strengths as a teacher and the more they become an extension of herself, the better those comments will be. Different teachers, tapping on different strengths, will make vastly different strategies work—and work well. We need to respect these differences and even celebrate them, since successful response, like successful teaching, seems so much a matter of individual work between teacher and student.

This is not to say, however, that one style of response is as good as another or that any style of response that fits the teacher's demeanor and classroom style is effective. Not at all. Even if there is not one right way to respond to student writing, even if successful response is a matter of individual style, surely there are better and worse ways to respond—and even wrong ways to respond. At one extreme, some comments are overly harsh or disrespectful, and usurp control over student writing, making sweeping editorial changes and dictating what should be said or how it should be presented from top to bottom. At the other extreme, some teacher comments are so minimal and generic that they become detached and offer no help, no real response. Both extremes ought to be avoided. Students must be allowed to develop their own ideas and encouraged to take responsibility for their writing; they must be allowed to make their own writing decisions and learn to make better choices. Comments that recognize the integrity of the student as a learning writer and that look to engage him in substantive revision are better than those that do not.

If we are going to make sure our comments are working as well as they can, we need to look at what we are doing with the way we present our comments on the page. All of us, it seems to me, would do well, then, to take a close, hard look at the comments we make, consider whether they are doing the kind of work we want them to do, and make whatever changes we can to make them work better. When all is said and done, our response styles are not determined by our personality. They are not determined by our institutional setting. They do not follow automatically from our attitudes or intentions. They are not inseparable from our classroom context. And they are not set in stone. We create our styles by the choices we make on the page, in the ways we present our comments. We have an opportunity to recreate, modify, or refine this style every time we write a new set of comments, by attending to what we comment on, how much we address, and how we present our comments. From time to time, we would do well to ask our students to respond to our responses and see how they understand, react to, and make use of different kinds of comments—and then find ways to make our comments more productive. We would also do well to develop a repertoire of responses—and learn to use different strategies for different students and different classroom situations.

The best responding styles will not feature certain focuses and modes of commentary and exclude certain others. The best responding styles will create us on the page in ways that fit in with our classroom purposes, allow us to take advantage of our strengths as teachers, and enable us to interact as productively as we can with our students. Ultimately, they will allow us to make comments that are ways of teaching.

Notes

1.   In *Rhetorical Traditions and the Teaching of Writing*, Knoblauch and Brannon spell out the distinctions between these two styles of response. Directive comments are designed "either simply to label the errors in writing or to define restrictively what a student would (or will) have to do in order to perfect it in the teacher's eyes" (125). Some examples they give: "Rephrase," "This is obvious—cut it out." In facilitative commentary, by contrast, the teacher tries "to create motivation for immediate and substantive revision by describing a careful reader's uncertainties about what a writer intends to say," as in the following response:

> How important are these factors? Do you imply that they are relative or that they don't always matter? Is your essay going to be about these factors?

These comments are designed to lead the student to reflect on her choices as a writer, not to tell her what to do. They provide her with information that she "is free to consider though not constrained to adopt" (126).

2.   In many ways, the social turn in composition has fueled our resistance to defining different types of commentary in terms of specific textual strategies. Influenced by poststructural theory, we have moved away from a close scrutiny of the written text and focused increasingly on the social conditions and practices that inform writing. Thus, according to Brannon and Knoblauch, the main difference between directive and facilitative response does not lie in the outward appearance of the comments, but in the teacher's attitude, in what the teacher generally strives to do in his comments: to direct students to make changes or allow them to retain control over the writing. Consequently, they forego the analysis of individual comments based on how they appear on the page. They seem to assume that if a teacher takes on a given attitude or posture, her responses will naturally reflect the purpose she has in mind.

3.   Not all comments in a given category imply the same degree of control. The comment "This sentence makes no sense" is more controlling than "This sentence is not well-structured," though both of them are evaluations. Moreover, the comments from one category may shade into the gradations of control of another category. The spectrum suggests the *typical* degrees of control implied in various ways of framing comments, not a firm hierarchy. Notably, the meaning and control of any given comment may be influenced by the surrounding comments. A question that follows a harsh criticism will tend to be more controlling than the

same question when it follows a comment that praises the student's writing:

> This is at best a questionable argument. Should we make all things that are dangerous illegal?
>
> I think you've got a good point here about not legalizing things that are dangerous. Should we make all things that are dangerous illegal?

It is also important to note that a teacher's control is more than just a matter of the focuses and modes he employs. The number of comments he makes, the range of those comments, and the agenda he brings to his reading, among other things, also influence teacher control.

4. Different forms of the "same" response, I am suggesting, amount to different comments. Consider the following comments. They all deal with the same issue and can be seen as having the same general goal—to lead the writer to revise his statement that "you shouldn't legalize something that is dangerous." But they are cast in different modes and function in different ways:

- Make it clear that you're talking only about dangerous drugs. (imperative)
- I'd try to make it clear that you're talking about dangerous drugs, so you don't suggest that anything that is dangerous should be illegal. (advisory)
- This is an over-statement. (evaluative)
- This may be making a stronger claim than you need. (qualified evaluative)
- I'm wondering about bungee jumping, race-car driving, boxing, and cigarette smoking. They are dangerous, yet they are not illegal. (reader response)
- Aren't there a lot of drugs out there that are not dangerous? (closed question)
- How much are you concerned with the danger illegal drugs pose to society? How much are you concerned with the danger they pose to individual users? (open questions)

Only the first comment, "Make it clear that you're talking only about dangerous drugs," immediately directs the student to make a change. The other versions offer advice, present evaluations, or ask the student to consider certain changes.

Works Cited

Bazerman, Charles. "Reading Student Texts: Proteus Grabbing Proteus." *Encountering Student Texts: Interpretive Issues in Reading Student Writing*, 139-46. Ed. Bruce Lawson, Susan Sterr Ryan, and W. Ross Winterowd. Urbana: NCTE, 1989.

Brannon, Lil, and C.H. Knoblauch. "On Students' Rights to Their Own Texts: A Model of Teacher Response." *College Composition and Communication* 33 (May 1982): 157-66.

Elbow, Peter, and Pat Belanoff. *Sharing and Responding.* New York: Random House, 1989.

Flynn, Elizabeth. "Learning to Read Student Papers from a Feminist Perspective." *Encountering Student Texts: Interpretive Issues in Reading Student Writing,* 49-58. Ed. Bruce Lawson, Susan Sterr Ryan, and W. Ross Winterowd. Urbana: NCTE, 1989.

Fuller, David. "Teacher Commentary That Communicates: Practicing What We Preach in the Writing Class." *Journal of Teaching Writing* 6 (Fa/Wi 1987)): 307-17.

Horvath, Brooke. "The Components of Written Response: A Practical Synthesis of Current Views." *Rhetoric Review* 2 (January 1984): 136-56.

Knoblauch, C.H., and Lil Brannon. "Teacher Commentary on Student Writing: The State of the Art." *Freshman English News* 10 (Fall 1981): 1-4.

Knoblauch, C.H., and Lil Brannon. *Rhetorical Traditions and the Teaching of Writing.* Upper Montclair, NJ: Boynton/Cook, 1984.

Krest, Margie. "Monitoring Student Writing: How Not to Avoid the Draft." *Journal of Teaching Writing* 7 (Sp/Su 1988): 27-39.

Moxley, Joseph. "Responding to Student Writing: Goals, Methods, Alternatives." *Freshman English News* 17 (Spring 1989): 3-4, 9-10.

Probst, Robert E. "Transactional Theory and Response to Student Writing." *Writing and Response: Theory, Practice, Research,* 68-79. Ed. Chris Anson, Urbana: NCTE, 1989.

Purves, Alan. "The Teacher as Reader: An Anatomy." *College English* 46 (March 1984): 259-65.

Rule, Rebecca. "Conferences and Workshops: Conversations on Writing in Process." *Nuts and Bolts: A Practical Guide to Teaching College Composition,* 43-65. Ed. Thomas Newkirk. Portsmouth, NH: Boynton/Cook, Heinemann, 1993.

Sommers, Jeffrey. "The Writer's Memo: Collaboration, Response, and Development." *Writing and Response: Theory, Practice, Research,* 174-86. Ed. Chris Anson. Urbana: NCTE, 1989.

Sommers, Nancy. "Responding to Student Writing." *College Composition and Communication* 33 (May 1982): 148-56.

Straub, Richard, and Ronald F. Lunsford. *Twelve Readers Reading: Responding to College Student Writing.* Cresskill, NJ: Hampton Press, 1995.

Learning to Praise

Donald A. Daiker

In *A Moveable Feast*, Ernest Hemingway recounts his first meeting with F. Scott Fitzgerald. One night while Hemingway is sitting with friends at the Dingo Bar in Paris, Fitzgerald unexpectedly walks in, introduces himself, and proceeds to talk nonstop about Hemingway's writing, especially "how great it was." Hemingway reports that he was embarrassed by Fitzgerald's lavish compliments—not because he felt flattered by them, but because he and his fellow expatriates "still went under the system, then, that praise to the face was open disgrace" (150).

The distrust of praise among American writers abroad seems to have rubbed off on composition teachers at home. In a 1985 study at Texas A&M University, Sam Dragga analyzed forty freshman essays that had been graded and marked by four randomly chosen and traditionally trained teaching assistants. They wrote a total of 864 comments on the essays, but only 51 of them were comments of praise. This means that 94% of the comments focused on what students had done poorly or incorrectly, only 6% on what had been done well. The same pattern apparently prevails in high school as well. A study of responses by thirty-six secondary English teachers revealed that although 40% of their end-of-paper comments were positive, the percentage of positive marginal comments was a meager .007% (Harris).

The conclusion that college composition teachers find error more attractive than excellence is consistent with a pilot study of my own conducted in 1982 at Miami University (Daiker). I asked twenty-four colleagues to grade and comment on "Easy Street," a student essay chosen because it combines strength with weakness in both content and style. I asked my colleagues to mark the essay as if it had been submitted in their freshman composition course. They made a total of 378 separate markings or comments on the student essay: 338, or 89.4%, of them cited error or found fault; only 40, or 10.6%, of them were comments of praise. What may make the predominance of correction over commendation even more significant is that during the previous month, a departmental memorandum reported scholarly consensus on two matters of grading: (1) an instructor should not mark every writing error, because students cannot psychologically cope with a deluge of deficiencies; and (2) an instructor should use praise and positive reinforcement as a major teaching strategy.

Scholarship notwithstanding, composition teachers have traditionally withheld praise from papers they have considered less than perfect. A case in point is the well-known "Evaluating a Theme," published in the *Newsletter of the Michigan Council of Teachers of English* (Stevens). The issue consists of twenty-five responses—twenty-one by college teachers, four by secondary teachers—to a single composition, and the issue's popularity carried it through sixteen printings. According to my figures, the proportion of criticism to praise is roughly the same as in the Texas A&M and Miami studies; the Michigan teachers identified nine errors or problems for every instance of praiseworthy writing. Just as important, fifteen of the twenty-five teachers found nothing in the paper deserving of praise. In three of those instances, college professors sufficiently skilled to ferret out thirty flaws apiece in a brief essay could not—or would not—identify a single source of strength. Their wholly negative comments reminded me of a grade-appeal procedure in which I was asked to evaluate eight   compositions written for a colleague's freshman English class. I read the compositions in order, paper one through paper eight, and I read them with increasing despair—not because of what the student had written, but because in responding to a semester's worth of writing, my colleague had offered not a single word of praise. Not an idea, not an example, not a sentence or clause or phrase or punctuation mark—nothing, apparently, merited a compliment. I began to wonder why the student was appealing only a grade, and I had visions of Bartleby the scrivener at work in a dead-letter office.

Francis Christensen observed a quarter century ago that there are two sharply contrasting points of view toward the teaching of English (Christensen 1962). The first he calls the "school" tradition, the second the "scholarly" tradition. The school tradition, nourished by a view of language that regards all change as decay and degeneration, encourages instructors to respond to student writing primarily by identifying and penalizing error. Because of the school tradition, it has long been common to speak of "correcting" themes. There is no clearer embodiment of the negative and narrowly conformist values of the school tradition than the popular correction chart. The 1985 "Harbrace College Handbook Correction Chart," to take a recent example of the species, provides seventy-one correction symbols for instructors to use and students to interpret. Why are correction symbols needed? Why write "d" rather than "diction," or "frag" rather than "This is not a complete sentence because it lacks a verb"? Presumably because instructors find so many errors to mark that not enough time remains for them to use whole words or complete sentences themselves. Significantly, what the correction charts never include is a symbol for approval or praise.

To become teachers of English in a "positive, joyous, creative, and responsible sense," Christensen urges us to replace the inert, rule-encumbered school tradition with more enlightened scholarly views. For several decades now, composition scholars have reported the value of praise in improving student writing. Paul B. Diederich, senior research associate for the Educational Testing Service, concluded from his research in evaluation that "noticing and praising whatever a student does well improves writing more than any kind or amount of correction of what he does badly, and that it is especially important for the less able writers who need all the encouragement they can get" ("Measuring" 20).

Since writing is an act of confidence, as Mina Shaughnessy reminds us (85), it is not surprising that the scholarly tradition emphasizes responding with encouragement. Ken Macrorie recommends that we "encourage and encourage, but never falsely" (688). E. D. Hirsch, who believes that written comments may turn out to be "the most effective teaching device of all" (159), agrees that "the best results are likely to be produced by encouragement" (161). For William F. Irmscher, "the psychology of positive reinforcement . . . should be the major resource for every writing teacher" (150). All of these individuals would support Diederich's statement that "The art of the teacher—at its best—is the reinforcement of good things" ("Praise" 58).

Praise may be especially important for students who have known little encouragement and, in part for that reason, suffer from writing apprehension. Writing apprehension is a measure of anxiety established through the research of John Daly and Michael Miller. According to these researchers, the highly apprehensive writer is one for whom anxiety about writing outweighs the projection of gain from writing. Because they fear writing and its consequences, "high apprehensives" seek to avoid writing situations: they are reluctant to take courses in writing, and they choose academic majors and occupations with minimal writing requirements. When they do write, they use language that is significantly less intense than people with low writing apprehension; that is, they are more reluctant to take a stand or to commit themselves to a position. They try to play it safe not only by embracing neutrality, but by saying less: in response to the same assignment, high apprehensives write fewer words and make fewer statements than low apprehensives (Daly and Miller "Apprehension"; Daly "Effects"; Daly and Shamo; Holland). The problem for highly apprehensive writers is circular. Because they anticipate negative consequences, they avoid writing. Yet the avoidance of writing—the lack of practice—leads to further negative consequences: writing of poor quality that receives low grades and unfavorable comments.

One's attitude toward the act of writing, Daly concludes, clearly affects not only how one writes and how often one writes, but even how others evaluate that writing (Daly "Effects"). What may be equally important—since writing is a powerful and perhaps even unique mode of learning (Emig)—is that by systematically avoiding writing situations, high apprehensives close off opportunities for learning and discovery.

But the cause of writing apprehension may suggest its cure—or at least its treatment. A major cause of writing apprehension is past failure or a perception of past failure; high apprehensives perceive their writing experiences as significantly less successful than low apprehensives. Daly says that the "highly apprehensive writer expects, due to a history of aversive responses, negative evaluations for writing attempts. This expectation likely becomes self-fulfilling" ("Effects" 571). These "aversive responses" include negative comments on assignments and low grades on papers and in writing courses. The connection between writing apprehension and teacher response is supported by the research of Thomas Gee. Working with 139 eleventh graders, Gee found that students whose compositions received either criticism alone or no commentary at all developed significantly more negative attitudes toward writing than students whose compositions received only praise. Moreover, after just four weeks, students who received only negative comments or none at all were writing papers significantly shorter than those of students who were praised.

Since positive reinforcement, or its lack, is so crucial to a student's level of writing apprehension (Daly and Miller "Studies"), one way of reducing apprehension is by allowing students to experience success with writing. They will experience success, of course, whenever their writing is praised. For students who do not share their writing with others—and high apprehensives fear negative responses from their peers as well as their instructors—the writing teacher is likely their only potential source of praise.

But praise, however beneficial as a remedy for apprehension and as a motivator of student writing, is more easily enjoined than put into practice. Dragga notes in his study, for instance, that the four teaching assistants trained in praiseworthy grading all experienced "difficulty in labeling and explaining the desirable characteristics of their students' writing." He concludes that teacher training must emphasize explicit criteria for praiseworthy grading. The title of this article implies that praise does not flow readily from the marking pens of writing teachers; it must be learned.

Still, an instructor's conscious decision to praise the work of students is a promising starting point. Sometimes all that's needed is a gimmick. My own method is to allow myself nothing but positive comments during an initial reading of a student paper; I lift my pen to write words of praise only. Another practice is to ask, just before moving to another essay, "Have I told Melissa two or three things about her paper that I like?" R. W. Reising's technique is even more effective: he has developed a grading form that requires him to write one to three positive comments before he even considers noting a weakness (43).

But sometimes what we need is not a gimmick but understanding. We need to understand that what deserves praise is, for a teacher of writing, a relative and not an absolute question. As Ben Jonson says, "I will like and praise some things in a young writer which yet, if he continue in, I cannot but justly hate him for the same" (617). Following relative standards, we are in no sense dishonest or condescending in praising one writer for what we might ignore or criticize in another—even within the same class. Diederich urges us to praise everything a student has done that is "even a little bit above his usual standard" ("Measuring" 20).

After all, we follow relative standards in most of the teaching we do outside the classroom. In helping children learn how to talk or how to color or how to swim, we don't hold them up to the absolute standards of Demosthenes, van Gogh, or Mark Spitz; we don't even expect them to match their older friends or siblings. In fact, we praise them for the most modest achievements. I still remember trying to help my six-year-old daughter Pam learn how to hit a softball in our backyard on Withrow Avenue. Although I pitched the ball as gently as I knew how, trying to make it eminently hittable, Pam just could not get her bat on the ball. We tried all sorts of minor adjustments in her batting stance—hands held closer together, feet placed further apart, head turned at a more acute angle—but Pam kept missing. Despite my encouragement, she was losing heart in the enterprise. Finally, on perhaps the thirtieth pitch, Pam did hit the ball—nothing like solid contact, but still a distinctly audible foul tip. Of course, I jumped up and down; of course, I shouted, "Way to go, Pammy!"; and of course, she smiled. I praised her lots more when she managed first a foul pop, then a dribbler to the mound, and then a genuine ground ball. As a high school student, Pam started at first base for the varsity softball team.

Even with relative standards, a commitment to positive reinforcement, and perhaps a gimmick or two, most of us could benefit from some practice in praise. For that purpose, let's work with an essay written several years ago by a Miami University freshman in response to an open assignment.

Easy Street

The crowd screams and chants, as a bewildered contestant nervously jumps up and down in search of help. Excitedly, Monty Hall comments on the washer and dryer behind box number two in trade for the big curtain where Carol Marroll is standing. The contestant, with glamour and greed in her eyes; wildly picks the curtain. But when raised there stands a 300 pound cow munching on a bail of hay. Embarrassed and sad, the woman slowly sits down.

The old American ideal of hard work and get ahead had traditionally been one followed by many men. But with the arrival of the twentieth century, their seems to be a new way to get ahead. The new American ideal of something for nothing. It seems to have taken the place of honest work. In our popular television game shows, the idea of being able to win prizes and cash by just answering a few simple questions seems to thrill the average American. It is so popular and fascinating that the morning hours are consumed with five to six hours of the programs. The viewer is thrown into a wonderland where everything is free for the taking. The reason for such interest in these programs is that they show life as most of us really wish it be to be–soft, easy, free. Our society now enjoys the simplicities of life, and our television game shows exemplify that.

One of the newest of all American dreams is to win a state lottery. What easier way is there to become a millionaire with such a small investment? The state makes it as easy as just reading a couple of numbers off a card, or scratching away a secret spot. Who hasn't at least once in their life, dreamed of hitting the big one, and living off the fat the rest of their life; without ever having to work again? Our country clubs, local junior football teams, even our churches have lotteries now thriving on that dream.

In our whole vocabulary their is no word that can command as much attention as the word "free." It sums up our modern culture and feelings. Advertisers use the word as frequently as possible knowing its strong effect on the public. The idea of giving something away without the consumer having to pay for it has made many a company successful.

The old American ideal seems to have moved over for the new. No longer does a man have to work late or get up early. By just guessing the right tune in five notes; he could be ordering caviar in the morning rather than toast.

When "Easy Street" was evaluated by college instructors, grades ranged from B to F, with C and C- by far the most common. But my colleagues found much to praise even in an essay they rated average or slightly below average in quality. Their comments of praise are categorized below, according to the four levels Nina Ziv used in her study of teacher response: conceptual, structural, sentential, and lexical.

A. Conceptual level.

1. "Your thesis—that the new American ideal is 'something for nothing'—is strong and clear."

2. "Your thesis is interesting and clear, and your use of particular, graphic details to support the thesis greatly aids your reader's understanding. The conversational tone of your paper also helps the reader understand you."

3. "The content of this paper is interesting & to the point, the essay is fairly well unified, and you show the ability to use effective details."

4. "There is much that is strong here; your sense of detail is good and your ideas are insightful."

5. "You have provided some excellent examples which capture the essence of the 'new' American ideal."

6. "Your ideas are brilliant, and the way you have argued your point is convincing. Keep up with original and thought-provoking ways of looking at life, around you."

7. "I like the scope of your commentary, which moves from the initial, interest-provoking example, to the statement of American ideals in paragraph #2, to the further example—of the state lottery—in paragraph #3."

8. "You come across as being perceptive and as concerned about an important trend in our culture."

9. "Your ideas here are strong and clear" (refers to second paragraph).

10. "Your paper has fine unity and some precise illustrations."

B. Structural level.

1. "The paper is well-organized and well-focused, with some nice paragraph transitions."

2. "Good details" (refers to next-to-last sentence of first paragraph and to middle sentence of third paragraph).

3. "An effective opening paragraph—good detail!"

4. "Well put, effective use of specific detail" (refers to last sentence of third paragraph).

5. "A superb choice of topic—and a good natural organization from specific to general—from private to public—and from analysis to significance."

6. "Effective introduction—your detailed description gets the reader interested and draws him into your analysis."

7. "Good strategy for your opening: you caught my attention."

8. "Good details here" (refers to opening sentences of third prgh).

9. "I like this" (refers to the whole of first paragraph).

10. "I got a good first impression of this paper. You've started off well with an anecdote that gives the reader a good visual picture and gets her into your thesis."

C. Sentential level.

1. "Good sentences" (refers to middle sentences of second prgh).

2. "Good parallelism" (refers to third sentence of third paragraph and to first two sentences of last paragraph).

3. "Very nice pair of sentences—clear and concise" (refers to first two sentences of fourth paragraph).

4. "Effective closing image. Good!"

5. "Nice structure" (refers to last sentence of fourth paragraph).

D. Lexical level.

1. "Good—effective word choice here" (refers to "chants, as a bewildered contestant").

2. "You have a vigorous and full vocabulary."

3. "Nice title."

4. "Nice series—good climax" (refers to "soft, easy, free" of second paragraph).

5. "Nice phrase" (refers to "with glamour and greed in her eyes").

Although these positive comments show that "Easy Street" has much to praise, instructors marking the paper more readily recognized error than they identified strengths, especially on the sentential and lexical levels. For example, many instructors pointed out the dangling modifier in the next-to-last sentence of the first paragraph ("But when raised"), but no one applauded the effective use of appositive adjectives ("Embarrassed and sad") as modifiers in the following sentence. It seems clear that we have been better trained to spot comma splices and fragments and other syntactic slips than to notice when students take risks: Only one of two dozen evaluators commended the student for "soft, easy, free," a notable instance of series variation with the coordinating conjunction eliminated. Instructors routinely called attention to the misused semicolon in "By just guessing the right tune in five notes; he could be ordering caviar in the morning rather than toast." Far fewer heard the interesting sentence rhythms created by the sophisticated use of repetition.

So perhaps we need to go back to school ourselves to learn how to recognize what merits praise in student writing. A good starting point for syntax are the chapters on free modifiers in *Notes toward a New Rhetoric* (Christensen and Christensen) and in *The Writer's Options* (Daiker, Kerek, and Morenberg), and the articles on coordination by Winston Weathers and Robert L. Walker. But probably even more useful are sessions at conferences, at department meetings, and at workshops for teaching assistants in which we help each other learn what to praise and how to praise. But, if we listen to students, the "how" may not be all that important. At the same time that students tell us that criticism must be specific to work—a comment like "diction" or "logic" or "awkward" is almost always misunderstood unless explained in detail—they receive even vague compliments like "nice" and "good" and "well written" with gratitude and thanksgiving (Hayes and Daiker). Don Murray once casually remarked at a Wyoming Conference on Freshman and Sophomore English that one of his favorite responses to student writing begins with the five words "I like the way you." He told us we could complete the sentence in any way we chose: "I like the way you use dialogue here" or "I like the way you started your paper with a story" or "I like the way you repeated the key word *animal* in this paragraph."

In his preface to John Gardner's *On Becoming a Novelist*, Raymond Carver recalls his experience as a college freshman in Gardner's creative writing class at Chico State College. Carver remembers, above all, that Gardner lavished more attention and care on his work than any student had a right to expect. Although Gardner would cross out what he found unacceptable in Carver's stories and add words and even sentences of his own, he was always looking to find something to praise. When there was a sentence, a line of dialogue, or a narrative passage that he liked, something that he thought "worked" and moved the story along in some pleasant or unexpected way, he'd write "Nice" in the margin or else "Good!" And seeing these comments, my heart would lift. (xvi-xvii)

It's a good bet that genuine praise can lift the hearts, as well as the pens, of the writers who sit in our own classrooms, too.

Works Cited

Carver, Raymond. Preface to John Gardner's *On Becoming a Novelist*, xvi-xvii. New York: Harper, 1983.

Christensen, Francis. "Between Two Worlds." Paper delivered to the California Association of Teachers of English, San Diego, 1962. Rpt. *Notes toward a New Rhetoric*. Ed. Bonniejean Christensen. New York: Harper and Row, 1967, 1978.

Christensen, Francis. *Notes toward a New Rhetoric: Nine Essays for Teachers*, 2nd ed. Ed. Bonniejean Christensen. New York: Harper and Row, 1967, 1978.

Daiker, Donald A. "The Teacher's Options in Responding to Student Writing." Paper presented at the annual Conference on College Composition and Communication, Washington, D.C., 1983.

Daiker, Donald A., Andrew Kerek, and Max Morenberg. *The Writer's Options: Combining to Composing*, 3rd ed. New York: Harper, 1986.

Daly, John A. "The Effects of Writing Apprehension on Message Encoding." *Journalism Quarterly* 54 (1977): 566-72.

Daly, John A., and Michael D. Miller. "Apprehension of Writing as a Predictor of Message Intensity." *The Journal of Psychology* 89 (1975): 175-77.

Daly, John A., and Michael D. Miller. "The Empirical Development of an Instrument to Measure Writing Apprehension." *Research in the Teaching of English* 9 (1975): 242-49.

Daly, John A., and Michael D. Miller. "Further Studies on Writing Apprehension: SAT Scores, Success Expectations, Willingness to Take Advanced Courses and Sex Differences." *Research in the Teaching of English* 9 (1975): 250-56.

Daly, John A., and Wayne Shamo. "Academic Decisions as a Function of Writing Apprehension." *Research in the Teaching of English* 12 (1978): 119-26.

Diederich, Paul B. "In Praise of Praise." *NEA Journal* 52 (1963): 58-59.

Diederich, Paul B. *Measuring Growth in English*. Urbana: NCTE, 1974.

Dragga, Sam. "Praiseworthy Grading: A Teacher's Alternative to Editing Error." Paper presented at the Conference on College Composition and Communication, New Orleans, 1986.

Emig, Janet. "Writing as a Mode of Learning." *College Composition and Communication* 28 (1977): 122-28.

Gee, Thomas C. "Students' Responses to Teacher Comments." *Research in the Teaching of English* 6 (1972): 212-21.

Harris, Winifred Hall. "Teacher Response to Student Writing: A Study of the Response Pattern of High School Teachers to Determine the Basis for Teacher Judgment of Student Writing." *Research in the Teaching of English* 11 (1977): 175-85.

Hayes, Mary F., and Donald A. Daiker. "Using Protocol Analysis in Evaluating Responses to Student Writing." *Freshman English News* 13 (1984): 1-4, 10.

Hemingway, Ernest. *A Moveable Feast*. New York: Scribners, 1964.

Hirsch, E. D., Jr. *The Philosophy of Composition*. Chicago: University of Chicago Press, 1977.

Holland, M. "The State of the Art: The Psychology of Writing." Paper presented at the Inland Area Writing Project's Summer Writing Conference, University of California at Riverside, 1980.

Irmscher, William F. *Teaching Expository Writing*. New York: Holt, Rinehart, and Winston, 1979.

Jonson, Ben. "Timber, or Discoveries." *Ben Jonson*, vol. 8. Ed. C.H. Herford Percy and E. Simpson. Oxford, England: Clarendon, 1947.

Macrorie, Ken. "To Be Read." *English Journal* 57 (1968): 688-92.

Reising, R. W. "Controlling the Bleeding." *College Composition and Communication* 24 (1973): 43-44.

Shaughnessy, Mina. *Errors and Expectations: A Guide for the Teacher of Basic Writing*. New York: Oxford UP, 1977.

Stevens, A. K., ed. "Evaluating a Theme." *Newsletter of the Michigan Council of Teachers of English* 5 (1958): 6.

Walker, Robert L. "The Common Writer: A Case for Parallel Structure." *College Composition and Communication* 21 (1970): 373-79.

Weathers, Winston. "The Rhetoric of the Series." *College Composition and Communication* 17 (1966): 217-22.

Ziv, Nina. D. "The Effect of Teacher Comments on the Writing of Four College Freshmen." *New Directions in Composition Research*. Ed. Richard Beach and Lillian S. Bridwell, 362-80. New York: Guilford, 1984.

Talking About Text: The Use of Recorded Commentary in Response to Student Writing

Chris M. Anson

The process of reading and responding to students' work often places us, as teachers, in the role of judges. Typically, we imagine a certain response to our assignments that might count as "excellent" or "accomplished," and then read the actual papers against that ideal. Because we have limited time to write on students' papers, we usually focus on the most important shortcomings relative to the ideal, hoping that students will learn by trial and error to avoid the same problems in future assignments.

This role and purpose often yields a formal, authoritative, and judgmental style of response. Early in my own teaching, I felt uneasy using this style in my written comments when my classroom demeanor was more casual and personal. When I commented on students' writing, it was as if I distanced myself from them and turned into a juror, casting legalistic verdicts on their work. Even when I tried to write more openly, in a questioning or supportive way, the very existence of my own text, layered over the students' words and often correcting their errors or even editing their work, seemed controlling and dictatorial.

My discomfort with this type of response was explained, if not eased, by research and theory in the newly developing field of composition studies that showed the importance of making writers' learning processes more central in the classroom. At the time, teachers still typically assigned papers and then judged them when they came in. The process movement showed how teachers could provide support for writers at various stages during the development of their papers, especially between successive drafts. But even with the help of my revision guides and the use of small groups in which students shared drafts of their papers, my response to their work, which I continued to offer in writing at the end of the process, seemed to change little.

Then, halfway through a course one of my students had eye surgery and was told to read as little as possible for a few days. Not wanting to fall behind in her work, she asked if I would be willing to tape-record my comments about a paper she had turned in before the surgery. I agreed, and set to work that night.

The experience of talking to my student about her paper on a cassette tape entirely changed the way I respond to students' written work in most of the classes I teach. The method itself is quite simple; it involves substituting or supplementing the usual written commentary we give to students (in the margins or at the end of their papers) with oral commentary given to them on cassette tapes. When students turn in a draft of a final paper, they provide an inexpensive blank cassette tape, appropriately labeled, which can be put into a small carrying case or cassette storage box available at most discount stores. On the day the papers are returned, the students also get back their cassette tape with the teacher's commentary, which they can then listen to when they look over their work.

Tape-recording my comments on students' papers didn't remove the responsibility of making judgments. I was still using my expertise to weigh the students' successes and shortcomings and, on final papers, reach a verdict about their quality. But the tone and style of my comments seemed different. Because I was literally *talking* to each student, I felt a social dimension to my commentary that had been less present in my short, often corrective written remarks. My comments had a narrative quality, and were framed with personal remarks. I found myself starting with brief openers: "Hi, Mark, how's it going? Hey, I love this title!" My written comments, in contrast, lacked context and seemed impersonal— a kind of shorthand. Because I couldn't take the time to write out thoughts that didn't seem highly focused on the student's text, my written comments were terse and unelaborated: "Explain more?," "How so?," "Yes, good point," "Edit?," "Would everyone agree?," "Syntax." Of course, I could have written much more than such comments, perhaps even including some more personal statements of encouragement or engagement, but the editorial nature of written comments just didn't lend itself to such expansion. In constrast, on the tapes, I could loop back to issues earlier in the paper, or explain myself in detail, or allude to class sessions. I could show something of my own reading process, the way I interpreted the student's words or the way I tried to construct meaning from the student's text. Even though I was in most cases grading students' work on the tapes, I also felt a change in my purpose, as what had been correcting and judging eased gently into coaching and advising. I began feeling more like a mentor, a teacher in the true sense of the word. My students seemed to learn more from me, and I learned much more from them—about themselves and what was happening to them over the progress of my courses.

As I experimented with the tape method, I also found that I no longer dreaded the process of reading my students' work. For one thing, I was more comfortable with my role; I felt better about who I was in relation to my students. But I was also astonished to see how much more help I

was giving students in my taped comments than in my written margina-
lia. In just a few minutes, I could offer advice or give readerly response
that would have taken me a great deal of time to write out by hand. A
typical tape of five or ten minutes represented pages of material I would
have been incapable of offering in text form for a class of 25 students. As
I evaluated the method, I also found that students not only preferred
taped commentary but rated my overall teaching more highly. The tapes
were revealing something about me as a teacher that my students weren't
getting from my written comments.

In the fifteen years since I began using this method, I have found
myself experimenting with various styles and techniques in search of the
"best" approach. The experimentation was worthwhile because it showed
me the great variety of ways in which we can use our voices to help students. But it also showed me that the "best" method is at best relative: we
must learn to adapt approaches like taped-recorded response to the specific contexts in which we teach. The following are some of the more
important issues I consider before I use the method.

- **Decide whether to comment on drafts or final papers, or both.**
Comments on final papers are often evaluative. The response explains a
grade or other assessment of the writing, sometimes correcting errors or
pointing out problems in logic, organization, the adherence to norms of
the field, or other concerns. The writing becomes a kind of test—of accu-
mulated knowledge, of the ability to use certain methods of intellect or
scholarship, or of the ability to create clear, readable prose. Taped comments can more readily provide a more thorough, detailed explanation of
your assessment, so that students can understand how you arrived at it
and can learn from your counsel.

But you can use taped comments even more productively during the
students' process of writing a paper, especially when that paper is long
and complex. The most effective moment is when a student has finished
a full rough draft of a paper. If you build in a requirement for students to
submit a rough draft a week or more before the deadline for the final
draft, you may find that what they turn in looks surprisingly like what
they would have turned in as their final paper. But now, using the tapes,
you can provide comments that lead to an improved paper. The learning
that results from this intervention is much greater than what students
learn from final comments, which they sometimes ignore in their haste to
see only the grade.

A student in an advanced course in "Writing About Science," for
example, submitted a draft of a paper on natural selection which included the following paragraph:

Natural selection can effect behavior in the way that people strive to be the best and become selected. Therefore you can change your behavior to get into the selection process. The environment is always changing and we adapt our behavior to the environment. So we are often changing to the environment so we become more a part of the natural selection process.

In his recorded commentary, the teacher said this:

I like the way you're moving from the biological to the, I guess you could call it the social meaning of natural selection in this paragraph, but the leap may be too big here. Maybe you could explain what you mean by being selected, and by getting into the selection process. What would happen if someone was not well-suited for the environment, you know, in a biological way, but still got selected? And on getting selected, do you mean by this something social, like being chosen for a team, or something biological, along the lines of animal competition during mate selection? I'm just feeling a little confused at this point.

• **Decide ahead on your investment of time.** Talking out loud about a student's paper seems to spark many spontaneous discoveries that lead to more explanation and more talk. It is easy to spend twenty or thirty minutes on a tape and still feel less than "talked out." Depending on how many students you may have or how long and complex their papers are, you may want to limit your talk to a specific amount of time. I usually aim for five minutes of actual taping once I have read through the paper, glancing at my watch when I start. As I see the time running out, I wrap up my commentary with a list of the four or five most important issues in the student's paper.

• **Decide how you will organize your comments.** The actual process of talking about a student's text can be quite varied, and each method has different consequences. I have discovered two general approaches: *organizing your commentary* and *reading "live."*

Organizing your commentary means knowing what you want to say before you say it. Reading the paper first quickly to get a sense of its contents and structure will help you to formulate your thoughts before turning on the tape-recorder. You can even jot down some marginal shorthand during your initial skimming to jog your memory later when you begin to talk (I often use checks, question marks, or circles for this purpose). Then, as you talk, you can focus on the most important issues you noticed during your initial reading. For example, if you discover that a student has not offered any evidence to support a main assertion in a paper, you can address that problem from the start, and suggest ways to revise the draft.

Organizing your thoughts in advance allows you to give students clear, concise commentary usually moving from the most to least important concerns in the paper. What it gains in these features, however, it often loses in its lack of spontaneity. Tape-recorded commentary also offers you a chance to *show* students what happens in readers' minds as they construct meaning from a piece of writing. In this process, you can read a small part of the paper, usually a paragraph or a section, then comment on what it has done to advance a line of thought or move a paper forward. The pause button on some tape recorders lets you stop to read the next chunk of text and then continue sharing your experience as a reader. Some users of taped commentary actually read the paper aloud, commenting on it as they read and giving voice to their otherwise internal thoughts and reading experiences. This method clearly takes more time, but is especially effective for writers who lack experience reading their own texts.

The difference between these two approaches can be illustrated in excerpts from two teachers' taped commentary on papers in a course called "Writing the Large Academic Paper." The first excerpt is from the start of one teacher's comments on a paper written by a senior; the paper is about the decentralization of political leadership in Senegal. After some opening remarks and a few comments praising the student's progress, the teacher says this:

> *OK, what I'd like to do here is to focus on three key, um, three main areas that you should probably consider as you prepare the next draft. First, structure. Second, elaboration, especially in the section on the 1990 reform and the role of PS in the political process. Third, the style of the section describing your research site. OK. On the structure question, I really like your use of these subheadings, but at times I think you've almost got too many. If you take a look on, on page 14 . . . .*

For this rather long project, and perhaps because the draft had already undergone some development, the teacher decided it would be best to read the entire paper and then organize his comments into three areas for revision. In contrast, another teacher of the same course chose to use the "reading live" approach. The following excerpt is from about halfway through this teacher's taped response on a paper about the role of the United Nations in promoting international peace. The student had begun each new section with a news headline about the United Nations:

> *OK. I've moved on now and read the next section on neutrality. One thing I'm noticing right away is the absence of the news item as a leading, ah, as a way to give some background to the section. Do you want to be consistent with this device? Because maybe your reader starts expecting them, you know, I certainly, after five or six of these, I'm really enjoying them and sort of looking for them. You might check my reaction about this against some other readers. See if they feel the same way. OK, I'm also, at this point, I'm thinking, "she's going to link the good offices concept with neutrality . . . ."*

In contrast to her colleague, this teacher uses her own experience as a reader to show her student what works or doesn't work for her as she reads. Perhaps because it is not organized in advance, this commentary also seems to put much of the responsibility for decision making back on the student, who must now weigh her teacher's reactions against those of other readers and make choices for revision.

• **Include contextual remarks when appropriate.** Written comments on students' papers rarely link the paper to other work, allude to progress in the course, or include remarks about other matters of the classroom context. Taped comments don't guarantee that these more contextual issues enter into a teacher's commentary, but their oral and interpersonal nature offer more opportunities to do so. In their narrative quality, taped comments let you mentor students in the full context of your class. Comments can focus on the progress a student has made between the last paper and the one being discussed. It is also easier to focus on the strategies a student has employed to create a paper, especially if you have seen a draft in progress. In a response to a series of persuasive papers in an introductory composition course, a teacher said the following:

> *You've really got the hang of setting up the main claim early on, and this one is a lot clearer than in your last assignment. What I'd work on now is deciding which details to include in the supporting section, because this seems long, I mean, there are a whole lot of ideas here but you don't really say much about some of them, so I can't tell as a reader what's important and what's not important to the main line of reasoning.*

• **Use the opportunity for explanation.** Draining of time and energy, written comments can encourage a brevity that may not always be helpful to students. The marginal label "awk" (for "awkward") identifies a place where you stumbled over the students' badly crafted language; but the label tells the student nothing about why the passage seems awkward, or about how to rethink its wording. When they are strategically placed in a rough draft, such abbreviated comments can help to put the responsibility back on a student for working out a revision. On final drafts, however, students may be puzzled by them or simply ignore them. As a result, they learn little.

In taped comments, consider offering some brief descriptions of specific problems. Most helpful are "reader-like" explanations—simply talking through your actual experience reading something that is confusing, illogical, poorly worded, or otherwise problematic. In a response to a rough draft of a research paper on Native American schools, a teacher said this:

> *Now, when I got to this line, I stumbled a little. Let me read it to you, OK? "The American Board of Commissioners provided funding for the establishment of permanent missionary schools sponsoring education for Cherokees." I guess I'm wondering if the funding is sponsoring this, or the schools? If it's the schools, as a reader I'm wondering what it means to sponsor education? See the confusion here?*

• **Provide helpful strategies.** Perhaps because they take so much time, written comments rarely offer students helpful techniques or strategies for revision, for future writing assignments, or for classwork. In just a few seconds on a tape, you can show students how to overcome difficulties that are apparent in their writing. In a paper that made use of observational data, a teaching assistant said this:

> *Try organizing the observations from most to least important; then draw a line in the list at the point when they stop being essential to your conclusions.*

And in a paper written in "Writing in the Social Sciences," another teacher made this comment:

> *I guess I want to believe you here but you haven't given me enough reason. I think the issue is causality—what evidence is there that proximity actually causes aggression? So what you might try next time is naming each possible cause on the left side of a piece of paper; then write down the evidence of causality on the right side. Put a question mark next to any items where the research evidence conflicts. Then when you make an assertion, you can say whether it's supported in some way.*

• **Consider students' concerns.** Although academic papers are usually supposed to "stand on their own," our role as teachers allows us to carry on dialogues with students *about* their papers. Yet we often miss opportunities for such dialogue when we read students' papers. Students may create a paper in isolation, and we may read it similarly cloistered, the quickly written marginal comments standing as our only real connection with the student. Students' concerns, intentions, and goals are invisible to us, sometimes leading to comments that they perceive to be less than relevant or useful.

Tapes give us the chance to hear students' concerns before we read their work. This can be effective at both the draft and final stages of writing. In my smaller classes, I usually ask students to talk to me on their tape for a maximum of three minutes, focusing on their uncertainties or on the specific issues they would like me to address. After quickly reading a student's paper, I then listen to his or her brief comments and record my response to those comments, along with any other important issues not raised by the student. The following excerpt comes from Melissa, one of my own students in an introductory composition course. Melissa's paper compared two young children's attitudes toward TV violence:

> . . . *I'm also wondering if I've said enough about Jamie's, about the interview with Jamie. I mean, it sounds to me like I kind of lurch into the next kid without really finishing with him. It just seems incomplete or something. But then by now it's so darned long, I just can't see adding two pages to the analysis.*

Clearly, Melissa is raising important concerns about her draft, concerns I can then address helpfully in my own taped response to her.

Encouraging students to focus on what they perceive to be the problems in their drafts also helps them to build the skills of critical reflection and revision. You can "answer" well-founded concerns, offering your expert perspectives and suggestions.

• **Consider student dialogues.** Revision groups and peer conferences are a staple of writing courses. Students usually read and respond to the drafts of one or two peers, using a list of questions provided by the teacher. In one model, classes are cancelled for one or two sessions so that students can meet in revision groups outside of class, usually with the teacher as facilitator. In the "in-class" model, the students discuss their reactions to each other's papers in class, offering "readings" that are especially useful in the revision process.

In some courses, out-of-class revision groups may be impossible to arrange, and in others even in-class groups may be difficult to fit in. In such cases, consider having students tape-record their responses to each other's drafts, swapping the tapes in class. Hand out a list of guidelines for the taped commentary (how much time to spend, what comments are appropriate, and so on). Such student-to-student dialogues can be excellent ways to build collaborative learning into a course without sacrificing a lot of time during class sessions.

Spoken Response and New Technologies

Before the advent of cassette-tape technology, taped responses would have been impractical; most students didn't own reel-to-reel tape recorders, and they were too bulky and awkward in any case. But almost all students now have a cassette tape player at home or in their car, and all colleges and universities can provide them. The small, uniform size of the cassettes makes them no more difficult to handle than students' papers themselves.

In the context of computer technology, we are at a moment in history much like the transition to cassette tapes from reel-to-reel tapes. Consequently, we still may be looking somewhat skeptically on the potential of computers to offer useful alternative methods for responding to students' work: they are too bulky or complicated; access is too limited; there are too many different kinds of programs and equipment.

But it is, in fact, just a moment. It is now estimated that over half of American college students have their own personal computer. Within a few years, microcomputer technology will be at the fingertips of virtually every college student, either personally or on campus, and converting disks into different formats and programs will be simple. How or whether we make use of this technology for enhancing our methods of reading students' work is very much up to us, if we can guide and control the process.

Most newer models of personal computers now have the capability to record and/or play back voice recordings, allowing the concept of tape-recorded commentary to be adapted to word-processing. In an evolving draft of a long paper on physical therapy, for example, Jennie, one of my students, wrote the following paragraph:

> Balgrist rehabilitation center is located at the University of Zurich in the city of Zurich which is one of the largest cities in Switzerland. Balgrist specializes in rehabilitation for disabilities from paralysis known as paraplegia and tetraplegia in Swiss German or paraplegic and quadriplegic in English.

◁)) It is one of the best rehabilitation centers for people with paralysis disorders. Paraplegikers stay for 4-6 months and tetra-plegikers stay up to 1 year if needed.

After opening Jennie's disk on my computer and locating the install-ment in which this paragraph appeared, I skimmed through her intro-duction (which was unchanged since my last commentary) and began to read her new text. When I reached this paragraph, I placed my cursor at the beginning of the paragraph and accessed the "voice record" function in my computer. Clicking on "record," I then spent about 45 seconds talk-ing to her about the information she was providing in this paragraph. Deposited at the start of the paragraph (as shown) was an icon notifying Jennie that a recorded comment was embedded in her text. I then placed the cursor toward the end of the paragraph and offered her some sug-gestions about the style of her sentences (which tend to stack up modi-fied information awkwardly). A second icon appeared at that point (as shown).

Opening her file on her own, less sophisticated computer at home, Jennie could see my icons in her text. Although she did not have a voice-record function on her own computer, she could still click on the icons and hear a playback of my voice. Later, she could simply delete the icons (and the recording) from the text when she no longer needed them.

In addition to increasingly sophisticated sound capabilities, comput-ers will eventually involve both the recording and playback of video. Microcomputers are available with tiny video cameras that record the user's face for later playback. Using such technology, a student would be able to open up a paper on a disk, click on an icon, and then both hear and see the teacher, whose image appears in a box at the top of the screen. While this option may seem almost ridiculous to us now, it won't be long before the quality of images improves and their size increases. The tech-nology will offer us something approaching a student-teacher conference.

No method of response—written marginal annotations, taped com-ments, even a one-way computerized conference in multimedia—will ever surpass the centuries-old method of sitting down with a writer to discuss his or her work. Nor should it. But as our roles and responsibili-ties become more diverse and more complex, we should be prepared to use available resources in an educationally rich way in those situations in which they are most useful and practical. For me, taped response has pro-vided one such way to reach out to students through something more than red marks layered over their own words.

Ranking, Evaluating, and Liking: Sorting Out Three Forms of Judgment

Peter Elbow

This essay is my attempt to sort out different acts we call assessment—some different ways in which we express or frame our judgments of value. I have been working on this tangle not just because it is interesting and important in itself but because assessment tends so much to drive and control *teaching*. Much of what we do in the classroom is determined by the assessment structures we work under.

Assessment is a large and technical area and I'm not a professional. But my main premise or subtext in this essay is that we nonprofessionals can and should work on it because professionals have not reached definitive conclusions about the problem of how to assess writing (or anything else, I'd say). Also, decisions about assessment are often made by people even less professional than we, namely legislators. Pat Belanoff and I realized that the field of assessment was open when we saw the harmful effects of a writing proficiency exam at Stony Brook and worked out a collaborative portfolio assessment system in its place (Belanoff and Elbow; Elbow and Belanoff). Professionals keep changing their minds about large-scale testing and assessment. And as for classroom grading, psychometricians provide little support or defense of it.

The Problems with Ranking and the Benefits of Evaluating

By ranking I mean the act of summing up one's judgment of a performance or person into a single, holistic number or score. We rank every time we give a grade or holistic score. Ranking implies a single scale or continuum or dimension along which all performances are hung.

By evaluating I mean the act of expressing one's judgment of a performance or person by pointing out the strengths and weaknesses of different features or dimensions. We evaluate every time we write a comment on a paper or have a conversation about its value. Evaluation implies the recognition of different criteria or dimensions—and by implication different contexts and audiences for the same performance. Evaluation requires going *beyond* a first response that may be nothing but a kind of ranking ("I like it" or "This is better than that"), and instead

looking carefully enough at the performance or person to make distinctions between parts or features or criteria.

It's obvious, thus, that I am troubled by ranking. But I will resist any
temptation to argue that we can get rid of all ranking—or even should.
Instead I will try to show how we can have *less* ranking and *more* evaluation in its place.

I see three distinct problems with ranking: it is inaccurate or unreli-
able; it gives no substantive feedback; and it is harmful to the atmosphere
for teaching and learning.

(1) First the unreliability. To rank reliably means to give a *fair* number, to
find the single quantitative score that readers will agree on. But readers
don't agree.

This is not news—this unavailability of agreement. We have long
seen it on many fronts. For example, research in evaluation has shown
many times that if we give a paper to a set of readers, those readers tend
to give it the full range of grades (Diederich). I've recently come across
new research to this effect—new to me because it was published in 1912.
The investigators carefully showed how high school English teachers
gave different grades to the same paper. In response to criticism that this
was a local problem in English, they went on the next year to discover an
even greater variation among grades given by high school geometry
teachers and history teachers to papers in their subjects. (See the summary of Daniel Starch and Edward Elliott's 1913 *School Review* articles in
Kirschenbaum, Simon, and Napier 258-59.)

We know the same thing from literary criticism and theory. If the best
critics can't agree about what a text means, how can we be surprised that
they disagree even more about the quality or value of texts? And we
know that nothing in literary or philosophical theory gives us any
agreed-upon rules for settling such disputes.

Students have shown us the same inconsistency with their own con-
trolled experiments of handing the same paper to different teachers and
getting different grades. This helps explain why we hate it so when students ask us their favorite question, "What do you want for an A?": it
rubs our noses in the unreliability of our grades.

Of course, champions of holistic scoring argue that they get *can* get
agreement among readers—and they often do (White). But they get that
agreement by "training" the readers before and during the scoring sessions. What "training" means is getting those scorers to stop reading the
way they normally read—getting them to stop using the conflicting criteria and standards they normally use outside the scoring sessions. (In an

impressive and powerful book, Barbara Herrnstein Smith argues that whenever we have widespread inter-reader reliability, we have reason to suspect that difference has been suppressed and homogeneity imposed— almost always at the expense of certain groups.) In short, the reliability in holistic scoring is not a measure of how texts are valued by real readers in natural settings, but only of how they are valued in artificial settings with imposed agreements.

Defenders of holistic scoring might reply (as one anonymous review- er did) that holistic scores are not perfect or absolutely objective readings but just "judgments that most readers agree are the appropriate ones given the purpose of the assessment and the system of communication." But I have been in and even conducted enough holistic scoring sessions to know that even that degree of agreement doesn't occur unless "pur- pose" and "appropriateness" are defined to mean acceptance of the sin- gle set of standards imposed on that session. We know too much about the differences among readers and the highly variable nature of the read- ing process. Suppose we get readings only from academics, or only from people in English, or only from respected critics, or only from respected writing programs, or only from feminists, or only from sound readers of my tribe (white, male, middle-class, full professors between the ages of fifty and sixty). We *still* don't get agreement. We can sometimes get agree- ment among readers from some subset, a particular community that has developed a strong set of common values, perhaps *one* English depart- ment or *one* writing program. But what is the value of such a rare agree- ment. It tells us nothing about how readers from other English depart- ments or writing programs will judge—much less how readers from other domains will judge.

(From the opposite ideological direction, some skeptics might object to my skeptical train of thought: "So what else is new?" they might reply. "Of *course* my grades are biased, 'interested' or 'situated'—always partial to my interests or the values of my community or culture. There's no other possibility." But how can people consent to give grades if they feel that way? A single teacher's grade for a student is liable to have substan- tial consequences—for example, on eligibility for a scholarship or a job or entrance into professional school. In grading, surely we must not take anything less than genuine fairness as our goal.)

It won't be long before we see these issues argued in a court of law, when a student who has been disqualified from playing on a team or rejected from a professional school sues, charging that the basis for his plight—teacher grades—is not reliable. I wonder if lawyers will be able to make our grades stick.

(2) Ranking or grading is woefully uncommunicative. Grades and holistic scores are nothing but points on a continuum from "yea" to "boo"—with no information or clues about the criteria behind these noises. They are 100 percent evaluation and 0 percent description or information. They quantify the degree of approval or disapproval in readers but tell nothing at all about what the readers actually approve or disapprove of. They say nothing that couldn't be said with gold stars or black marks or smiley-faces. Of course, our first reactions are often nothing but global holistic feelings of approval or disapproval, but we need a system for communicating our judgments that nudges us to move beyond these holistic feelings and to articulate the basis of our feeling—a process that often leads us to change our feeling. (Holistic scoring sessions sometimes use rubrics that explain the criteria—though these are rarely passed along to students—and even in these situations, the rubrics fail to fit many papers.) As C. S. Lewis says, "People are obviously far more anxious to express their approval and disapproval of things than to describe them" (7).

(3) Ranking leads students to get so hung up on these oversimple quantitative verdicts that they care more about scores than about learning—more about the grade we put on the paper than about the comment we have written on it. Have you noticed how grading often forces us to write comments to justify our grades?—and how these are often *not* the comment we would make if we were just trying to help the student write better? ("Just try writing several favorable comments on a paper and then giving it a grade of D" [Diederich 21].)

Grades and holistic scores give too much encouragement to those students who score high—making them too apt to think they are already fine—and too little encouragement to those students who do badly. Unsuccessful students often come to doubt their intelligence. But oddly enough, many "A" students also end up doubting their true ability and feeling like frauds—because they have sold out on their own judgment and simply given teachers whatever yields an A. They have too often been rewarded for what they don't really believe in. (Notice that there's more cheating by students who get high grades than by those who get low ones. There would be less incentive to cheat if there were no ranking.)

We might be tempted to put up with the inaccuracy or unfairness of grades if they gave good diagnostic feedback or helped the learning climate; or we might put up with the damage they do to the learning climate if they gave a fair or reliable measure of how skilled or knowledgeable students are. But since they fail dismally on both counts, we are faced with the striking question of why grading has persisted so long.

There must be many reasons. It is obviously easier and quicker to express a global feeling with a single number than to figure out what the strengths and weaknesses are and what one's criteria are. (Though I'm heartened to discover, as I pursue this issue, how troubled teachers are by grading and how difficult they find it.) But perhaps more important, we see around us a deep *hunger to rank*—to create pecking orders: to see who we can look down on and who we must look up to, or in the military metaphor, who we can kick and who we must salute. Psychologists tell us that this taste for pecking orders or ranking is associated with the authoritarian personality. We see this hunger graphically in the case of IQ scores. It is plain that IQ scoring does not represent a commitment to looking carefully at people's intelligence; when we do that, we see different and frequently uncorrelated *kinds* or *dimensions* of intelligence (Gardner). The persistent use of IQ scores represents the hunger to have a number so that everyone can have a rank. ("Ten!" mutter the guys when they see a pretty woman.)

Because ranking or grading has caused so much discomfort to so many students and teachers, I think we see a lot of confusion about the process. It is hard to think clearly about something that has given so many of us such anxiety and distress. The most notable confusion I notice is the tendency to think that if we renounce ranking or grading, we are renouncing the very possibility of judgment and discrimination—that we are embracing the idea that there is no way to distinguish or talk about the difference between what works well and what works badly.

So the most important point, then, is that *I am not arguing against judgment or evaluation*. I'm just arguing against that crude, oversimple way of *representing* judgment—distorting it, really—into a single number, which means ranking people and performances along a single continuum.

In fact I am arguing *for evaluation*. Evaluation means looking hard and thoughtfully at a piece of writing in order to make distinctions as to the quality of different features or dimensions. For example, the process of evaluation permits us to make the following kinds of statements about a piece of writing:

- The thinking and ideas seem interesting and creative.
- The overall structure or sequence seems confusing.
- The writing is perfectly clear at the level of individual sentences and even paragraphs.
- There is an odd, angry tone of voice that seems unrelated or inappropriate to what the writer is saying.

- Yet this same voice is strong and memorable and makes one listen even if one is irritated.

- There are a fair number of mistakes in grammar or spelling: more than "a sprinkling" but less than "riddled with."

To rank, on the other hand, is to be forced to translate those discriminations into a single number. What grade or holistic score do these judgments add up to? It's likely, by the way, that more readers would agree with those separate, "analytic" statements than would agree on a holistic score.

I've conducted many assessment sessions where we were not trying to impose a set of standards but rather to find out how experienced teachers read and evaluate, and I've had many opportunities to see that good readers give grades or scores right down through the range of possibilities. Of course good readers sometimes agree—especially on papers that are strikingly good or bad or conventional, but I think I see difference more frequently than agreement when readers really speak up.

The process of evaluation, because it invites us to articulate our criteria and to make distinctions among parts or features or dimensions of a performance, thereby invites us further to acknowledge the main fact about evaluation: that different readers have different priorities, values, and standards.

The conclusion I am drawing, then, in this first train of thought is that we should do less ranking and more evaluation. Instead of using grades or holistic scores—single number verdicts that try to sum up complex performances along only one scale—we should give some kind of written or spoken evaluation that discriminates among criteria and dimensions of the writing—and if possible that takes account of the complex context for writing: who the writer is, what the writer's audience and goals are, who we are as readers and how we read, and how we might differ in our reading from other readers the writer might be addressing.

But how can we put this principle into practice? The pressure for ranking seems implacable. Evaluation takes more time, effort, and money. It seems as though we couldn't get along without scores on writing exams. Most teachers are obliged to give grades at the end of each course. And many students—given that they have become conditioned or even addicted to ranking over the years and must continue to inhabit a ranking culture in most of their courses—will object if we don't put grades on papers. Some students, in the absence of that crude gold star or black mark, may not try hard enough (though how hard is "enough"—and is it really our job to stimulate motivation artificially with grades—and is grading the best source of motivation?).

It is important to note that there are certain schools and colleges that do *not* use single-number grades or scores, and they function successfully. I taught for nine years at Evergreen State College, which uses only written evaluations. This system works fine, even down to getting students accepted into high quality graduate and professional schools.

Nevertheless we have an intractable dilemma: that grading is unfair and counterproductive but that students and institutions tend to want grades. In the face of this dilemma there is a need for creativity and pragmatism. Here are some ways in which I and others use *less ranking* and *more evaluation* in teaching—and they suggest some adjustments in how we score large-scale assessments. What follows is an assortment of experimental compromises—sometimes crude, seldom ideal or utopian—but they help.

a.   Portfolios. Just because conventional institutions oblige us to turn in a single quantitative course grade at the end of every marking period, it doesn't follow that we need to grade individual papers. Course grades are more trustworthy and less damaging because they are based on so many performances over so many weeks. By avoiding frequent ranking or grading, we make it *somewhat* less likely for students to become addicted to oversimple numerical rankings—to think that evaluation always translates into a simple number—in short, to mistake ranking for evaluation. (I'm not trying to defend conventional course grades since they are still uncommunicative and they still feed the hunger for ranking.) Portfolios permit me to refrain from grading individual papers and limit myself to writerly evaluative comments—and help students see this as a positive rather than a negative thing, a chance to be graded on a body of their best work that can be judged more fairly. Portfolios have many other advantages as well. They are particularly valuable as occasions for asking students to write extensive and thoughtful explorations of their own strengths and weaknesses.

A midsemester portfolio is usually an informal affair, but it is a good occasion for giving anxious students a ballpark estimate of how well they are doing in the course so far. I find it helpful to tell students that I'm perfectly willing to tell them my best estimate of their course grade—but only if they come to me in conference and only during the second half of the semester. This serves somewhat to quiet their anxiety while they go through seven weeks of drying out from grades. By midsemester, most of them have come to enjoy not getting those numbers and thus being able to think better about more writerly comments from me and their classmates.

Portfolios are now used extensively and productively in larger assessments, and there is constant experimentation with new applications (Belanoff and Dickson; *Portfolio Assessment Newsletter; Portfolio News*).

b.   Another useful option is to make a strategic retreat from a wholly negative position. That is, I sometimes do a *bit* of ranking even on individual papers, using two "bottom-line" grades: H and U for "Honors" and "Unsatisfactory." I tell students that these translate to about A or A- and D or E. This practice may seem theoretically inconsistent with all the arguments I've just made, but (at the moment, anyway) I justify it for the following reasons.

First, I sympathize with a *part* of the students' anxiety about not getting grades: their fear that they might be failing and not know about it— or doing an excellent job and not get any recognition. Second, I'm not giving *many* grades; only a small proportion of papers get these H's or U's. The system creates a "non-bottom-line" or "non-quantified" atmosphere. Third, these holistic judgments about best and worst do not seem as arbitrary and questionable as most grades. There is usually a *bit* more agreement among readers about the best and worst papers. What seems most dubious is the process of trying to rank that whole middle range of papers—papers that have a mixture of better and worse qualities so that the numerical grade depends enormously on a reader's priorities or mood or temperament. My willingness to give these few grades goes a long way toward helping my students forgo most bottom-line grading.

I'm not trying to pretend that these minimal "grades" are truly reliable. But they represent a very small amount of ranking. Yes, someone could insist that I'm really ranking every single paper (and indeed if it seemed politically necessary, I could put an OK or S [for satisfactory] on all those middle range papers and brag, "Yes, I grade everything.") But the fact is that I am doing *much less sorting* since I don't have to sort them into five or even twelve piles. Thus there is a huge reduction in the total amount of unreliability I produce.

(It might seem that if I use only these few minimal grades I have no good way for figuring out a final grade for the course—since that requires a more fine-grained set of ranks. But I don't find that to be the case. For I also give these same minimal grades to the many other important parts of my course such as attendance, meeting deadlines, peer responding, and journal writing. If I want a mathematically computed grade on a scale of six or A through E, I can easily compute it when I have such a large number of grades to work from—even though they are only along a three-point scale.)

This same practice of crude or minimal ranking is a big help on larger assessments outside classrooms, and needs to be applied to the process of assessment in general. There are two important principles to emphasize. On the one hand, we must be prudent or accommodating enough to admit that despite all the arguments against ranking, there are situations when we need that bottom-line verdict along one scale: which student has not done satisfactory work and should be denied credit for the course? which student gets the scholarship? which candidate to hire or fire? We often operate with scarce resources. But on the other hand, we must be bold enough to insist that we do far more ranking than is really needed. We can get along not only with fewer occasions for assessment but also with fewer gradations in scoring. If we decide what the *real* bottom-line is on a given occasion—perhaps just "failing" or perhaps "honors" too—then the reading of papers or portfolios is enormously quick and cheap. It leaves time and money for evaluation—perhaps for analytic scoring or some comment.

At Stony Brook we worked out a portfolio system where multiple readers had only to make a binary decision: acceptable or not. Then individual teachers could decide the actual course grade and give comments for their own students—so long as those students passed in the eyes of an independent rater (Elbow and Belanoff; Belanoff and Elbow). The best way to begin to wean our society from its addiction to ranking may be to permit a tiny bit of it (which also means less unreliability)—rather than trying to go "cold turkey."

c.   Sometimes I use an analytic grid for evaluating and commenting on student papers. An example is given in Figure 1.

Strong   OK   Weak

			CONTENT, INSIGHTS, THINKING, GRAPPLING WITH TOPIC
			GENUINE REVISION, SUBSTANTIVE CHANGES, NOT JUST EDITING
			ORGANIZATION, STRUCTURE, GUIDING THE READER
			LANGUAGE, SYNTAX, SENTENCES, WORDING, VOICE
			MECHANICS: SPELLING, GRAMMAR, PUNCTUATION, PROOFREADING
			OVERALL [Note: this is not a sum of the other scores.]

Figure 1.

I often vary the criteria in my grid (e.g., "connecting with readers" or "investment") depending on the assignment or the point in the semester.

Grids are a way I can satisfy the students' hunger for ranking but still not give in to conventional grades on individual papers. Sometimes I provide nothing but a grid (especially on final drafts), and this is a very quick way to provide a response. Or, on midprocess drafts I sometimes use a grid in addition to a comment: a more readerly comment that often doesn't so much tell them what's wrong or right or how to improve things but rather tries to give them an account of what is *happening to me* as I read their words. I think this kind of comment is really the most useful thing of all for students, but it frustrates some students for a while. The grid can help these students feel less anxious and thus pay better attention to my comment.

I find grids extremely helpful at the end of the semester for telling students their strengths and weaknesses in the course—or what they've done well and not so well. Besides categories like the ones above, I use categories like these: "skill in giving feedback to others," "ability to meet deadlines," "effort," and "improvement." This practice makes my final grade much more communicative.

d.   I also help make up for the absence of ranking—gold stars and black marks—by having students share their writing with each other a great deal both orally and through frequent publication in class magazines. Also, where possible, I try to get students to give or send writing to audiences outside the class. At the University of Massachusetts at Amherst, freshmen pay a ten dollar lab fee for the writing course, and every teacher publishes four or five class magazines of final drafts a semester. The effects are striking. Sharing, peer feedback, and publication give the best reward and motivation for writing, namely, getting your words out to many readers.

5.   I sometimes use a kind of modified *contract grading*. That is, at the start of the course I pass out a long list of all the things that I most want students to do—the concrete activities that I think most lead to learning—and I promise students that if they do them *all* they are guaranteed a certain final grade. Currently, I say it's a B—it could be lower or higher. My list includes these items: not missing more than a week's worth of classes; not having more than one late major assignment; *substantive* revising on all major revisions; good copy editing on all final revisions; good effort on peer feedback work; keeping up the journal; and substantial effort and investment on each draft.

I like the way this system changes the "bottom-line" for a course: the intersection where my authority crosses their self-interest. I can tell them, "You have to work very hard in this course, but you can stop worrying about grades." The crux is no longer that commodity I've always hated and never trusted: a numerical ranking of the quality of their writing along a single continuum. Instead the crux becomes what I care about most: the *concrete behaviors* that I most want students to engage in because they produce more learning and help me teach better. Admittedly, effort and investment are not concrete observable behaviors, but they are no harder to judge than overall quality of writing. And since I care about effort and investment, I don't mind the few arguments I get into about them; they seem fruitful. ("Let's try and figure out why it looked to me as though you didn't put any effort in here.") In contrast, I hate discussions about grades on a paper and find such arguments fruitless. Besides, I'm not making fine distinctions about effort and investment—just letting a bell go off when they fall palpably low.

It's crucial to note that I am *not* fighting evaluation with this system. I am just fighting ranking or grading. I still write evaluative comments and often use an evaluative grid to tell my students what I see as strengths and weaknesses in their papers. My goal is not to get rid of evaluation but in fact to emphasize it, enhance it. I'm trying to get students to listen *better* to my evaluations—by uncoupling them from a grade. In effect, I'm doing this because I'm so fed up with students *following* or *obeying* my evaluations too blindly—making whatever changes my comments suggest but doing it for the sake of a grade; not really taking the time to make up their own minds about whether they think my judgments or suggestions really make sense to them. The worst part of grades is that they make students obey us without carefully thinking about the merits of what we say. I love the situation this system so often puts students in: I make a criticism or suggestion about their paper, but it doesn't matter to their grade whether they go along with me or not (so long as they genuinely revise in some fashion). They have to think; to decide.

Admittedly this system is crude and impure. Some of the really skilled students who are used to getting A's and desperate to get one in this course remain unhelpfully hung up about getting those H's on their papers. But a good number of these students discover that they can't get them, and they soon settle down to accepting a B and having less anxiety and more of a learning voyage.

The Limits of Evaluation and the Benefits of Evaluation-Free Zones

Everything I've said so far has been in praise of evaluation as a substitute for ranking. But I need to turn a corner here and speak about the *limits* or *problems* of evaluation. Evaluating may be better than ranking, but it still carries some of the same problems. That is, even though I've praised evaluation for inviting us to acknowledge that readers and contexts are different, nevertheless the very word *evaluation* tends to imply fairness or reliability or getting beyond personal or subjective preferences. Also, of course, evaluation takes a lot more time and work. To rank you just have to put down a number; holistic scoring of exams is cheaper than analytic scoring.

Most important of all, evaluation harms the climate for learning and teaching—or rather *too much* evaluation has this effect. That is, if we evaluate *everything* students write, they tend to remain tangled up in the assumption that their whole job in school is to give teachers "what they want." Constant evaluation makes students worry more about psyching out the teacher than about what they are really learning. Students fall into a kind of defensive or on-guard stance toward the teacher: a desire to hide what they don't understand and try to impress. This stance gets in the way of learning. (Think of the patient trying to hide symptoms from the doctor.) Most of all, constant evaluation by someone in authority makes students reluctant to take the risks that are needed for good learning—to try out hunches and trust their own judgment. Face it: if our goal is to get students to exercise their own judgment, that means exercising an immature and undeveloped judgment and making choices that are obviously wrong to us.

We see around us a widespread hunger to be evaluated that is often just as strong as the hunger to rank. Countless conditions make many of us walk around in the world wanting to ask others (especially those in authority), "How am I doing, did I do OK?" I don't think the hunger to be evaluated is as harmful as the hunger to rank, but it can get in the way of learning. For I find that the greatest and most powerful breakthroughs in learning occur when I can get myself and others to *put aside* this nagging, self-doubting question ("How am I doing? How am I doing?")—and instead to take some chances, trust our instincts or hungers. When everything is evaluated, everything counts. Often the most powerful arena for deep learning is a kind of "time out" zone from the pressures of normal evaluated reality: make-believe, play, dreams—in effect, the Shakespearian forest.

In my attempts to get away from too much evaluation (not from all evaluation, just from too much of it), I have drifted into a set of teaching practices which now feel to me like the *best* part of my teaching. I realize now what I've been unconsciously doing for a number of years: creating "evaluation-free zones."

a.   The paradigm evaluation-free zone is the ten minute, nonstop freewrite. When I get students to freewrite, I am using my authority to create unusual conditions in order to contradict or interrupt our pervasive habit of always evaluating our writing. What is essential here are the two central features of freewriting: that it be private (thus I don't collect it or have students share it with anyone else); and that it be nonstop (thus there isn't time for planning, and control is usually diminished). Students quickly catch on and enter into the spirit. At the end of the course, they often tell me that freewriting is the most useful thing I've taught them (see Belanoff, Elbow, and Fontaine).

b.   A larger evaluation-free zone is the single unevaluated assignment—what people sometimes call the "quickwrite" or sketch. This is a piece of writing that I ask students to do—either in class or for homework—without any or much revising. It is meant to be low stakes writing. There is a bit of pressure, nevertheless, since I usually ask them to share it with others and I usually collect it and read it. But I don't write any comments at all—except perhaps to put straight lines along some passages I like or to write a phrase of appreciation at the end. And I ask students to refrain from giving evaluative feedback to each other—and instead just to say "thank you" or mention a couple of phrases or ideas that stick in mind. (However, this writing-without-feedback can be a good occasion for students to discuss the *topic* they have written about—and thus serves as an excellent kick-off for discussions of what I am teaching.)

c.   These experiments have led me to my next and largest evaluation-free zone—what I sometimes call a "jump start" for my whole course. For the last few semesters I've been devoting the first three weeks *entirely* to the two evaluation-free activities I've just described: freewriting (and also more leisurely private writing in a journal) and quickwrites or sketches. Since the stakes are low and I'm not asking for much revising, I ask for *much more* writing homework per week than usual. And every day we write in class: various exercises or games. The emphasis is on getting rolling, getting fluent, taking risks. And every day all students read out loud something they've written—sometimes a short passage even to the whole class. So despite the absence of feedback, it is a very audience-filled and sociable three weeks.

At first I only dared do this for two weeks, but when I discovered how fast the writing improves, how good it is for building community, and what a pleasure this period is for me, I went to three weeks. I'm curious to try an experiment with teaching a whole course this way. I wonder, that is, whether all that evaluation we work so hard to give really does any more good than the constant writing and sharing (Zak).

I need to pause here to address an obvious rejoinder: "But withholding evaluation is *not* normal!" Indeed, it is not normal—certainly not normal in school. We normally tend to emphasize evaluations—even bottom-line ranking kinds of evaluations. But I resist the argument that if it's not normal we shouldn't do it.

The best argument for evaluation-free zones is from experience. If you try them, I suspect you'll discover that they are satisfying and bring out good writing. Students have a better time writing these unevaluated pieces; they enjoy hearing and appreciating these pieces when they don't have to evaluate. And *I* have a much better time when I engage in this astonishing activity: reading student work when I don't have to evaluate and respond. And yet the writing improves. I see students investing and risking more, writing more fluently, and using livelier, more interesting voices. This writing gives me and them a higher standard of clarity and voice for when we move on to more careful and revised writing tasks that involve more intellectual pushing—tasks that sometimes make their writing go tangled or sodden.

The Benefits and Feasibility of Liking

Liking and disliking seem like unpromising topics in an exploration of assessment. They seem to represent the worst kind of subjectivity, the merest accident of personal taste. But I've recently come to think that the phenomenon of liking is perhaps the most important evaluative response for writers and teachers to think about. In effect, I'm turning another corner in my argument. In the first section I argued against ranking—with evaluating being the solution. Next I argued not *against* evaluating—but for no-evaluation zones in *addition* to evaluating. Now I will argue neither against evaluating nor against no-evaluation zones, but for something very different in addition, or perhaps underneath, as a foundation: liking.

Let me start with the germ story. I was in a workshop and we were going around the circle with everyone telling a piece of good news about their writing in the last six months. It got to Wendy Bishop, a good poet (who has also written two good books about the teaching of writing), and she said, "In the last six months, I've learned to *like* everything I write."

Our jaws dropped; we were startled—in a way scandalized. But I've been chewing on her words ever since, and they have led me into a retelling of the story of how people learn to write better.

The old story goes like this: We write something. We read it over and we say, "This is terrible. I *hate* it. I've got to work on it and improve it." And we do, and it gets better, and this happens again and again, and before long we have become a wonderful writer. But that's not really what happens. Yes, we vow to work on it—but we don't. And next time we have the impulse to write, we're just a *bit* less likely to start.

What really happens when people learn to write better is more like this: We write something. We read it over and we say, "This is terrible.... But I *like* it. Damn it, I'm going to get it good enough so that others will like it too." And this time we don't just put it in a drawer, we actually work hard on it. And we try it out on other people too—not just to get feedback and advice but, perhaps more important, to find someone else who will like it.

Notice the two stories here—two hypotheses. (a) "First you improve the faults and then you like it." (b) "First you like it and then you improve faults." The second story may sound odd when stated so baldly, but really it's common sense. Only if we like something will we get involved enough to work and struggle with it. Only if we like what we write will we write again and again by choice—which is the only way we get better.

This hypothesis sheds light on the process of how people get to be published writers. Conventional wisdom assumes a Darwinian model: poor writers are unread; then they get better; as a result, they get a wider audience; finally they turn into Norman Mailer. But now I'd say the process is more complicated. People who get better and get published really tend to be driven by how much *they* care about their writing. Yes, they have a small audience at first—after all, they're not very good. But they try reader after reader until finally they can find people who like and appreciate their writing. I certainly did this. If someone doesn't like her writing enough to be pushy and hungry about finding a few people who also like it, she probably won't get better.

It may sound so far as though all the effort and drive comes from the lonely driven writer—and sometimes it does (Norman Mailer is no joke). But, often enough, readers play the crucially active role in this story of how writers get better. That is, the way writers *learn* to like their writing is by the grace of having a reader or two who likes it—even though it's not good. Having at least a few appreciative readers is probably indispensable to getting better.

When I apply this story to our situation as teachers I come up with this interesting hypothesis: *good writing teachers like student writing* (and like students). I think I see this borne out—and it is really nothing but common sense. Teachers who hate student writing and hate students are grouchy all the time. How could we stand our work and do a decent job if we hated their writing? Good teachers see what is only *potentially* good, they get a kick out of mere possibility—and they encourage it. When I manage to do this, I teach well.

Thus, I've begun to notice a turning point in my courses—two or three weeks into the semester: "Am I going to like these folks or is this going to be a battle, a struggle?" When I like them everything seems to go better—and it seems to me they learn more by the end. When I don't and we stay tangled up in struggle, we all suffer—and they seem to learn less.

So what am I saying? That we should like bad writing? How can we see all the weaknesses and criticize student writing if we just like it? But here's the interesting point: if I *like* someone's writing it's *easier* to criticize it.

I first noticed this when I was trying to gather essays for the book on freewriting that Pat Belanoff and Sheryl Fontaine and I edited. I would read an essay someone had written, I would want it for the book, but I had some serious criticism. I'd get excited and write, "I really like this, and I hope we can use it in our book, but you've got to get rid of this and change that, and I got really mad at this other thing." I usually find it hard to criticize, but I began to notice that I was a much more critical and pushy reader when I liked something. It's even fun to criticize in those conditions.

It's the same with student writing. If I like a piece, I don't have to pussyfoot around with my criticism. It's when I don't like their writing that I find myself tiptoeing: trying to soften my criticism, trying to find something nice to say—and usually sounding fake, often unclear. I see the same thing with my own writing. If I like it, I can criticize it better. I have faith that there'll still be something good left, even if I train my full critical guns on it.

In short—and to highlight how this section relates to the other two sections of this essay—liking is not the same as ranking or evaluating. Naturally, people get them mixed up: when they like something, they assume it's good; when they hate it, they assume it's bad. But it's helpful to uncouple the two domains and realize that it makes perfectly good sense to say, "This is terrible, but I like it." Or, "This is good, but I hate it." In short, I am not arguing here *against* criticizing or evaluating. I'm merely arguing *for* liking.

Let me sum up my clump of hypotheses so far:

- It's not improvement that leads to liking, but rather liking that leads to improvement.
- It's the mark of good writers to like their writing.
- Liking is not the same as evaluating. We can often criticize something better when we like it.
- We learn to like our writing when we have a respected reader who likes it.
- Therefore, it's the mark of good teachers to like students and their writing.

If this set of hypotheses is true, what practical consequences follow from it? How can we be better at liking? It feels as though we have no choice—as though liking and not-liking just happen to us. I don't really understand this business. I'd love to hear discussion about the mystery of liking—the phenomenology of liking. I sense it's some kind of putting oneself out—or holding oneself open—but I can't see it clearly. I have a hunch, however, that we're not so helpless about liking as we tend to feel.

For in fact I can suggest some practical concrete activities that I have found fairly reliable at increasing the chances of liking student writing:

1.   I ask for lots of private writing and merely shared writing, that is, writing that I don't read at all, and writing that I read but don't comment on. This makes me more cheerful because it's so much easier. Students get *better* without me. Having to evaluate writing—especially bad writing—makes me more likely to hate it. This throws light on grading: it's hard to like something if we know we have to give it a D.

2.   I have students share lots of writing with each other—and after a while respond to each other. It's easier to like their writing when I don't feel myself as the only reader and judge. And so it helps to build community in general: it takes pressure off me. Thus I try to use peer groups not only for feedback, but for other activities too, such as collaborative writing, brainstorming, putting class magazines together, and working out other decisions.

3.   I increase the chances of my liking their writing when I get better at finding what *is* good—or *potentially* good—and learn to praise it. This is a skill. It requires a good eye, a good nose. We tend—especially in the academic world—to assume that a good eye or fine discrimination means *criticizing*. Academics are sometimes proud of their tendency to be both-

ered by what is bad. Thus I find I am sometimes looked down on as dumb and undiscriminating: "He likes bad writing. He must have no taste, no discrimination." But I've finally become angry rather than defensive. It's an act of discrimination to see what's good in bad writing. Maybe, in fact, this is the secret of the mystery of liking: to be able to see potential goodness underneath badness.

Put it this way. We tend to stereotype liking as a "soft" and sentimental activity. Mr. Rogers is our model. Fine. There's nothing wrong with softness and sentiment—and I love Mr. Rogers. But liking can also be hard-assed. Let me suggest an alternative to Mr. Rogers: B. F. Skinner. Skinner taught pigeons to play ping-pong. How did he do it? Not by moaning, "Pigeon standards are falling. The pigeons they send us these days are no good. When I was a pigeon . . . ." He did it by a careful, disciplined method that involved close analytic observation. He put pigeons on a ping-pong table with a ball, and every time a pigeon turned his head 30 degrees toward the ball, he gave a reward (see my "Danger of Softness").

What would this approach require in the teaching of writing? It's very simple . . . but not easy. Imagine that we want to teach students an ability they badly lack, for example, how to organize their writing or how to make their sentences clearer. Skinner's insight is that we get nowhere in this task by just telling them how much they lack this skill: "It's disorganized. Organize it!" "It's unclear. Make it clear!"

No, what we must learn to do is to read closely and carefully enough to show the student little bits of *proto*-organization or *sort of* clarity in what they've already written. We don't have to pretend the writing is wonderful. We could even say, "This is a terrible paper and the worst part about it is the lack of organization. But I will teach you how to organize. Look here at this little organizational move you made in this sentence. Read it out loud and try to feel how it pulls together this stuff here and distinguishes it from that stuff there. Try to remember what it felt like writing that sentence—creating that piece of organization. Do it some more." Notice how much more helpful it is if we can say, "Do *more* of what you've done here," than if we say, "Do something *different* from anything you've done in the whole paper."

When academics criticize behaviorism as crude it often means that they aren't willing to do the close careful reading of student writing that is required. They'd rather give a cursory reading and turn up their nose and give a low grade and complain about falling standards. No one has undermined behaviorism's main principle of learning: that reward produces learning more effectively than punishment.

d.   I improve my chances of liking student writing when I take steps to get to know them a bit as people. I do this partly through the assignments I give. That is, I always ask them to write a letter or two to me and to each other (for example about their history with writing). I base at least a couple of assignments on their own experiences, memories, or histories. And I make sure some of the assignments are free choice pieces—which also helps me know them.

In addition, I make sure to have at least three conferences with each student each semester—the first one very early. I often call off some classes in order to keep conferences from being too onerous (insisting nevertheless that students meet with their partner or small group when class is called off). Some teachers have mini-conferences with students during class—while students are engaged in writing or peer group meetings. I've found that when I deal only with my classes as a whole—as a large group—I sometimes experience them as a herd or lump—as stereotyped "adolescents"; I fail to experience them as individuals. For me, personally, this is disastrous since it often leads me to experience them as that scary tribe that I felt rejected by when I was an eighteen-year-old—and thus, at times, as "the enemy." But when I sit down with them face to face, they are not so stereotyped or alien or threatening—they are just eighteen-year-olds.

Getting a glimpse of them as individual people is particularly helpful in cases where their writing is not just bad, but somehow offensive—perhaps violent or cruelly racist or homophobic or sexist—or frighteningly vacuous. When I know them just a bit I can often see behind their awful attitude to the person and the life situation that spawned it, and not hate their writing so much. When I know students I can see that they are smart behind that dumb behavior; they are doing the best they can behind that bad behavior. Conditions are keeping them from acting decently; something is holding them back.

e.   It's odd, but the more I let myself show, the easier it is to like them and their writing. I need to share some of my own writing—show some of my own feelings. I need to write the letter to them that they write to me—about my past experiences and what I want and don't want to happen.

f.   It helps to work on my own writing—and work on learning to *like* it. Teachers who are most critical and sour about student writing are often having trouble with their own writing. They are bitter or unforgiving or hurting toward their own work. (I think I've noticed that failed PhDs are often the most severe and difficult with students.) When we are stuck or sour in our own writing, what helps us most is to find spaces free from evaluation such as those provided by freewriting and journal writing. Also, activities like reading out loud and finding a supportive reader or two. I would insist, then, that if only for the sake of our teaching, we need to learn to be charitable and to like our own writing.

A final word. I fear that this sermon about liking might seem an invitation to guilt. There is enough pressure on us as teachers that we don't need someone coming along and calling us inadequate if we don't *like* our students and their writing. That is, even though I think I am right to make this foray into the realm of feeling, I also acknowledge that it is dangerous—and paradoxical. It strikes me that we also need to have permission to hate the dirty bastards and their stupid writing.

After all, the conditions under which they go to school bring out some awful behavior on their part, and the conditions under which we teach sometimes make it difficult for us to like them and their writing. Writing wasn't meant to be read in stacks of twenty-five, fifty, or seventy-five. And we are handicapped as teachers when students are in our classes against their will. (Thus high school teachers have the worst problem here, since their students tend to be the most sour and resentful about school.)

Indeed, one of the best aids to liking students and their writing is to be somewhat charitable toward ourselves about the opposite feelings that we inevitably have. I used to think it was terrible for teachers to tell those sarcastic stories and hostile jokes about their students: "teacher room talk." But now I've come to think that people who spend their lives teaching *need* an arena to let off this unhappy steam. And certainly it's better to vent this sarcasm and hostility with our buddies than on the students themselves. The question, then, becomes this: do we help this behavior function as a venting so that we can move past it and not be trapped in our inevitable resentment of students? Or do we tell these stories and jokes as a way of staying stuck in the hurt, hostile, or bitter feelings—year after year—as so many sad teachers do?

In short I'm not trying to invite guilt, I'm trying to invite hope. I'm trying to suggest that if we do a sophisticated analysis of the difference between liking and evaluating, we will see that it's possible (if not always easy) to like students and their writing—without having to give up our intelligence, sophistication, or judgment.

Let me sum up the points I'm trying to make about ranking, evaluating, and liking:

- Let's do as little ranking and grading as we can. They are never fair and they undermine learning and teaching.

- Let's use evaluation instead—a more careful, more discriminating, fairer mode of assessment.

- But because evaluating is harder than ranking, and because too much evaluating also undermines learning, let's establish small but important evaluation-free zones.

- And underneath it all—suffusing the whole evaluative enterprise—let's learn to be better likers: liking our own and our students' writing, and realizing that liking need not get in the way of clear-eyed evaluation.

Works Cited

Diederich, Paul. *Measuring Growth in English*. Urbana: NCTE, 1974.

Belanoff, Pat, and Peter Elbow. "Using Portfolios to Increase Collaboration and Community in a Writing Program." *WPA: Journal of Writing Program Administration* 9 (Spring 1986): 27-40. (Also in *Portfolios: Process and Product*. Ed. Pat Belanoff and Marcia Dickson. Portsmouth, NH: Boynton/Cook-Heinemann, 1991.)

Belanoff, Pat, Peter Elbow, and Sheryl Fontaine, eds. *Nothing Begins with N: New Investigations of Freewriting*. Carbondale: Southern Illinois UP, 1991.

Bishop, Wendy. *Something Old, Something New: College Writing Teachers and Classroom Change*. Carbondale: Southern Illinois UP, 1990.

Bishop, Wendy. *Released into Language: Options for Teaching Creative Writing*. Urbana: NCTE, 1990.

Elbow, Peter. "The Danger of Softness." *What Is English?*, 197-210. New York: MLA, 1990.

Elbow, Peter, and Pat Belanoff. "State University of New York: Portfolio-Based Evaluation Program." *New Methods in College Writing Programs: Theory into Practice*, 95-105. Ed. Paul Connolly and Teresa Vilardi. New York: MLA, 1986. (Also in *Portfolios: Process and Product*. Ed. Pat Belanoff and Marcia Dickson. Portsmouth, NH: Boynton/Cook-Heinemann, 1991.)

Gardner, Howard. *Frames of Mind: The Theory of Multiple Intelligences*. New York: Basic, 1983.

Kirschenbaum, Howard, Simon Sidney, and Rodney Napier. *Wad-Ja-Get? The Grading Game in American Education*. New York: Hart Publishing, 1971.

Lewis, C. S. *Studies in Words*, 2nd ed. London: Cambridge UP, 1967.

Portfolio Assessment Newsletter. Five Centerpointe Drive, Suite 100, Lake Oswego, Oregon 97035.

Portfolio News. c/o San Dieguito Union High School District, 710 Encinitas Boulevard, Encinitas, CA 92024.

Smith, Barbara Herrnstein. *Contingencies of Value: Alternative Perspectives for Critical Theory*. Cambridge: Harvard UP, 1988.

White, Edward M. *Teaching and Assessing Writing*. San Francisco: Jossey-Bass, 1985.

Zak, Frances. "Exclusively Positive Responses to Student Writing." *Journal of Basic Writing* 9 (1990): 40-53.

Options for Responding to Student Writing

Peter Elbow

The main point of this memo is to give some simple, concrete, practical guidelines for commenting on student papers. But these will make most sense if I start off with a few larger observations.

It's clear that students learn from doing extensive writing. It's not clear that they learn from our comments on their writing. Extensive research has shown that when students read our comments, they frequently misunderstand what we have written.

The reasons are easy to see. First there are the unhelpful conditions under which we write our comments. Writing was not meant to be read in stacks of twenty or forty papers on the same topic—often a single topic specified by us. These conditions tempt us to read not as most readers do (to find out what the writer has to say that might be useful or entertaining), but rather to hold up papers against an ideal text in our heads. Besides, we often write our comments late at night, perhaps tired, even grumpy, sometimes using incomplete sentences, and we almost never do the main thing we ask our students to do, namely to revise.

Then there are the conditions in which students read. They come to our comments with idiosyncratic assumptions and expectations from their past experiences with comments from teachers. When they read what we write they are liable to be defensive or annoyed or insecure or fragile and ready to stop trying. Students often interpret *any* comment as a criticism.

If this weren't enough, there is also a larger problem. To grade or comment on a student paper is to interpret a text. We know that good scholars tend to disagree not only in their estimates of value but even in their interpretations of what a text means—texts they've read carefully and countless times. And we know that nothing in literary or philosophical theory gives us any agreed-upon rules for settling these disputes. To reflect on this is to realize how little we can trust what we or any teacher writes on a student paper.

We have reason then to be humble in our commenting—and also to try to be as strategic as we can: to try to figure out how to spend our efforts in ways most likely to be of use–and least likely to be a waste of time. To put it differently, we should follow the dictum of our better paid fellow professionals, "At least do no harm."

The fact is, there is no right or best way to respond to student writing. The right or best comment is the one that will help *this* student on *this* topic on *this* draft at *this* point in the semester—given her character and experience. My best chance of figuring out what is right for this student at any given point depends on knowing about what was going on for her as she was writing. (Did she think she was supposed to sound detached and uninvolved or is this timidity? Was she struggling hard on this paper or getting confused or just being lazy?) If I am responding to the paper in a face-to-face conference with the student, I can probably learn some of these things. Responding in conference is very helpful. I try to do it frequently. But often I am commenting in solitude with only the text before me. I find the following guidelines helpful:

—In order to know more about what was going on for the student, I always ask for a piece of "process writing" with every main assignment. This can be in the form of a "writer's log" or a "cover letter" to the reader. I usually invite something informal—even handwritten. I ask them to tell me things like: what they see as their main points; the story of how they went about writing and what it was like for them as they were writing; how did they get their ideas; what were some of the choices they made; which parts went well or badly for them; were there any surprises; and above all what questions they have for readers. If it is a revision it's particularly helpful to ask what changes they made and why. Reading the cover letter usually helps me decide what to say in my comment. Often I can agree with much of what the student has said—sometimes even being more encouraging about the essay than the student was. With process writing, my comment is not the initiation of discourse but an answer to discourse that the student started. Process writing is not so easy for lots of students. But this self-reflective sort of writing is worth working on. It helps them learn to see their own thinking and writing more clearly and to be more aware of their writing process. In the beginning I often do practice sessions in class on the day that a paper is due.

—Similarly, it's helpful if I can glance through some peer responses before commenting. I can often second what was said by others and help the student take peer response more seriously—and feel less dependent on my responses.

—I find commenting much easier if I read the whole piece before making any comments—except sometimes putting straight and wiggly lines where I am pleased or somehow bothered. I save lots of time by reminding myself that students can seldom benefit from criticism of more than two or three problems. The most crucial decision in commenting is which problems to focus on, and I can't make that decision till I read the whole paper through. Most of my bad commenting comes from jumping in with marginal comments as I am reading: I am more likely to waste my time on something that turns out to be a minor issue; or make some passing remark that the student misunderstands; or say something that's actually wrong ("you obviously don't understand X"—when later on it's clear that he does understand X); or get caught up in a little spasm of unhelpful irritation. If I settle for just making straight and wiggly lines during my first reading, these serve as reminders when I am trying to decide at the end what are the few main things I need to say. Even when I want to give movies of my mind—to tell the story of my reactions as I was in the process of reading—I can usually do this more clearly and helpfully by waiting till I've read the whole piece.

—I try not to mess up students' papers (especially final drafts) by writing on them. When I put anything on them I write only in light pencil, never ink—usually making just straight and wiggly lines and at most a couple of phrases (e.g., "I stumbled here"). I prefer commenting on a separate sheet not only because I can write more quickly and neatly on my computer, but also because this method makes me comment as a *reader* about effects rather than as an *editor* trying to fix the text. Not putting ink on their papers sends an important message about *them* owning and being in charge of their own text, them being writers—and most of all a message about me not trampling on their texts.

—When I return papers to students with comments, I find it very helpful sometimes to take five minutes right then and ask them to write me a short note telling what they heard me saying and how they are reacting to it. This helps me learn when my comments are unclear or when students misinterpret my words or react in ways I don't expect. These are often fascinating short pieces of writing.

—One of the most useful kinds of response is often overlooked because it seems too simple: to *describe* the paper as well as I can: what are its main points, its subsidiary points, how is it structured?

—When I comment on a draft, I can make my comments positive suggestions for revising rather than negative points in an autopsy. Even when I am commenting on a final version, I can frame my comments in a positive, forward looking way—"Here's what to work on in your next paper"—instead of just saying, "Here's what didn't work."

A Down-to-Earth Note on Epistemology

When students don't read or heed our comments very well, I don't think we should necessarily assume carelessness or ineptness. I think students understand—sometimes consciously, sometimes not—how untrustworthy our comments can be. They may not talk about epistemology, but they see different teachers asking for very different things but calling it "good writing."

Let me point then finally to an important source of trustworthiness or epistemological validity we can call on when we write comments. We can write comments that are at least *true*, if we tell our reactions and frankly acknowledge their subjectivity—even if they are true only for one reader. (Examples: "I started out sympathetic to what you were saying, but in the third paragraph I began fighting you—getting irritated and starting to disagree with the very point I was ready to accept in the beginning." Or, "For the whole first page I was wondering what your opinion was about this volatile issue, and I couldn't tell. But it wasn't bothering me; it was kind of intriguing. I was hoping you wouldn't plop down with a flat-footed black or white position, and it was a great relief to see you torn or conflicted.")

When we write comments that purport to be true in general or true for other readers, we are very likely to be wrong. (Examples: "You have too many asides and anecdotes." Or, "You should move this third paragraph to the beginning.") Even when we write "unclear" we are saying what some other good readers would quarrel with. But when we write about what happened to us in reading, we are paying students the intellectual respect of trying to avoid lies.

There is an enormous pedagogical power that comes from this truth-telling. Students often fight our more impersonal "verdicts"—in part because they sense how questionable they are. Often we win such disputes only by resorting to institutional authority—which further undermines our students' shaky faith in teacher judgments. When, on the other hand, we simply tell the truth about what happened to us as we were reading, students cannot doubt or quarrel with us: what we say has a higher chance of being actually listened to.

If we are willing to say, "Unconvincing for me," instead of "Unconvincing," students are more likely to pause, listen, and think—instead of just resisting, or else unthinkingly giving in to authority. Besides, magisterial shorthand words like "Awkward" are often extremely unclear. I've been trying to learn to translate that word into what is more accurate and honest with phrases like, "I stumbled here," or "I'm lost," or "This felt roundabout." Even though it sometimes costs me a few more words, I try to avoid an impersonal God/truth voice in my comments.

Besides, when we give students our frankly acknowledged subjective reactions, we are treating them as writers: "Here are my reactions: you decide what to do about them." By treating students as writers, we help them learn to treat us as real readers instead of just sources of impersonal verdicts. And interestingly enough, our subjective reactions are often surprisingly universal.

To sum up. Writing comments is a dubious and difficult enterprise. In my view, these are the things that in the end are least likely to waste our time or cause harm: to get students to want to write; to read what they write with good attention and respect; to show them that we understand what they have written—even the parts where they had trouble getting their meaning across; and respecting them and the dialogue to tell them some of our thoughts on what they are writing about. Surely what writers need most is the experience of being heard and a chance for dialogue.

More Options For Responding to Student Writing

There is no single best way to respond to student papers. The best comment is always *what this particular student needs to hear on this particular occasion*. Therefore we can comment better and more easily when our minds fill quickly with *many* different things, even conflicting things, that we *might* say about a paper. Then we have more options. Most bad commenting comes from relying on only one or two habitual modes of commenting or settling for the first thing that comes to mind. What follows is an artificial exercise you obviously cannot use on all papers. But if you practice it now and then, your mind will fill with more options when you are writing actual comments and you're short of time.

Straight and wavy lines. Put straight lines underneath words and alongside sections that come through strongly or effectively. Put wavy lines where you feel some kind of resistance or dissatisfaction. You can give this feedback nearly as quickly as you can read—and it is surprisingly helpful.

Movies of the reader's mind—first quick version—just for yourself, not for the student. Quick notes will do. What was going on in you as you were reading the paper? It is particularly important to notice what you were *feeling*—as a way to help you prevent your actual comment to the student from being too skewed by unaware feelings.

Praise the text—first quick version. What worked? What strengths do you see?

Describe the text. What would most observers agree is actually "there"— that they actually see? That is, describe the text as accurately and dispassionately as possible. This is discourse analysis. Examples: describe the genre; the topic; the main point; the main sub-points; the organization (which parts perform which functions?); describe the syntax (e.g., long and short sentences and where); the diction (e.g., kinds of words—and where); the voice; the point of view; and so on. Obviously, pure objectivity is not possible, but if you make an honest effort to disengage yourself as far as you can from judging or interpreting, you are giving a gesture of respect: treating students as writers and taking their writing seriously as "texts." The effort also helps you *see* the text better and almost invariably leads to new understandings of it and possibilities for good feedback of other sorts.

"Reply" to the text as a human being, not as a teacher. This too is a crucial act of respect: to take the writer's view seriously enough to reply to *what* she says—instead of ignoring or sidestepping the message with a meta-comment about *how* she says it. Many students have never had a *reply* of this sort to anything they have written. To reply makes us human readers, not just evaluators.

Make inferences about process—about what was happening in the writer as he or she was writing this paper. Examples: "I had a feeling you got a little bored with your topic during the last half." Or "I sensed that in the beginning you felt your topic was X, but by the end you were actually more interested in Y." Or, "Could it be that as you revised, you started to have doubts about your main point?" Of course these inferences are risky guesswork. But even wrong guesses can be productive if you invite the student to disagree with them. For example, if you guess that he was bored and he tells us he was not, this leads to a useful discussion about the words and how they worked on at least one reader. And if you are accurate in your inference, this kind of feedback can have a more helpful impact on how the student goes about writing in the future than if you made a perfect diagnosis of faults and advice.

Praise the text—second try. You can almost certainly see more to praise now that you have carefully described it, replied to it, and made inferences about the student's process. In addition to noting actual strengths, you can note *potential* strengths the student might exploit in revising. Well focused praise—even for small successes—produces more learning than criticism of failures: Telling someone to stop doing X doesn't help them learn how to do X.

Find the fruitful problem. Try to figure out the *one problem* that might be most useful to work on.

Back to movies—this time for the student. Even though you might need to leave out *some* of your actual reactions, an honest process account of what was happening to you as you read can often be surprisingly effective. For example students often ignore me when I tell them clearly about explicit problems in an argument, but they usually perk up their ears and take me more seriously when I say, "I nodded my head in agreement with your main point when you described it at the beginning of your paper, but when you started arguing for it, I found I myself resisting and even fighting you."

So what will your comment be? Now, after trying out these options, write the actual comment you guess might be most appropriate for this student on this occasion.

Using Scoring Guides to Assess Writing

Edward M. White

It is hard to say who dislikes grading more, teachers or students. Yet assessment is a necessary part of learning. In sports, the assessment occurs when the tennis ball hits the net or the basketball misses the basket. We make correction in our swing or our shot until a new assessment (the ball went in) tells us we have done it right. Then we try to keep doing it right. With writing, the assessment usually comes from a trained writing teacher and even then there is no single "right" way to do it. We still need assessment if we are to improve, but we need to have confidence that the assessment is professional, fair, and honest, that is, in sports terms, that the height of the net stays the same, or in assessment terms, that the measurement is valid and reliable. If we are doing the assessing, we need to know a great deal about the teaching and learning of writing so that our assessments are appropriate and helpful as well.

We do not need to assess every piece of writing that students give us. Sometimes an encouraging word or a simple check mark indicating satisfactory work is more appropriate than a grade. But encouragement and praise are only part of teaching; it is a self-deceiving illusion to imagine that we can avoid judgment as part of our work. We are required to inscribe grades for students at the end of the term and those symbols are a powerful response to students about the quality of what they have done. And most students are concerned enough about how they are doing to keep asking if we try to put them off. We should not condemn them for this; it is a perfectly professional and sound question for any diligent learner to ask. If we are wise teachers, we do not allow concern for the grade to replace the drive to improve; the assessments are means to an end, not ends in themselves. Judgment is tough to do and tough to take, but unless we do it we are not professional; it comes with the territory. The reading of papers always awaits us. The problem is to find ways of assessing student work that are fair, consistent, public, clear, and responsible—grades that support teaching and learning rather than substitute for them.

Using Scoring Guides to Improve Assignments and Teacher Grading

Scoring guides, developed originally for large-scale assessment of writing, have unexpectedly become a powerful teaching tool as classroom teachers have adapted them for responding to student writing. The scoring guide describes with some detail the textual features that lead to particular scores or grades. Here is an example of one that has been widely used for grading essay questions:

Score of 6: Superior

- Addresses the question fully and explores the issues thoughtfully
- Shows substantial depth, fullness, and complexity of thought
- Demonstrates clear, focused, unified, and coherent organization
- Is fully developed and detailed
- Evidences superior control of diction, syntactic variety, and transition; may have a few minor flaws

Score of 5: Strong

- Clearly addresses the question and explores the issues
- Shows some depth and complexity of thought
- Is effectively organized
- Is well developed, with supporting detail
- Demonstrates control of diction, syntactic variety, and transition; may have a few flaws

Score of 4: Competent

- Adequately addresses the question and explores the issues
- Shows clarity of thought but may lack complexity
- Is organized
- Is adequately developed, with some detail
- Demonstrates competent writing; may have some flaws

Score of 3: Weak

- May distort or neglect parts of the question
- May be simplistic or stereotyped in thought
- May demonstrate problems in organization
- May have generalizations without supporting detail or detail without generalizations; may be undeveloped
- May show patterns of flaws in language, syntax, or mechanics

Score of 2: Inadequate

- Will demonstrate serious inadequacy in one or more of the areas specified for the 3 paper

Score of 1: Incompetent

- Fails in its attempt to discuss the topic
- May be deliberately off-topic
- Is so incompletely developed as to suggest or demonstrate incompetence
- Is wholly incompetent mechanically

–Edward M. White, *Teaching and Assessing Writing*, 1994

This example illustrates many features common to all scoring guides. It uses numerical scoring rather than letter grades, a useful shift in symbolism for students carrying a burden of self-doubt from years of more or less arbitrary alphabetic assessments. It employs the 6-point scale, now the most commonly used one, with its generally acceptable upper half scores centered around the 5 and its generally unacceptable lower half scores centered around the 2. Each score descriptor follows a similar pattern, listing a set of criteria in order of importance. Here, the first descriptor has to do with the content of the response, in relation to the question asked; the second deals with depth and complexity of thought; the third with organization; the fourth with development; and the last with correctness. Scoring is based on an overall impression of the student writing as a whole (thus, "holistic" scoring) with an understanding that strengths in one of the criteria will compensate in part for weaknesses in another.

But this scoring guide is probably more useful for proficiency exams than for classroom assignments, since it is so general in nature. Here is a well-conceived first-year composition assignment, designed for the first paper in the course, for which a scoring guide will be very helpful:

> Describe a person you knew well when you were a child. Use enough detail so your readers can picture the person clearly from the child's perspective. At the same time, try to make your readers understand from the tone of your description the way you felt about the person you describe.

It is worth a moment to notice why this is a particularly good assignment to start a writing course. It has a clear purpose (to help students learn to use detail as evidence) and will help move students from personal experience writing to analytical writing, but it is also interesting and accessible to insecure young students. Even though it is accessible to everyone with memories, it contains challenges for the best writers: to use the child's perspective without falling into a child's voice, to control point of view and tone, to convey feelings only by means of selected detail. Discussion of these matters in class will help students understand the complexity of the assignment, despite its clear demand and focus. And that discussion can lead naturally to the creation of a scoring guide.

If the class is unusually worried about grades, all that may be needed is a 2-point scale, reflecting satisfactory or unsatisfactory work, depending on whether the assignment is fulfilled. But we might choose to call those score points 5 and 2, with the intention of developing a 6-point scoring guide. A writing class will be ready, after some discussion, to come up with something like the following:

> Score of 5: These papers give enough detail so that the reader can visualize the character. They also describe the narrator and give enough interaction between the two to allow the reader to understand an aspect of their relationship. Writing errors do not distract the reader.

> Score of 2: These papers give little or no detail, telling us generalizations about a person ("he was very nice") instead of describing one ("he was always smiling"). The focus may be almost entirely on the narrator or a situation, the language may be vague, and there may be more than an occasional spelling or grammatical error.

It would not be hard to expand these descriptors or to fill in the scores on either side of them. For example, the 6 writer would have enough confidence in the descriptions to allow the reader to draw appropriate conclusions. The 4 paper would accomplish the job but in a minimal way. Meanwhile, the center upper-half paper, the 5, does everything well but states the attitude of the writer instead of allowing the details and the tone of the description to do so. Again, the 3 paper might have just a bit of detail and an unclear attitude, while the 1 paper just doesn't understand or address the task, or perhaps is a mechanical disaster. The score of 1 will mean different things for different classes, depending on the background and abilities represented by the students.

A good scoring guide will open up possibilities of writing for students, not close them down. If the focus of the discussion, and the creation of the scoring guide, is on the writing task and its creative possibilities, the guidelines in the scoring guide do not become formulaic or restrictive; they wind up describing the ongoing work of the class. Thus they actually become liberating, since students can see what excellent work will look like and they can aim for it. A poorly developed scoring guide, on the other hand, can force student writers into narrow patterns, such as the five-paragraph theme or other formulaic ways of meeting goals. One scoring guide, in use by a school district, for example, actually defines a well-organized paragraph as one containing three complete sentences, whether or not those sentences have anything to do with each other or make any sense. Teachers need to use scoring guides to help students discover and shape meaning, not to establish patterns which all students must follow.

As these examples demonstrate, the creation of a scoring guide is much more complicated than it seems. The scoring guide is a kind of test of the writing assignment, which too often has unclear purposes. You cannot create, or work with your students to create, a scoring guide until you are yourself clear on what the assignment is asking students to do and what it will be teaching them. Furthermore, no class assignment exists without a context of class discussion, reading assignments, papers already completed and to come—that is, the assignment is part of the class curriculum. Thus the assignment in question needs to fit in with overall course goals and the particular goals for that time in the course. If it does not, the vagueness of the assignment's purpose will become glaringly evident when you attempt to put together a scoring guide.

This problem of making clear an assignment's purpose becomes clear when we try to write a scoring guide for the assignment that directed Nancy to write the essay "What if Drugs Were Legal?" (presented earlier in this collection). Here is the assignment:

> Select from a journal, magazine, or newspaper, a recent article on an issue you are interested in, one that presents a view you disagree with or that you find some problem with. In an essay intended for the same publication, write a response to the article. You may respond to the article as a whole or to parts of it. Your task is not to review the article for its own sake but to express your views on what this writer has to say. Your final draft should identify the author, title, and issue you are responding to and summarize what the author says about it, and then present your response.

If we wait until we have received the weak essay that Nancy has produced to this assignment (see 28-29), we have a difficult problem deciding how to respond. As we analyze just what the essay is calling for, and what it was supposed to teach, among all the writing issues this assignment presents, we wind up in the same muddle that the writer found herself in. What will we focus on and value enough for commentary? What, in other words, is the product that Nancy has tried to turn out supposed to accomplish? What is the process that the writer should have gone through to get there? And how will we know if she has learned whatever the assignment is out to teach?

We are likely to be tempted to blame Nancy for writing such a bad paper and scoff at her own sense that she is a good writer. But as we start to write the scoring guide, we notice that there are four major tasks for Nancy to accomplish in very little space: first, she must select, understand, and (at least in part) summarize an article; second, she must use her understanding of the article, and quotations from it, to develop her own ideas on the same topic; third, she must understand the difference between asserting her ideas or referring to her chosen author's ideas, on the one hand, and developing her own ideas, on the other; and fourth, she must have information and ideas on her topic that are not entirely superficial, though no research or further reading is suggested. It is clear from Nancy's writing that she needs instruction in all four areas; it is also clear that she is not aware of this need. We're also left to wonder, finally, if the teacher who composed the assignment was aware of the many different kinds of demands it makes on the student writer.

At this point, we need to decide what we really intend to teach. If the goal is principally the first I listed above—to help students learn to make use of outside texts—we'll have to set aside class time to practice these activities. Some work in locating appropriate material, writing a summary, using quotations properly, and accurate referring to positions with which one disagrees would all be useful as part of the teaching and learning involved with this essay. If the second goal is the principal one here, then we should arrange some instruction and practice in analysis of argument, so that Nancy can show where the argument in the article is wrong. Without such instruction, students are likely to do what Nancy does here, that is, simplify or distort the argument presented, say it is wrong without much consideration of why, and then assert her own views without giving contrasting evidence. But perhaps course work in both those matters has taken place (though Nancy gives no signs that it has) and the third goal is what matters for the assignment: development of Nancy's own ideas. If so, then Nancy needs instruction in the difference between asserting (and reasserting) ideas, on the one hand, and developing ideas using argument, definitions, and evidence, on the other. Finally, if we are looking at the critical thinking issues in the assignment rather than the rhetorical ones, we need to engage Nancy in some discussion of the arguments for and against legalization of drugs: the history of drugs, the lessons of prohibition of alcohol, the experiments with legalization in places such as the Netherlands, and so on. It is difficult to construct an argument without much information.

Is it reasonable or fair to expect Nancy to know enough in the four areas I have just outlined to be able to accomplish the writing task set out? I don't think so. Nancy thinks she is a good writer and she may indeed be one; but this assignment is in fact asking for superficial arguments and analysis; it is asking for the poor writing that it elicits. By speaking in a casual and superficial way about its very complex demands, the assignment suggests that an equally casual and superficial response is good enough. Until we attempt to compose a fuller, more detailed writing assignment and devise a scoring guide for the assignment, its complexity and difficulties are not apparent; we might be tempted to blame the weak writing on Nancy and (no doubt) her fellow students, or perhaps the schools, which never teach their students as much as we wish. But as we start to unpack the various tasks the assignment demands and notice how many advanced skills are needed for the task, we see that an entire curriculum is adumbrated by the apparently simple task. In this way, the creation of a scoring guide demands that we articulate our criteria and goals for the assignment and understand how it fits into the purposes of our course as a whole.

We could profitably spend class time and preparatory writing assignments on each of the four major tasks involved, and then, more reasonably, have high expectations for the completion of the larger writing task. The writing assignment then would be a natural part of the class work and the class goals, and everyone involved would be well aware of these connections. Because the teacher had made clear the various components of the assignment, the students would be able to work on each and on bringing them together coherently.

If we wanted to use this assignment, after some genuine instruction in the various rhetorical and research skills it involves, we could put together a scoring guide for it. All we need at this point is a set of criteria for the scores of 5 and 2:

Score of 5: These papers will demonstrate an ability to construct and develop an argument in response to an article from a magazine or journal. Specifically, they will:

- Clearly and fairly summarize an article on a controversial topic
- Analyze the argument of the article to demonstrate its strengths and weaknesses
- Respond to the article by showing how and why the writer of the paper disagrees with the views expressed in the article
- Develop the views of the writer of the paper in an organized way, using personal experience and other sources, to demonstrate a conclusion

Score of 2: These papers do not accomplish the four tasks set out in the assignment or they do so in a superficial and unsupported way. Specifically, they will:

- Select a weak or superficial article and/or fail to summarize it with clarity and fairness
- Instead of analysis of the article, present quotations or summaries without much discussion
- Allude casually or not at all to the article in presenting the opinions of the writer of the essay
- Present assertions of opinion without organized development or evidence

Again, it would be easy enough to develop the additional score points, through elaboration of the criteria already set out. As the students work through a series of drafts moving toward completion of the assignment, the clear set of criteria become a yardstick for them to use on their own work, especially if the teacher will respond to drafts using the scoring guide. If asked to rate Nancy's present draft, for instance, we could expect students to see it in the 2/3 range, since it is weak in all four criteria, but shows signs of development towards the upper half, at least potentially. The result of this use of a scoring guide, as any teacher who has followed this process will attest, is remarkable. Once students see and understand what is expected, they can usually produce it, given enough time and support. Instead of encouraging superficiality and failure, the scoring guide helps students work toward and achieve success.

Using Scoring Guides in Peer Group Assessment

Once the criteria for grading have become clear enough to the teacher and to the class, they become a natural part of the writing assignment itself. The students will be liberated from their usual worries about "psyching out the teacher" if they can know from the outset the standards by which their work will be judged. Some teachers make sure to involve the students themselves in the creation of the scoring guide, so that they can see the quality standards as partly of their own devising. Teachers who use scoring guides in this way spend more time working constructively with students as they write their papers, since the standards for performance are clear and public and the students are more ready to seek help in meeting them.

This application of scoring guides opens new possibilities for the efficient use of student and teacher time. Since the standards for judgment are out in the open, and since they have at least in part been developed by the class, the teacher can now ask the class members to respond to and even grade the papers written by their peers. Since the students now have both a vocabulary and a scale to use for discussing and evaluating the writings they examine, they need no longer deliver only the vague and unhelpful comments common to unstructured peer groups. Instead, they can (and in fact do) hold the other students' essays to the standards set out in the scoring guide. Moreover, by learning how to read and evaluate the papers written by other students, they learn how to read their own. This procedure has the magical value of increasing student learning at the same time it decreases the teacher's paper load. Although few teachers will want to use peer evaluation and response for final drafts or for crucial decisions on course grades, many teachers find it a constructive and economical way to help students read and assess their early drafts.

Using Scoring Guides to Help Students Assess Their Own Work

One of the paradoxes of teaching writing is that the most experienced and professional writers will revise time and time again, sometimes dozens of drafts, while the least experienced writers are usually perfectly happy with their first drafts. Teachers nowadays speak of the necessity of revision as part of the process of writing, but we are notoriously unsuccessful at convincing our students to undertake genuine revision. Diligent students will edit their work, particularly if we have marked up their drafts, in accordance with teacher demands. But a genuine revision, one that reconsiders and changes in substance what has been said in an early draft, is rare indeed. Why is this?

There are, of course, many reasons, including simple laziness and more interesting competing activities. But even diligent and serious students rarely revise their work and the tyranny of the first draft undercuts most teacher efforts to help students improve their work. One answer to this persistent problem is related to the absence of public assessment criteria: students do not revise their work because, in their heart of hearts, they don't really think there is anything wrong with it. All writers have some difficulty reading their own drafts and the least experienced writers have the most trouble of all.

This is at heart an assessment problem. If students could learn to assess their own work, they would be much more likely to adopt the work habits of professional writers, who usually consider the first draft as working copy to get them started, not the end of the line. The difference is not that professional writers turn out wonderful first drafts (though all writers occasionally do) but that professionals are good enough at assessing their own work to know how to delete, move text, change direction, and turn out new drafts. If we could help our students assess their own work, we will be helping them develop writing habits that will lead to better work throughout their lives.

Working in class with scoring guides looks to help students change the way they produce texts. Instead of producing a draft the night before it is due and praying that the teacher will be kind, the students will have a set of clear criteria before them from the time the assignment is given. They will be expected to participate in drawing up those criteria and to apply them to the drafts they and their peers turn out well in advance of the due date.

Conclusion: Scoring Guides and the Teaching of Writing

Scoring guides help teachers teach more effectively, first, by supporting simple fairness in teacher grading; second, as a means of restoring credibility to grades by making the criteria clear and public; and, finally, as a way for students to internalize standards for their peers and themselves. We need to be cautious and thoughtful in our use of them, however, for they can as easily become formulas for text production instead of liberating influences for writers. But as part of a thoughtful curriculum with well-conceived writing assignments, scoring guides offer teachers ways to help students understand revision and make useful discriminations about writing. They form a link between general statements of what constitutes good writing and specific textual features that can lead to much improved student writing. They also demonstrate the power of grading to promote instruction. As writing teachers, we need all the help we can get, and scoring guides are a particularly helpful classroom device for us.

A Selected Bibliography on Teacher Response

Books and Collections

Anson, Chris, ed. *Writing and Response: Theory, Practice, Research*. Urbana: NCTE, 1989.

Elbow, Peter, and Pat Belanoff. *Sharing and Responding*. New York: Random House, 1989.

Freedman, Sarah Warshauer. *Response to Student Writing*. Urbana: NCTE, 1987.

How to Handle the Paper Load. Classroom Practices in Teaching English 1979-1980. Urbana: NCTE, 1979.

Judine, Sister I. H. M., ed. *A Guide for Evaluating Student Composition*. Urbana, IL: NCTE, 1965; ERIC ED 033 948.

Lawson, Bruce, Susan Sterr Ryan, and W. Ross Winterowd, eds. *Encountering Student Texts: Interpretive Issues in Reading Student Writing*. Urbana: NCTE, 1989.

Sorcinelli, Mary Deane, and Peter Elbow. *Writing to Learn: Strategies for Assigning and Responding to Writing Across the Disciplines*. San Francisco: Jossey-Bass, 1997.

Straub, Richard, and Ronald F. Lunsford. *Twelve Readers Reading: Responding to College Student Writing*. Cresskill, NJ: Hampton Press, 1995.

Reviews of Scholarship

Griffin, C.W. "Theory of Responding to Student Writing: The State of the Art." *College Composition and Communication* 33 (October 1982): 296-301.

Horvath, Brooke. "The Components of Written Response: A Practical Synthesis of Current Views." *Rhetoric Review* 2 (Janurary 1984): 136-56. Rpt. in Gary Tate, Edward P.J. Corbett, Nancy Myers, ed. *The Writing Teacher's Sourcebook*, 3rd ed. New York: Oxford UP, 1994.

Jerabek, Ross, and Daniel Dietrich. "Composition Evaluation: The State of the Art." *College Composition and Communication* 26 (May 1975): 183-86.

Knoblauch, C.H., and Lil Brannon. "Teacher Commentary on Student Writing: The State of the Art." *Freshman English News* 10 (Fall 1981): 1-4. Rpt. in Richard Graves, ed. *Rhetoric and Composition: A Sourcebook for Teachers and Writers*. Upper Montclair, NJ: Boynton/Cook, 1984.

Assigning and Responding to Student Writing

Elbow, Peter. "High Stakes and Low Stakes in Assigning and Responding to Writing." *Writing to Learn: Strategies for Assigning and Responding to Writing Across the Disciplines*, 5-13. See Sorcinelli and Elbow, 1997.

Larson, Richard L. "Making Assignments, Judging Writing, and Annotating Papers: Some Suggestions." *Training the New Teacher of College Composition*, 109-16. Ed. Charles W. Bridges. Urbana: NCTE, 1986.

Lindemann, Erika. "Making and Evaluating Writing Assignments." *A Rhetoric for Writing Teachers*, 2nd ed., 191-223. New York: Oxford UP, 1987.

Young, Art. "Mentoring, Modeling, Monitoring, Motivating: Response to Students' Ungraded Writing as Academic Conversation." *Writing to Learn: Strategies for Assigning and Responding to Writing Across the Disciplines*, 27-38. See Sorcinelli and Elbow, 1997.

Responding Theory and Practice

Anson, Chris. "The Artificial Art of Evaluating Writing." *Journal of Teaching Writing* 1 (Fall 1982): 159-69.

Anson, Chris, Joan Graham, David Jolliffe, Nancy Shapiro, Carolyn Smith. "Responding to Student Writing." *Scenarios for Teaching Writing: Contexts for Discussion and Reflective Practice*, 34-62. Urbana: NCTE, 1993.

Auten, Janet Gebhart. "Power and the Teacher's Pen: Talking about Teacher Response to Student Writing." *The CEA Forum* 28 (Summer 1998): 1-4.

Baumlin, James, and Tita French Baumlin. "Paper Grading and the Rhetorical Stance." *Encountering Student Texts*, 171-82. See Lawson, 1989.

Bazerman, Charles. "Reading Student Texts: Proteus Grabbing Proteus." *Encountering Student Texts*, 139-46. See Lawson, 1989.

Berkenkotter, Carol. "Student Writers and Their Sense of Authority over Texts." *College Composition and Communication* 35 (October 1984): 312-19.

Brannon, Lil, and C.H. Knoblauch. "On Students' Rights to Their Own Texts: A Model of Teacher Response." *College Composition and Communication* 33 (May 1982): 157-66.

Chiseri-Strater, Elizabeth. "Evaluation as Acts of Reading, Response, and Reflection." *Nuts and Bolts: A Practical Guide to Teaching College Composition*, 179-202. Ed. Thomas Newkirk. Portsmouth, NH: Boynton/Cook, Heinemann, 1993.

Connors, Robert J., and Andrea Lunsford. "Teachers' Rhetorical Comments on Student Papers." *College Composition and Communication* 44 (May 1993): 200-24.

Connors, Robert J., and Cheryl Glenn. "Responding to and Evaluating Student Essays." *The St. Martin's Guide to Teaching Writing*, 3rd ed. New York: St. Martin's, 1995.

Daiker, Donald. "Learning to Praise." *Writing and Response: Theory, Practice, Research*, 103-13. See Anson, 1989.

Danis, M. Francine. "The Voice in the Margins: Paper-Marking as Conversation." *Freshman English News* 15 (Winter 1987): 18-20.

Flynn, Elizabeth. "Learning to Read Student Papers from a Feminine Perspective." *Encountering Student Texts*, 49-58. See Lawson, 1989.

Fuller, David. "Teacher Commentary That Communicates: Practicing What We Preach in the Writing Class." *Journal of Teaching Writing* 6 (Fa/Wi 1987): 307-17.

Haswell, Richard. "Minimal Marking." *College English* 45 (October 1983): 600-04.

Hodges, Elizabeth. "Negotiating the Margins: Some Principles for Responding to Our Students' Writing, Some Strategies for Helping Students Read Our Comments." *Writing to Learn: Strategies for Assigning and Responding to Writing Across the Disciplines*, 77-89. See Sorcinelli and Elbow, 1997.

Hodges, Elizabeth. "The Unheard Voices of Our Responses to Students' Writing." *Journal of Teaching Writing* 11 (1992): 203-18.

Johnston, Brian. "Non-Judgmental Responses to Students' Writing." *English Journal* 71 (April 1982): 50-3.

Kehl, D. G. "The Art of Writing Evaluative Comments on Student Themes." *English Journal* 59 (1970): 972-80.

Knoblauch, C.H., and Lil Brannon. "Responding to Texts: Facilitating Revision in the Writing Workshop." *Rhetorical Traditions and the Teaching of Writing*, 118-50. Upper Montclair, NJ: Boynton/Cook, 1984.

Knoblauch, C.H., and Lil Brannon. "Teacher Commentary on Student Writing: The State of the Art." *Freshman English News* 10 (Fall 1981): 1-4.

Krest, Margie. "Monitoring Student Writing: How Not to Avoid the Draft." *Journal of Teaching Writing* 7 (Sp/Su 1988): 27-39.

Lees, Elaine. "Evaluating Student Writing." *College Composition and Communication* 30 (December 1979): 370-74.

Lunsford, Ronald F. "When Less Is More: Principles for Responding in the Disciplines." *Writing to Learn: Strategies for Assigning and Responding to Writing Across the Disciplines*, 91-104. See Sorcinelli and Elbow, 1997.

Mandel, Barrett John. "Teaching Without Judgment." *Ideas for English 101: Teaching Writing in College*. Ed. Richard Ohmann and W. B. Coley. Urbana: NCTE, 1975.

Moxley, Joseph. "Responding to Student Writing: Goals, Methods, Alternatives." *Freshman English News* 17 (Spring 1989): 3-4, 9-10.

Moxley, Joseph. "Teachers' Goals and Methods of Responding to Student Writing." *Composition Studies: Freshman English News* 20 (Spring 1992): 17-33.

Murray, Patricia Y. "Teachers as Readers, Readers as Teachers." *Encountering Student Texts,* 73-85. See Lawson, 1989.

Onore, Cynthia. "The Student, the Teacher, and the Text: Negotiating Meanings through Response and Revision." *Writing and Response,* 231-60. See Anson, 1989.

Phelps, Louise Wetherbee. "Images of Student Writing: The Deep Structure of Teacher Response." *Writing and Response,* 37-66. See Anson, 1989.

Podis, Leonard A., and Joanne M. Podis. "Improving Our Responses to Student Writing: A Process-Oriented Approach." *Rhetoric Review* 5 (Fall 1986): 90-8.

Probst, Robert. "Transactional Theory and Response to Student Writing." *Writing and Response,* 68-79. See Anson, 1989.

Purves, Alan. "The Teacher as Reader: An Anatomy." *College English* 46 (March 1984): 259-65.

Robertson, Michael. "'Is Anybody Listening?': Responding to Student Writing." *College Composition and Communication* 37 (1986): 87-91.

Rothgery, David. "'So What Do We Do Now?' Necessary Directionality and the Writing Teacher's Response to Racist, Sexist, Homophobic Papers." *College Composition and Communication* 44 (May 1987): 87-91.

Schwegler, Robert. "The Politics of Reading Student Papers." *The Politics of Writing Instruction: Postsecondary,* 203-26. Ed. Richard Bullock and John Trimbur. Portsmouth: Boynton/Cook, 1991.

Searle, Dennis, and David Dillon. "The Message of Marking: Teacher Written Responses to Student Writing at Intermediate Grade Levels." *Research in the Teaching of English* 14 (October 1980): 233-42.

Smith, Summer. "The Genre of the End Comment: Conventions in Teacher Responses to Student Writing." *College Composition and Communication* 48 (May 1997): 249-68.

Sommers, Nancy. "Responding to Student Writing." *College Composition and Communication* 33 (May 1982): 148-56.

Straub, Richard. "Teacher Response as Conversation: More than Casual Talk, An Exploration." *Rhetoric Review* 14 (1996): 374-98.

Straub, Richard. "The Concept of Control in Teacher Response: Defining the Varieties of 'Directive' and 'Facilitative' Commentary." *College Composition and Communication* 47 (May 1996): 223-51.

Welch, Kathleen. "Sideshadowing Teacher Response." *College English* 60 (April 1998): 374-95.

White, Edward M. "Post-Structural Literary Criticism and the Response to Student Writing." *College Composition and Communication* 35 (May 1984): 186-95.

Zak, Frances. "Exclusively Positive Responses to Student Writing." *Journal of Basic Writing* 9 (1990): 40-53.

Alternative Methods of Teacher Response

Anson, Chris. "In Our Own Voices: Using Recorded Commentary to Respond to Writing." *Writing to Learn: Strategies for Assigning and Responding to Writing Across the Disciplines*, 105-13. See Sorcinelli and Elbow, 1997.

Carnicelli, Thomas. "The Writing Conference: A One-to-One Conversation." *Eight Approaches to Teaching Composition*, 101-31. Ed. Timothy Donovan and Ben McClelland. Urbana: NCTE, 1980.

Harris, Muriel. *Teaching One-to-One: The Writing Conference*. Urbana: NCTE, 1986.

Hawisher, Gail, and Charles Moran. "Responding to Writing On-Line." *Writing to Learn: Strategies for Assigning and Responding to Writing Across the Disciplines*, 115-25. See Sorcinelli and Elbow, 1997.

Lauer, Janice. "Interpreting Student Writing." *Encountering Student Texts*, 121-28. See Lawson, 1989.

Murray, Donald. "The Listening Eye: Reflections on the Writing Conference." *Learning by Teaching*. Montclair, NJ: Boynton/Cook, 1982.

Newkirk, Thomas. "The First Five Minutes: Setting the Agenda in a Writing Conference." *Writing and Response*, 317-31. See Anson, 1989.

Rose, Alan. "Spoken versus Written Criticism of Student Writing: Some Advantages of the Conference Method." *College Composition and Communication* 33 (October 1982): 326-31.

Sommers, Jeffrey. "The Effects of Tape-Recorded Commentary on Student Revision: A Case Study." *Journal of Teaching Writing* 8 (Fall/Winter 1989): 49-75.

Sommers, Jeffrey. "The Writer's Memo: Collaboration, Response, and Development." *Writing and Response*, 174-86. See Anson, 1989.

Tobin, Lad. "Responding to Student Writing: Productive Tension in the Writing Conference." *Writing Relationships: What Really Happens in the Composition Class*, 40-56. Portsmouth, NH: Boynton/Cook, Heinemann, 1993.

Rule, Rebecca. "Conferences and Workshops: Conversations on Writing in Process." *Nuts and Bolts: A Practical Guide to Teaching College Composition*, 43-65. Ed. Thomas Newkirk. Portsmouth, NH: Boynton/Cook, Heinemann, 1993.

Effects of Teacher Comments

Burkland, Jill and Nancy Grimm. "Motivating Through Responding." *Journal of Teaching Writing* 5 (Fall 1986): 237-46.

Dohrer, Gary. "Do Teachers' Comments on Students' Papers Help?" *College Teaching* 39 (1991): 48-54.

Dragga, Sam. "The Effects of Praiseworthy Grading on Students and Teachers." *Journal of Teaching Writing* 7 (1988): 41-50.

Gee, Thomas. "Students' Responses to Teacher Comments." *Research in the Teaching of English* 6 (Fall 1972): 212-21.

Lynch, Catherine, and Patricia Klemans. "Evaluating Our Evaluations." *College English* 40 (October 1978): 166-80.

Sperling, Melanie, and S.W. Freedman. "A Good Girl Writes Like a Good Girl: Written Responses to Student Writing." *Written Communication* 4 (1987): 343-69.

Straub, Richard. "Students' Reactions to Teacher Comments: An Exploratory Study." *Research in the Teaching of English* 31 (February 1997): 91-119.

Ziv, Nina. "The Effect of Teacher Comments on the Writing of Four College Freshmen." *New Directions in Composition Research*, 362-80. Ed. Richard Beach and Lillian Bridwell. New York: Guilford, 1984.

Reading and Evaluating Student Writing

Coles, William E., Jr., and James Vopat. *What Makes Writing Good: A Multiperspective.* Lexington, MA: Heath, 1985.

Cooper, Charles R., and Lee Odell, eds. *Evaluating Writing: Describing, Measuring, Judging.* Urbana: NCTE, 1977.

Crowley, Sharon. "On Intention in Student Texts." *Encountering Student Texts*, 99-110. See Lawson, 1989.

Elbow, Peter. "Ranking, Evaluating, Liking: Sorting Out Three Forms of Judgment." *College English* 55 (1993): 187-206

Gere, Anne. "Written Composition: Toward a Theory of Evaluation." *College English* 31 (1980): 44-58.

Knoblauch, C.H., and Lil Brannon, "The Development of Writing Ability: Some Myths about Evaluation and Improvement." *Rhetorical Traditions and the Teaching of Writing*, 151-71. Upper Montclair, NJ: Boynton/Cook, 1984.

Thompson, Thomas. "Understanding Attitudes Toward Assessment: The Personality Factor." *Assessing Writing* 2 (1995): 191-206.

Winterowd, W. Ross. "The Drama of the Text." *Encountering Student Texts*, 21-33. See Lawson, 1989.

Grading

Corder, James. "Asking for a Text and Trying to Learn It." *Encountering Student Texts*, 89-98. See Lawson, 1989.

Elbow, Peter. "Grading Student Writing: Making It Simpler, Fairer, Clearer." *Writing to Learn: Strategies for Assigning and Responding to Writing Across the Disciplines*, 127-40. See Sorcinelli and Elbow, 1997.

Freedman, Sarah Warshauer. "Why Teachers Give the Grades They Do." *College Composition and Communication* 30 (May 1979): 161-64.

Irmscher, William F. "Evaluation." *Teaching Expository Writing*, 142-78. New York: Holt, Rinehart, and Winston, 1979.

Tobin, Lad. "Responding to Student Writing: What We Really Think About When We Think About Grades." *Writing Relationships: What Really Happens in the Composition Class*, 57-74. Portsmouth, NH: Boynton/Cook, Heinemann, 1993.

Additional Essays
For Response

Attention: Bass Fishermen
Context

BACKGROUND

This is the second rough draft of the third essay of the course, but it is the first time you have looked at the drafting toward this assignment. The strengths and problems you see in this paper are virtually the same ones you have seen in his earlier writing.

THE ASSIGNMENT

In your first two papers you tried to recreate a personal experience that was significant in your life. You concentrated on a single incident and tried to show what happened. In this paper, your first expository essay, your objective is to explain a subject to a reader. You will be concentrating, then, on presenting your understanding about an idea, process, or activity to someone who does not have this knowledge. Rather than talking about a single incident, say, a time when you vacationed in New England, you would be talking about the subject "vacationing." For instance, you might explain the pleasures of touring the New England states by car or describe New England's most enjoyable attractions.

Your assignment, then, is to select an idea, process, or activity that you know about but that many people are unfamiliar with. Assuming the stance of an expert writing a feature column for the school newspaper, write a 600-1000 word essay in which you explain this subject to readers.

Be careful to restrict your topic to a size that will be manageable in the assigned space. And try to develop your ideas with concrete examples and details so that your readers will be able to understand what you have to say about the subject.

You will take this paper through several drafts, and receive comments from either me or other students at the various stages.

Attention: Bass Fishermen
Rough Draft

Steve L.
Second Rough Draft

Attention: Bass Fishermen

If the feeling of a monster large-mouth bass on the end of your line sends the same feeling of excitement through your body as it does mine, the lakes of central Orlando are for you. Orlando is blessed with an extraordinary number of lakes to fish in. Almost all of these were formed by sink holes thousands of years ago. The sink holes were eventually filled with run-off from rain storms and formed some of the greatest natural fishing holes ever. During my early childhood the first   really fun thing I was taught to do by my grandfather was to fish for blue-gill. It wasn't until later that I acquired the skills to fish for large-mouth bass, but after I hooked my first bass I understood how exciting fishing really is. After spending the first ten years of my life on the bass infested lakes of Orlando, I took for granted the great fishing. Only after moving to Texas did I learn to appreciate the lakes of Orlando. I remember looking forward to summer vacation because we would always go to Orlando to visit my grandmother and grandfather for a couple of days before we would go to New Smyrna Beach. The drive from Texas was torture, because Florida's I-75 is lined with thousands of potential fishing holes. The temptation to stop and try my luck was almost unbearable. Every time I saw a lake I would tell myself it would be better to hold out until I got to Orlando, where I knew the monster bass would be lurking.

There is a certain lake in Orlando called Lake Ivenho that is my favorite place to fish. Lake Ivenho is actually a chain of four lakes   connected by links of water. I have an advantage over most people in fishing these lakes. I grew up on them and know most of the hidden underwater structures, like fallen trees and sand-bars that extend out into the lake. One of the things I love the most about this lake is that almost all the lake is fishable from the shoreline. This is a rare occurrence because on most lakes you can only fish in certain places unless you have a boat or waders. Lake Ivenho is unique because the only thing between you and the fish are the occasional patches of lillypads. The best solution to this problem is to work a top-water buzz bait in the early morning or late afternoon. I have hooked some big bass using this technique, but if the bass is big enough to give a good long fight it can be very difficult to get it through the lillypads. After fishing the lillypads that morning my next move was to work a plastic worm under the giant oak trees that hang out over much of Lake Ivenho. Bass like to hang out in these shady areas during the heat of the day so they can better spot unsuspecting prey swimming by. This didn't produce the monster bass I was looking for so my next move was to work a spinner-bait along the southeast bank of the lake where there is a three foot drop off at the shore line. This is a especially good place to fish during a change in barometric pressure. The reason bass do this is because they loose their sense of equilibrium and must move in close to static underwater structures to help maintain their sense of balance. This forces you to place the lure directly in front of the fish or it won't strike. After fishing for about another hour and a half, hot, hungry and tired from a long day of fishing I decided to call it a day even though I had failed to catch the "Monster Bass" I was looking for. After dinner, still wanting to catch a monster I decided to try night fishing, which has been known to produce some big fish. After putting on a big black worm I started to fish under a small bridge that went over the water that conncted two of the lakes. After fishing for about thirty minutes, I suddenly felt a tug at my line and because it was dark I couldn't tell if it had the worm in its mouth or not so I decided to wait for one more sign that it was still at the end of my line. A split second later I felt it and set the hook hard. It felt like I set the hook in a tree but the tree was fighting back. After fighting it in to the shoreline I reached down and pulled out my seven and a half pound monster.

Leukemia
Context

BACKGROUND

This personal experience essay is the third paper in a basic writing course. The first was a personal narrative, the second a personal experience essay.

THE ASSIGNMENT

For this essay please choose an event that has had an impact on you, either changing you in some way or teaching you an important lesson. In structuring this essay you will briefly summarize in the introduction the event that you will analyze. You can rely on the technique that many of you have already used—telling a brief anecdote (story) that shows in action, rather than reporting, the event that happened. The remainder of the essay will examine various ways in which the event affected you. You can think of effects in different ways: ways that you think or behave differently now, ways that you perceive the incident now, or things you have learned from this experience. The most important thing to remember is that the whole focus of this essay is on *how* you have been changed or affected by what has happened.

Leukemia
Final Draft

Kevin H.
Final Draft

Leukemia

In April of 1986 I was very sick. I always had a fever and some sort of a infection. I was very lathargic and I was tired all the time which led to having no energy most of the time. I was not very active and I did not like to do things like I did before I was sick. Later that month I had a very severe pain in my upper arm. The pain was unbearable. I also could not move my neck if I did it would hurt. My parents and I did not know what was causing this not even the doctor. My parents finally took me to another doctor that one of our friends suggested. He gave me a blood test and found out that my liver was enlarged. He admitted me into the hospital and he had another doctor look at me. The day after I was admitted the second doctor diagnosed mé as having Accute Lymphatic Leukemia. He explained it to my parents and I very throughly. He also said that this type of leukemia is the curable type of leukemia.

The whole family was shocked and they did not what to do or say. It finally came to them that I was really sick about a month later. They did not say much to me when they found out. At first when the doctor told me that I had leukemia I did not think much about it then. I did not know what leukemia was or what it did to people. I thought to myself, "Will I die?" I do not remember what I thought – I was just stunned. Later I found out that leukemia is a disease of the blood. The leukemia cells kills the white blood cells which weakens the immunitty system in the body. This is caused by the uncontroled increase in leukocytes. This is what causes the decreasing of white blood cells. The same day when the doctor diagnosed me as having leukemia he sent me to The Ohio State University Hospital, where I was to be admitted. When I first arrived there it seemed so big. The doctor at the hospital seemed really nice and friendly to me. There must have been at least three residents and interns that gave me a physical. It was not very pleasent to go through three physicals in one day.

A couple of days after I was admitted in the hospital my doctor wanted my family to have a blood test to see if their blood is the same type as my blood. Unfortonely they did not have the same type of blood. The reason why she (the doctor) wanted them to do this is because she wanted to check to see if I could have a bone marrow transplant. Because of my parents blood types and mine were not capable, I had to take chemotherapy treatments. I did not know what to expect from the treatments. All I knew was that people get very sick when they take it.

Before I could take any chemotherapy I had to sign a contract saying that I understood what I had read in the contract. I felt that I was making a big decision whether or not I wanted to take chemotherapy. My parents and a witness also had to sign the contract. The contract listed all of the types of chemo, the use of the chemo, and all of the side effects. When I read over the contract some of the treatments that they were going to do on me made me think twice before signing. The contract was for a protocal program which is connected with the nation for statistics.

There were three phases of treatment that I had to go through in it. The first was called the induction therapy treatments. It consisted of various types of chemotherapy. I had to take Prednisone during the whole thirty six days of induction therapy. I was all swollen and puffy which was caused by taking prednisone. At night I had severe cramps in my legs, feet, arms and hands. I really hated these cramps. There was nothing the doctor could do about them. All I could do was to relax where ever the cramps were and wish that the cramp would go away. I thought that there ought to be someway to releive me from the cramps, but they say they don't. I had to take different types of chemo such as Vincristine, and Adriamyacin.

The second therapy treatment was called the consolidation therapy period. This period was really long and I had to take some more types of chemotherapy. It lasted for about one hundred and fifty days. I had to take some new types of chemo called Ara-9 and many more types. The other phase of treatment is called the maintence therapy treatment. This is the longest of the three other phases of treatment, but it is the last one I will have to go through. This therapy period lasts for three years. Now I am in the Maintence therapy treatment phase, but I have two and a half years to go. Most of the chemotherapy that I have taken was given by IV and some of the chemo was taken by mouth which were pills.

Because my veins are hard to find to get blood tests and chemo, the doctor suggested that I get a Hickman Catheter placed in my chest. The catheter runs into the main artery that is in my chest. All the catheter is is a tube that was inserted in my shoulder and runs down out through my chest which is just dangling out. When ever I needed to get a blood test, receive blood products or get chemotherapy they would just inject it through the tube instead of poking at my arms trying to find a vein. I was very glad that they had something like this because I do not know what I would do if I had to go through four years of needles poking in my arms all of the time.

Now I am in the maintenance therapy phase. I do not have to stay in the hospital any more to receive treatments, but I do have to go to the clinic every week for a check up and to get new chemo. I am glad that I am out of the hospital. I have not yet gotten sick from the chemo in the maintence program yet, and I do not plan on it. I have to keep taking chemo for the next two years. I have a long road ahead of me.

Contributors

Chris Anson, North Carolina State University

Lil Brannon, University of North Carolina–Charlotte

Donald Daiker, Miami University

Peter Elbow, University of Massachusetts–Amherst

Anne Ruggles Gere, University of Michigan

C.H. Knoblauch, University of North Carolina–Charlotte

Glynda Hull, University of California–Berkeley

Richard Larson, Lehman College, City University of New York

Ronald F. Lunsford, University of North Carolina–Charlotte

Rebecca Mark, Tulane University

Ben McClelland, University of Mississippi

Pat McMahon, Tallahassee Community College

Cheryl Nims, New Mexico State University

Frank O'Hare, Ohio State University

Jane Peterson, Richland College

Nancy Sommers, Harvard University

Donald Stewart (late), Kansas State University

Patricia Stock, Michigan State University

Richard Straub, Florida State University

Edward White, California State University–San Bernardino

Tilly Warnock, University of Arizona

Printed in the United States
138303LV00001B/27/A

9 781572 732360